Advance Praise

"I met Mitch years ago when we both fell down the rabbit hole of watch collecting. You'll love reading [about his] watch collecting journey. He is a most interesting and multi-faceted guy; whip smart, curious, passionate, knowledgeable, demanding, and above all, a real kick in the ass! Enjoy!

"Mitch's book just keeps on ticking!"

—Edward Tonkin

"Our journey began in the watch industry and has evolved into an amazing friendship. It has been nothing short of extraordinary, from discovering hidden gems in obscure markets to attending exclusive launches. Our shared passion for timepieces has created unforgettable memories and a lasting friendship. Mitch gives you a unique perspective from a true collector's eye, looking at the inner workings of Swiss watch manufacturing."

—Ahmad Shahriar, President, North America and Canada, Breguet

"Mitch's capacity of intertwining personal accounts, with an immense wealth of technical knowledge about his time pieces, makes reading this book fun, educational, intriguing, and all around a marvelous experience."

—Nicola Cagliata, Jaeger-Le Coultre Boutique manager

"Mitch is some man for one man. We became friends through the work I was creating, and now I look forward to exploring and enjoying his."

—Stephen McGonigle, Watchmaker

"Rare is it that one comes across such a person as Mitch. He is to me, one of, if not the most, erudite friend I know. From his first interaction with me almost twenty years ago to now, the questions he asks and his quest for knowledge are insatiable. He has a need to continue on his path of gaining a better understanding of the Independent Watchmaker's world, and what makes them create their micro mechanical horological artform.

"He is a patron to many an Independent Watchmaker for the reason that he knows he makes a difference acquiring a piece. Maybe there is some selfish gain in having some of the world's most exclusive and desired timepieces in his remarkable collection, however, I'd argue on balance, his choices have a net benefit to those makers choosing that difficult path.

"I must add, Mitch's willingness to share his collection with like-minded individuals does an enormous service to those watchmaker's whose rare work he owns. No safe queens here! An honor and great pleasure to write this."

—**Tim Jackson**, Independent in Time

"Commissioning and making a handmade watch are the two sides of the same coin. It's a collaborative process between collector and watchmaker and very often results in a creation that neither fully expected.

"The other result is frequently an enduring friendship between two people who are passionate about all things watch related. The fact that projects are conceived and deals hammered out over a good meal or a nice pint makes this happenstance more likely.

"Mitch's book is an odyssey through the world of watches and their makers and the friendships that were forged along the way."

—**John McGonigle**, Watchmaker

Time
on
My Hands

A Collector's Journey
in a World of Watches

Mitch Katz

Cover Design by Anton Khodakovsky with http://bookcoversforall.com/

Kindlifresserbrunnen image from ID 259011914 | Kindlifresserbrunnen ©Olya Solodenko |Dreamstime.com

ISBN ebook: 978-1-964014-51-7
ISBN paperback: 978-1-964014-52-4
ISBN hardcover: 978-1-964014-53-1

Library of Congress Control Number 2024921577.

Published by Tasfil Publishing, LLC
Voorhees, New Jersey

TASFIL
Concierge Publishing

To my sons.

Table of Contents

Prologue

I have been collecting watches for well over twenty years. In the process, I have acquired some very interesting and unique pieces. My watches have provided me with endless enjoyment. Inspecting them, wearing them, sharing them with friends...the joy of possessing these mechanical marvels has been multifaceted.

Several years ago, I began paying attention to watch auctions. This was both a good and a bad thing. Being caught up in the vagaries of the hysteria created about certain watches, I was saddened by the commoditization of them. I am a firm believer that watches are mechanical art and not investment tools. Art and technology are the primary motivators for my collecting of watches. The results of the auctions, however, opened my eyes to the value of my collection and that quite a number of pieces in my possession are irreplaceable. With that I developed a new perspective and a greater sense of responsibility regarding the collection. I also came to the realization that my sons should be offered the opportunity to learn about the watches that might come into their possession at some point in the future.

There was a television series in the early 2000s, *Arrested Development*. The line frequently shared, "There's money in the banana stand," originated in that series. After my revelation about my collection, I called my sons and suggested that they needed to know what was in the safe deposit box in the bank, our "banana stand." They both said that they had no idea about my watch collection.

They knew quite well that I had a deep interest in watches. They knew the names of some of the watchmakers and even the names of some of the particular pieces in my collection. Agreeing with my desire to give them a better understanding about what was in the "banana stand," they requested that I give them information about the watches. I agreed and created a spreadsheet that listed all the watches in my collection with a rough valuation of each piece. Dutifully I sent that to them and have updated the listing periodically.

After sending them the spreadsheet, I felt unfulfilled. I was placing a financial value on the watches but not being true to what the watches meant to me. Creating the spreadsheet brought with it a flood of memories. I realized that most of the watches had one or more stories associated with them. These stories made each watch that more special and increased their individual value to me, maybe not monetarily but certainly on a personal level.

I decided that for my sons to truly understand their father's obsession with watches, it was important to me that they be provided with these stories and, as a result, an understanding of why I acquired these watches and not others. I want them to understand what makes each special to me. I also realized that by relating these stories, I hope to pass on the joy and passion of collecting, something applicable to any collector.

Around the time I was developing the idea of writing about my journey in the world of horology, I started considering the possibility of retirement. As the concept of stepping away from the profession I had dedicated myself to for the last fifty years became more of a reality, I decided that one of my initial projects would be to write the story of that journey. I would not start writing the book until I officially retired. In the intervening time, I began making notes and, most importantly, recalling stories and experiences that my wife and I have had in the world of watches. The day after I "dropped the mic" and formally retired, I donned my new work clothes, a t-shirt and shorts, and started page 1.

This is my story, to date.

Chapter 1
A Family Affair

I am part of a family of collectors.

My father was the first to manifest the collector gene. Stamp collecting was his passion. He devoted a lot of his free time to the pursuit of working with and furthering his collection. My mother collected pieces of china and teaspoons as souvenirs from their travels but never developed a consuming interest or desire to create a collection in the truest sense of the word. Products of the Depression, with modest resources, my parents were cautious when it came to spending money on non-essentials. However, that did not prevent my father from building his collection.

My sister collects in a different fashion. She frequents antique shops, yard sales, and second-hand stores. Possessing an uncanny ability to see the beauty and uniqueness of things that, to others, would be nothing more than pieces of bric-a-brac, she is able to take odd pieces of china, dolls, or fabric structures and create an admirable antique collection. She is an excellent practitioner of the saying that one man's trash is another's treasure.

Over the course of our years together, my wife, an avid tea drinker, has developed a collection of teapots. She does freely admit to being a collector of teapots. Some of the teapots are utilitarian while others are pure works of art. Building her collection has been a family affair. Whenever my father came for a visit during the summer, we would visit a gallery for their yearly exhibit of teapots. Traditionally, he bought her one handcrafted teapot on each visit. To repay his generosity, we gave him the invitation to the show. The postage used on the invitation was composed of stamps from the 1950s and 1960s. A win for both collectors.

Although my wife denies it, she also collects scarves. Wherever we might be, should she come upon a display of scarves, she is unable pass by without stopping and carefully inspecting the wares. Color, design, and texture are all variables that can tempt her. She shares this passion with our daughter-in-law, who has already benefited from my wife's collection. My wife insists that she is not a collector. But when someone has over a hundred scarves and shows no ability to walk away from a scarf that catches her eye, she definitely qualifies as a collector. She insists that since the collective monetary value of her scarves is less than one of my watches, she is not a collector. Sorry, my dear. No, that is not how it works. Being a collector is not defined by the inherent value of the items being collected.

From an early age, both of our sons have been collectors. Our older son started by collecting rocks. He, together with his brother, also began collecting what they labeled as "odds and ends." What exactly defined an "odd" versus an "end" my wife and I never could discern, but they knew.

Starting in second grade, our older son has had a love for baseball. For years he collected baseball cards and related paraphernalia. That passion served us, his parents, quite well as a tool to reward good behavior or as consolation for having teeth extracted. His collection remains in our house. We will not commit the same "crime" of discarding his cards and memorabilia as my mother did with mine.

In time, his collecting gene changed focus. He has always had a love of music and now has an ever-growing collection of guitars, amplifiers, and electronic gear. The "collecting gene" is strong in him, and we are seeing signs of passage to his son, who desires all things having to do with trains.

In high school, our younger son developed a deep interest in cars. The more exotic the better. Model cars became his passion throughout his high school years. In college, his collecting interests turned to denim. He, by his own admission, joined a collective of "denim nerds," people interested in the history of denim and who buy and trade samples of vintage denim. They also actively support artisans who currently work with denim. Recently, he has developed an appreciation of fine art (something shared with his parents). Time will tell if and to what he will turn his collecting eye. The collecting gene is strong in him, though he might not realize it at this time.

When speaking of collectors and collecting, it is necessary to define terms. What defines a collection can be debated, but it is reasonable to state that to be considered a collector there is the requirement that there be an element of ownership of the item of interest. The number of items possessed is not a part of the definition, but it is assumed that the collector will possess at least several of the particular category.

When trying to define who a collector is, there needs to be differentiation from the enthusiast and the "flipper." There are, of course, those who work on the commercial side of the business, but they are not part of this discussion. The definition of these categories—and there may be others to include, but for simplicity I am keeping it to these three general categories—can also be debated.

The "flipper" is someone who will purchase a collectible with the expectation of selling it in short order for a profit. This might be for financial gain, much like trading stocks, or to fund another purchase that will then be sold as well. This group is composed of people who see collectibles only as commodities, a source of income generation. There may be an appreciation for the objects that pass through their hands, but they have no strong desire for ownership. They may own a few of the collectibles, but their motivation is primarily financial. This group serves as a source of information for collectors when there is a desire to place a valuation on one's collection. Unfortunately, this group often detracts from the beauty of the collectibles by treating them merely as chattel and putting the monetary value far ahead of the appreciation of the artistry or intricacy of the particular piece. The interest regarding the workmanship is only in how it affects the financial return for the piece. For the purists, those who appreciate the work for what it is, this can be very distressing. Flippers can contribute to the creation of a false buzz and at times unwarranted inflated valuations and excess demand for particular models. Sadly, for the collectors, the insertion of the discussion of financial gains in collecting can put a cloud over the joys of collecting and diminish appreciation for other, more skillfully produced products. It is a constant challenge for collectors to try to counter the financial and hype-based discussion with education regarding what separates something of quality from others, emphasizing workmanship, artistry, technology, or the like.

The enthusiast is someone who has a true passion for a particular category of collectibles but does not extend their interest toward ownership. These are the people who read extensively, post on social media frequently, and at times develop a reputation for expertise. They might possess an encyclopedic knowledge of the subject and be an excellent reference source. Some may own a few of the particular category of collectibles, but for them the greater pleasure of the hobby is the ability to accumulate deep funds of knowledge rather than possession either because of personal preference or financial considerations.

The collector extends knowledge to actual possession. Some say that the collector is possessed by passion and obtains the collectibles with the goal of long-term ownership. At some level, the collector is someone who identifies one or more classes of objects that stimulate an interest and the desire for possession. Some collectors are of the belief that in order to be considered a collector, one must have a focus and go deep into one subset of a particular collectible category (with regard to watches, developing a single brand collection or a certain type of watch such as dive watches, military watches, or **chronographs**). Others consider a collector to be one who acquires pieces based on one's own criteria, no matter how eclectic the choices may be. (Special note: words in bold are defined in the glossary.)

When collecting something like stamps, coins, or baseball cards, there are a finite number of varieties produced, and it is easy to say what is owned and what is needed to complete a particular collection. Building such a collection is a process of acquisition of pieces that fill the empty slots in an album or allow checkboxes to be filled in (it is the old game of "need 'em, got 'em"). With regards to other collectibles, such as watches, there is a huge diversity to choose from. Millions of pieces are produced yearly, with different sizes, shapes, varieties, and price points. Building a collection takes a dedication to whatever principle fits a collector's objectives or passion. A watch collector may "need" a certain model or **complication** to fill out their collection, but more often the desire is more of a "want" when the particular piece speaks to the collector for a reason known to themselves: aesthetics, emotional, financial, technical, or the like. For me, my collection is dictated by my own guiding principles; I obtain what I like. I collect what appeals to me, whether it is based on uniqueness, technical innovation, artistry, story, or just fun. For whatever reason, a timepiece must resonate with me. Essential is the emotional response I experience whenever I put on the particular watch.

On the Importance of Making Connections with Your Collections

My wife and I collect art and have for decades. A number of years ago, we decided to look for a painting by a particular artist. We already owned several small pieces by her, but we wanted a larger one for a specific spot in our house. The owner of a gallery we frequent told us he had a painting by the artist that was an excellent representation of her genre. When we saw the piece in the gallery, we were interested. We thought that it would go well in our collection, and the gallerist allowed us to take it home so we could "live" with it for a couple of weeks.

We brought it home, and for the next two weeks the painting sat on the floor propped up against my desk, in front of the space we were looking to fill. We never hung it on the wall. After two weeks we realized that for some unexplained reason, we could not make an emotional connection with the painting even though it was exactly what we thought we wanted. Ultimately, we returned it to the gallery. The owner was fine with the return and accepted the painting back without question. As we were talking to him, he flipped through some transparencies of other artworks (yes, it was quite a while ago, when transparencies of artworks were still a thing). I spied a piece that I instantly recognized as one created by a different artist, whose work we also knew. I asked about it, and he told me it was in his bedroom in the back of the gallery. With his permission, I went to his bedroom, saw the piece, and immediately had to sit down on the floor as I was emotionally overcome by it. Within minutes my wife and I agreed to buy that piece of art, and it has been hanging in our study ever since. The emotional connection was instantaneous. I cannot express in words why one was right for us while the other was not. However, I have learned that if I trust my eye *and* my heart, I will not be led astray.

It is my opinion that many people do not have that trust in themselves. Too many want the "right" piece and worry too much about what others may think (made worse by the advent of "influencers" on social media telling us what to think, feel, and be). I believe that one must kiss a lot of frogs before one finds the prince. After frequent exposure to many possibilities, one slowly develops a sense of what appeals to them and what does not. With that, it will then be easier to start building one's own collection, if the trust and confidence is there.

Chapter 2
The Start of My Journey

As I said, my father was a stamp collector, a philatelist. It was his one hobby, a passion and a diversion from the stresses of everyday life. After dinner, he would disappear into the basement and immerse himself in paperwork for his practice, duties for his professional society, or the never-ending requirements of his ever-expanding stamp collection.

He was particularly interested in collecting mint, unused stamps from the United States, Israel, and the United Nations. He carefully put the stamps in special coverings and then mounted them in designated spaces within leather-bound albums. A few valuable ones were kept in a safe deposit box in the bank. For those special stamps, he mounted pictures in the album to signify ownership.

Besides his special interests, he had multiple other albums for collecting stamps from across the world, usually used or canceled ones. Although he enjoyed stamps from most countries, he took exception to the nations that printed indiscriminate numbers of variations for the express purpose, according to him, of generating revenue. Commemorative stamps, those memorializing a person or an historical event, were of particular importance to him, as they served as history lessons. He had a monthly subscription to *Linn's Stamp News* magazine, an essential periodical for all stamp collectors, and although he never seemed to concern himself with the financial value of his collection, he received multiple catalogs, including the yearly Scott Catalog, which listed the value of each stamp according to its condition.

The intricacies of philately are more complex than one would initially think. My father not only collected the individual stamps but also collected plate blocks. These are groupings of stamps that form the corner of each printed sheet. Each block has a serial number on the attached border. Its rarity makes it especially prized among collectors. We lived in Brooklyn and would, on occasion, drive into Manhattan to go to the main post office on a specific day so that my father could purchase a sheet of a newly released stamp and a first day cover, another prize for stamp collectors. The first day cover is a decoratively designed envelope that complements a newly released mint commemorative stamp that is mounted on the envelope, never to be used as mail. In addition, there is a very special cancellation mark with the date of release, also designed to celebrate whatever was being honored on the stamp.

As the pages of my father's albums became filled with the more modern and hence more affordable stamps, his collection needed to be backfilled with older and more expensive ones. My mother would buy him a stamp or a set of stamps once a year to fill in the gaps. Due to the expense, that gift for my father would account for all the gift-giving opportunities for him that year from my mother.

Known among friends, colleagues, and patients as an avid stamp collector, my father would be given bags filled with canceled stamps from all over the world. At times he would even purchase a bag with the hope of finding some to fill the gaps in his world collection. My job was to remove the stamps from the pieces of envelopes they were adhered to by soaking them in a bowl of water until the stamps floated free from the paper or could be easily peeled off. I would dry them, flatten them, and then mount them in the appropriate spot. It was fine for me to handle the canceled stamps but not the mint ones, as they required special treatment.

In New York City there was an annual stamp show at the Armory in upper Manhattan. There, my parents would cruise aisles filled with vendors and exhibits from all over the world. It was a pilgrimage that was never to be missed except in 1963, when the stamp show, scheduled for the weekend of November 22, was closed due to the assassination of President Kennedy.

As my parents perused the show for hours, I would wander around the hall looking at the exhibits or at the military vehicles parked in the building, as the Armory was still used by the National Guard. As an offshoot of the stamp show, there was always a small section dedicated to coin dealers. Gradually, I became interested in the coins, eventually spending most of my time at the stamp show sifting through rows of them. Ultimately, I made my foray into the world of collecting when I purchased several.

Hoping to encourage interest in stamp collecting, my father bought an album for me to start my own US stamp collection. Dutifully, I focused on canceled stamps. Mint stamps were not in my budget and besides, why compete with Dad? Although I did give some time to adding stamps to the album, it was not something that held my interest for very long. As I reflect on what it means to be a collector, with stamps I never experienced the passion that my father had or that I now have for watches. That said, stamp collecting did serve me well by helping me earn a merit badge when I was a Boy Scout.

Coin collecting replaced stamp collecting. I set aside the stamp albums and purchased books to mount US coins of different denominations dating back to the late nineteenth century. In short order, I was able to earn another merit badge, this time for coin collecting. When I was in high school, I attended coin shows on my own, and after going to several, I became friendly with some of the coin dealers. At one point, I was invited to go behind the exhibit tables and help a merchant arrange and maintain his stock during the show. I cannot remember if I actually sold anything, but I became friendly with a collector, and it was with him that I had my first paid job.

This collector paid me to accompany him and help him when he'd meet with coin dealers. I would take the subway to the Wall Street section of Manhattan on Saturday mornings and meet him at a particular place, where we would spend several hours looking through coins for ones to add to his collection. I was paid an hourly rate that nowadays would be comical, but it was a job that I got on my own. More memorable than the coins that I saw was the Chock Full of Nuts donut shop that I went to before meeting the collector. There I always had a cup of coffee and a sugar donut (I still remember the powdered sugar and the crunch of the donut). This went on for several months. I certainly did not make my fortune at the job, but it exposed me to the obsession that collecting could engender.

While I was not quite obsessed, collecting coins did become my main hobby. I inspected every coin that came my way to check its date and mint marks. I would also periodically inspect the coins in my mother's large change purse filled with pennies and dimes. In time, the slots in my books began to fill with the more common pennies, nickels, dimes, and quarters found in the change that I or family members received. Eventually, I started to buy coins, but my economics dictated that I had to rely mostly on searching through those that I happened upon in circulation. Occasionally, I experienced the excitement of finding a relatively uncommon coin. Coin collecting introduced me to the thrill of the hunt.

To foster my interest and collection, my parents periodically bought me proof sets. Proof sets are mint, unused coins of each denomination produced in a specific year and from a specific mint that are wrapped in clear cellophane or sealed in a plastic case. They were prized and quite special to me. Sadly, the books of coins and the book that contained the mint sets disappeared at some point, never to be seen again. I suspect that at the time of a move across the country, they were taken by some less-than-honest person. Even so, I still have several boxes containing coins that I have acquired over time. Contained within are some old foreign coins, a roll of mint pennies, and a bunch of wheat pennies and old dimes. Even to this day I check the dates of all the coins that I get as change. If I come upon a wheat penny or an old nickel or dime, I put it in one of the boxes for posterity.

Collecting coins and stamps were passing interests, but there was never any great passion. Certainly, there was the thrill of discovering an old coin, but the collecting spirit never enveloped me in the fashion I would later experience. In elementary school I collected baseball cards, but I was never able to get close to acquiring a full set of cards for a year. Baseball cards are released each year starting in the spring, around the time of spring training, and then they are released serially throughout the summer into the fall. However, my parents sent me to summer camp every year. For those eight weeks, I had no ability to purchase any packs of cards and, as a result, missed the opportunity to acquire a significant proportion of the released cards.

Regardless, there was great anticipation every year when the new edition of cards would come out, and there was joy in buying a pack. It was with equally great anticipation that I opened each pack and saw who was included in the five newly minted cards. Even now I still remember the smell of the stick of bubble gum included in Topps baseball cards. It was a wonderful smell that seemed to be infused into the cards. In the packs of cards also came checklists that would have, in numerical order, the number of each card and the associated player. Of course, we did not need any checklist. My friends and I memorized which cards we already had, and which were needed. At the time, monetary value of individual cards was not a factor, and certainly there were no merchants who assigned value to them or created a secondary market. The cards were to be studied (on the back of the cards there were valuable stories about the players, career statistics, and sometimes cartoons), traded (they were called trading cards), and, for us kids, flipped.

Flipping was not a commercial endeavor but rather a form of gambling that was not frowned upon by our parents. There were a number of different types of flipping games: tossing cards against a wall to see who could get closest to the wall; knocking down a propped coin; trying to match an opponent's card in any one of a number of ways, such as by positions, teams, or even the color on the card The end result was that fortunes (as defined by the number of cards possessed) were made and lost during countless hours of flipping.

I never had a large number of cards and to this day cannot remember if any of the cards that I had were particularly special or rare. My financial situation allowed me to get one or, at most, two packs at a time if I had a spare nickel or dime in my pocket. Fortunate were the kids who could buy a box at a time filled with twenty packs of cards. Also, I was usually not very lucky when it came to flipping and learned the hard way about winning and losing. In the end it was fine, as it was all part of the reason we collected baseball cards. At that time there was no inherent value placed on a certain card, except, perhaps, for bragging rights if one had a Mickey Mantle rookie card or the like.

Long after my card collecting days ended, they became a financial vehicle. With the advent of card dealers, specialized stores, and online sites, there seems to be a different spin on card collecting. The dollar value of a particular card has overtaken the sheer pleasure of collecting, and I cannot recall the last time I saw kids sitting around in a circle flipping cards. When my kids were in elementary school, Pogs were the rage. There were games involving Pogs, but they were frowned upon and were, in fact, outlawed in many schools, as it was seen as a form of gambling to which parents objected. In my view, the innocence of baseball card collecting was tarnished once adults got involved and the emphasis of collecting turned more toward the monetary gains. I will never know what I possessed at the end of my baseball collecting experience; at some point my mother threw out my remaining cards.

When I went to college, I was not in a position, nor did I have the interest, to collect anything. My next foray into collecting was after I started working and met my future wife. At the time we were living in New York City. The Greenwich Village art show occurred at the end of May on Memorial Day weekend. The show was an exhibit by many artists that filled the sidewalks of Greenwich Village, and it was during one of those shows that we bought our first piece of art. As we walked around the show, we came upon a watercolor of butterflies and flowers painted on silk by artist John Cheng from the Bronx. After much deliberation and with a fair degree of trepidation, we bought the piece for the huge price of thirty-five dollars. Never had we spent anything close to that for anything decorative. We enjoyed going to museums and looking at fine art, but we never thought that we would spend so much money on an original piece of art. We still have the painting and always will.

That nameless painting was our entry into the world of art collecting. We continue to haunt museums, galleries, and art exhibits, always enjoying the experience of broadening our exposure and continuing to define what art appeals to us. We are always on the lookout for the next piece that connects with us and "asks" to be brought home, although wall space in our house is now at a premium.

Enter Watches

Growing up, watches were a utilitarian accessory. As can be said about the majority of people, I understood very little about them. In college I had my share of Casios. My favorite was the one with the calculator. I wore that watch daily until one of the calculator buttons fell out. Without being able to perform mathematical functions, it ended its usefulness as anything other than a timepiece. When I finished my schooling and had a full-time job, I graduated to wearing Swatch watches. They were fun and cheap, and they reliably told the time. It was in the middle of the quartz crisis, a period of time in the 1970s and 1980s when quartz watch production all but decimated the Swiss watch industry. A common belief at the time was that the mechanical watch was a thing of the past.

I knew about Rolex watches back then, but I could not understand why anyone would spend so much money for a watch. I did not understand the allure that they held, much less care how a mechanical watch worked or what lay underneath the dial. At that time, I figured that a Rolex cost about three thousand dollars, while a Swatch watch cost about thirty. I decided I would wear a Swatch watch and change it when needed, expecting it to last months if not a year or two before it would need to be replaced. By that plan I could own one hundred Swatch watches for the price of a single Rolex. That was more than enough Swatch watches for a lifetime, I thought, and that way I would come out ahead. I stuck to that principle for several years and owned four Swatch watches in the process.

In the late 1980s, I realized that the Swatch idea was not giving me as much joy as I thought it would. It was just not portraying the professional image that I wanted. I decided to get a nicer watch and bought a Seiko quartz **chronograph**. It was certainly a step up from the "juvenile" Swatch watches.

Men's Quartz Chronograph by Seiko
(watches no longer in my possession are sketched)

Around that same time, my wife bought me my first dress watch, as on occasion I needed to dress nicely. A gold-plated Seiko quartz Mickey Mouse watch she purchased made for an appropriate accessory. Thin, gold, and nicely tucked under the sleeve, with a hint of humor, it was perfect for me at that time. To this day I still treasure it and will eventually pass it down to a grandchild, after the battery is changed, and if it still works.

Gold Tone Mickey Mouse by Seiko

Knocking off the Knock-Offs

I worked with someone who came from Thailand. He traveled to his home country once or twice a year to visit family and friends. When he returned, he would bring a handful of counterfeit Rolex watches as presents for coworkers. After one such trip, he gave me two "Rolex" watches, one for me and one for my wife. We would occasionally wear them but did not try to portray them as anything but what they were, "fakes."

Although he did own several authentic Rolex watches, he also wore his knock-offs interchangeably. One evening he stopped at a convenience store on his way home. While there, he was attacked and sustained quite a beating, and his watch, the object of the mugging, was stolen. What the attackers did not realize was that the stolen Rolex was a fake. The muggers saw the symbolic Rolex **crown** and went for the watch with no concern for the wearer's health or well-being. When he returned to work several days later, the bruising of his face and the story of the robbery left me with a lasting impression. That night my wife and I threw out our "Rolex" watches, and I decided I would never own a Rolex. Criminals know the Rolex **crown** and target people wearing those watches. Although I might wear a more valuable watch, it is much less likely that anyone, particularly the bad guys, would take notice of it because it does not have a **crown** on the dial. To be sure, Rolex does make a good product. I have spoken to a number of watchmakers who are very complimentary about the quality of the Rolex brand. In addition, the marketing strategies of Rolex are brilliant. The company produces nearly one million units per year, yet they are able to convince the watch-buying public of exclusivity, value (current and future), and status. None of those marketing ploys has ever appealed to me. Many watch collectors I know and respect as well as others I have met are very enthusiastic Rolex collectors. Just not me.

Entering the Big Leagues

In the later 1990s, I again upped my watch game. I bought my first expensive watch. I went to the watch store where I had purchased my Seiko **chronograph** and was talked into buying an Hublot Classic Fusion quartz watch. It had a steel case with a gold **bezel**, gold hands, and a black dial. The word "hublot" is French for porthole. It is constructed to look like a ship's porthole with six screws on the **bezel**. The watch came with a natural rubber strap which was revolutionary in the watch industry. It was the first time a fine watch came on a strap other than animal hide or on a metal bracelet. It provided me with my first experience of wearing a better watch. Very comfortable on the wrist, it was an experience I enjoyed.

Classic Fusion Quartz by Hublot

In the later part of 2001, I received a modest sum of money as part of my inheritance from my father's estate. Although not an inconsequential amount of money, it certainly was not a sum that would change my life in any way (little did I know that would be so untrue). I thought long and hard about what to do with the money. We owned a house, and the amount of money was not going to pay off the mortgage. Our sons' college education was budgeted. I am not a car guy, so using some of the money to buy a fancy car held no allure for me. Clothes are not long-lasting. What I wanted was something special, something that would last, and something that would be representative of my father's passion for collecting.

This was a recurrent topic of consideration until one day, while driving down the freeway, I told my wife that I wanted to buy a watch and explained how it met the criteria I'd established for at least a portion of the money that I had received. She was fine with the idea, and we drove to the watch store, The Watch Connection, where I had purchased the Hublot. Although I still enjoyed wearing the Hublot, I decided that I wanted a mechanical watch in order to honor my father. I knew nothing about mechanical watches. All I knew was that they did not require a battery, and I perceived them as long-lasting.

In the store, I inspected my options, going from showcase to showcase. In the words of the trade, I "walked the store." I was accompanied by Rob, a salesman who still works at The Watch Connection and who has become a good friend. Ultimately, I picked out a Maurice Lacroix Masterpiece Flyback Annuaire. The watch was two-toned with a steel case and gold **bezel** with Roman numerals on a lacquered dial. It was an **annual calendar** with a large date display at twelve o'clock and the month displayed between the four- and the five-hour **indicators**. It had a **flyback chronograph** with **sub-dials** to count the minutes and hours. The novice that I was, I underappreciated the complexity of the watch. In retrospect, it was good value for the price, especially as a first mechanical watch.

I am sure that I succumbed to some salesmanship; nonetheless, I selected the watch primarily because I liked the way that it looked. I liked the artistry and the complexity of the dial as well as its layout. It gave me joy to put it on. Despite all the positives, I was still unsure. I had no basis of comparison, no knowledge, and certainly no faith in myself. I walked out of the store into the sunlight to see how the watch looked on my wrist (something that I have never done since) and called a colleague of mine who I knew collected watches. He advised me that Maurice Lacroix was a credible brand, the piece was good value for the price, and, in fact, the price was fair. Hands shaking, nervous about making such a significant financial commitment, I again studied the watch. At that time, little did I realize that not only was I staring at the dial of a watch, but I was staring down into a deep, winding, branching rabbit warren. I thought that I was on the sidewalk of a shopping center, standing in the bright sun, but in fact

I was teetering on the precipice of a journey I have yet to complete, if I ever will.

Masterpiece Flyback Annuaire by Maurice Lacroix

Falling Down the Rabbit Hole

When I strapped on the watch, it felt good. There was a weight to the timepiece that I had not experienced previously. On the wrist, it felt special, and by extension, I felt special. It was a transcendent sensation. Ever since, the feeling of a watch on my wrist has become one of comfort and pleasure. In fact, I am incomplete if I am not wearing a watch. Previously, I would look forward to weekends, when I enjoyed taking my watch off my wrist and living the day without the dictates of time controlling my activities. Since the day I purchased my first mechanical watch, that is no longer the case. Now it is a matter of which watch I choose to wear that determines whether it is a workday or a weekend day.

I enjoyed wearing the Maurice Lacroix after the purchase and was quite excited by it. In truth, I had not descended fully into the rabbit hole. Not yet. A couple of months after acquiring the watch, my wife and I went away for a weekend to celebrate our wedding anniversary. We traveled to

Santa Barbara and had a wonderful room in a great bed-and-breakfast. As we walked down State Street, we came upon a newsstand. As they do, the newsstand had racks of magazines. There I found the October 2001 edition of *WatchTime*, with Terry Bradshaw, the former Pittsburgh Steelers quarterback, on the front cover. I read that magazine cover to cover; not one word was left unread. Although I knew I had much to learn about watches, I was stunned to find out that watches had oil reservoirs. So stunned, in fact, that after the weekend was over and we were back home, I burst into my son's room and blurted out my utter amazement: "Watches have oil reservoirs!" Of course, my son stared at me, speechless, as if I had lost my mind. Which I had.

The hook had been baited and implanted into my cheek, and now the fishing line was taut and ready to be pulled. To completely mix metaphors, I found myself descending into the mythical rabbit hole of watch collecting. Whatever analogy is appropriate, I was hooked or lost in an unending tunnel. I have yet to find myself free of the watch-collecting addiction. And that is okay.

.

Chapter 3
Education

Why do we collect? I am sure there are multiple explanations. Aside from financial considerations, collecting seems to be part of the human condition. Throughout history, we have chosen to collect things we treasure. The ancients even buried the dead with valuable items that could be considered as collectibles for use in the afterlife.

I believe that the collector is, to a certain degree, someone in pursuit of something that provides more than just a sense of ownership. The pleasure the collector experiences when obtaining a sought-after object may be more than pleasure that is behaviorally based reinforcement. There might very well be a neurological or hormonal basis to the high the collector experiences when "the hunt" for a desired object comes to fruition. The release of endorphins and the resultant pleasure experienced is certainly satisfying and possibly even addicting. Conceivably, that sensation, as occurs in any addictive condition, produces the desire to recreate the experience, setting the collector off on yet another hunt. My wife jokingly accuses me of having a watch addiction. I suspect that on a physiological basis, she may very well be correct. This addictive behavior that afflicts collectors is socially acceptable in comparison to other more nefarious addictions, but I wonder if there is more similarity between the two categories than we might wish to believe.

I do not know what specifically drew me to watches. My wife and I frequent galleries and museums and have an interest in collecting art. Watches represent mechanical art. To this day, the attraction I have to a particular watch is influenced at least in part by its design and artistry.

The features of the dial, such as its coloring, the **guilloché**, engraving, or layout are examples of what influences my decision about a particular watch. Too much writing on the dial, a displeasing color combination, inadequate finishing, or an unusual layout of **indicators**, on the other hand, can be a detractor, in my opinion, and I tend to shy away from pieces with those types of features. The watch collector spends as much time studying the movement, architecture, function, and finishing as he does the dial side of the piece when selecting a watch. A person can be readily identified as an enthusiast or collector if he or she immediately turns over a proffered watch in order to examine the movement, and particularly if they request a loupe to permit closer scrutiny. The shape of the minute and hour hands, the design of the case, the shape of the **lugs**, and how the watch lies on the wrist, as well as other minutia, are additional criteria that come into play when appreciating the artistry of the watch. These and other variables collectively influence my feelings about a particular watch.

Many watch collectors are also car enthusiasts. I am not. Watches are, like cars, machines. Car guys speak with wide-eyed wonderment about the workings of car engines, where clearances are measured in millimeters. A car is expected to function as designed in a reliable and efficient fashion for the duration of a particular journey. The journey can last minutes, hours, or even days. Many highly prized and collectible cars are built for performance but how often can these cars be put to the test and driven to the full extent to which they were designed? During the course of a typical day, driving a high-performance car on city streets does not permit the car to be operated as the designers and builders intended. It might get the driver to the next traffic light first, but it is not able to be pushed to its performance limits on city streets. With regard to luxury cars, they are designed to maximize comfort with various amenities that passengers get to enjoy. That said, the owner is typically the driver, who may not be able to fully enjoy the luxurious appointments of the car for which he or she has paid dearly. I am sure that the driver may, nonetheless, be happy with the huge, powerful engine that this car has under the hood. Modern cars are complicated machines with multiple computers that monitor functions in the engines and adjust the car's function to maximize performance efficiency. Regardless of the vehicle, it also comes with the requirement for fuel of some sort and the need for regular maintenance.

A luxurious car is a gift that keeps on giving. Regardless of the make and model of the car, it is built with the expectation to last a limited amount of time, whether it be ten or twenty years or even longer. At some point, most cars are relegated to a museum or personal collection, garage, or the crusher without the expectation of being driven any longer.

In comparison to cars, the movement of a watch, the equivalent to a car's engine, has tolerances measured in microns. When I spoke with a watch designer, he equated the difference between the tolerances in car engines and watches as the difference between the thickness of a penny and that of a strand of human hair. When a watch is wound and strapped upon the wrist, the movement is expected to function flawlessly, to its full capacity, for as long as it has power. If kept wound, it is expected to perform exactly as designed with an accuracy of plus or minus several seconds in a twenty-four-hour period every day for decades if not centuries. Watches will need servicing, but the intervals between services can be measured in years while for cars it is measured in months. It is true that there are time-measuring pieces (smart phones, quartz timepieces, radio-controlled clocks) that are more accurate, but the mechanical watch can be close in accuracy, and it is accomplished by virtue of pinions, gears, and springs without continuous computer-assisted input, all while housed in a case measured in millimeters. I am not an engineer, nor am I mechanically inclined, but I am fascinated by the workings of the watch. Innovative engineering is another factor that is considered when selecting a watch.

Associated with the watch itself is the story the particular watch represents, like how many of the paintings hanging in our house have stories attached to them. Often, when I look at a particular piece of art in our collection, I am transported to the time or situation that led to the acquisition of that piece. These stories are very personal and may have little significance to anyone other than my wife and me, but the memories are very special and live within the art. The same can be said for the watches that are in my collection. The stories associated with most of these watches add to their uniqueness and, no matter the inherent value, make them that much more valuable to me.

Furthering My Education

After I brought home the Maurice Lacroix and subsequently read through the *WatchTime* magazine, my quest for education regarding everything to do with watches and the watch industry took off.

People learn in different manners. Of the many different modalities possible, I tend to be more of an auditory learner. As such, I prefer to listen, learn, and thereafter incorporate the information. That said, I seek information about a specific subject in any available format, and over the years, my thirst for knowledge and understanding has taken me to different venues and led to many experiences and adventures.

To learn about watches, I subscribe to several magazines devoted exclusively to watches, and I also cruise magazine stands for additional content. From the time that I bought the Maurice Lacroix, I admit to having a thrill when seeing a watch that I own featured in an advertisement or in an article. It does stroke my ego to think that others thought enough about that particular watch to picture it in a publication.

I bought my first *Wristwatch Annual* in 2001 and have bought every annual edition since then. In that book, many watch companies have pictures of some of their products, particularly the latest releases, with technical descriptions of the dimensions of the case, movement, functions, and, of course, price. To this day, when that book arrives, I spend hours poring over the pages, studying the different releases, and I have, in the past, used it as a checklist much like the old checklists that came with baseball cards. Of course the list is not necessarily a shopping list (there is a limit to funds), but rather it is a guide to watches that, at a minimum, I want to see "in the metal" or consider for deeper investigation.

When reading a magazine dedicated to a specific genre, whether it be cars, watches, fashion, or the like, one must read it with some degree of caution. These magazines are supported in no small part through advertisements by the very companies whose products the contributors are reviewing. A modicum of skepticism should be included when reading these articles. It is very rare for there to be negative reviews of a model in such magazines. If that were to be the case, would the company then be willing to financially support the magazine? Accepting the limitation and possible inherent biases, these periodicals serve as valuable sources of information. It is up to the reader to validate the information that is provided in the articles.

In addition to magazines, annuals, and catalogs that I read cover to cover, I began to collect various books to further my education about different brands and watchmakers. Again, many of these books are written as marketing tools for brands, but they do give the history of the company and provide a better understanding of their philosophy and some detailed information regarding various models. Slowly, I built a small library of books written by nonaligned authors that discussed particular brands and others that provided profiles of individual watchmakers, their contributions to watchmaking, and their creations. The learning curve is steep and continues to this day.

The Collection Begins

The next watch that I brought home was the Delphis from Chronoswiss. Unlike the majority of watches I was seeing, the Delphis had a different way of displaying time. The hour, digitally displayed in a window, would change exactly on the hour, and the minutes were indicated by a hand that traveled, over the course of the hour, across an arc of 180 degrees. At the hour the minute hand "jumped" back to the beginning, and the hour number changed. Not only did the watch have a different way to tell time, but it also had a dial with a sunburst pattern created by machine-pressed **guilloché**. While the technology fascinated me, the dial served as my introduction to the art of **guilloché**. Learning about the Delphis, I discovered that the movement was a modified Enicar 165. From reading the catalog, I learned that Chronoswiss acquired all the Enicar stock movements when the movement company went out of business. The base movement became their in-house movement that they then modified as needed for different models.

That was how my education regarding movements, their derivation, and their features began. I learned how, in many watches, movements may have a brand designation but are actually off-the-shelf, commonly available ones. These movements are built by one of a number of specialized manufactures (such as ETA, Sellita, Vaucher, and others) and then modified to meet the particular brand's specifications. Even when modified, the basic functions and layout of the dials and gearing remain the same.

As I gained better understanding, I started to be able to identify the movement maker by inspecting the features of the movement. Not considered a significant watch in the pantheon of watches, the Delphis was probably the beginning of my greater appreciation for the art and technology of horology.

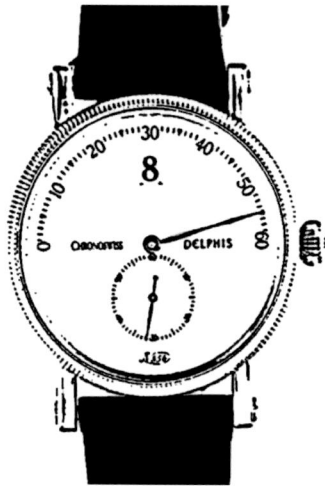

Delphis by Chronoswiss

My interest in watches continued to grow, but I still possessed an uneducated eye for quality and the finer points of watchmaking. To expand my base of knowledge, I took every opportunity to look at watches and began to make regular visits to several nearby watch stores. There, I was able to engage in discussions with salespeople about the different and, at times, unique features of various brands and individual models. Besides these stores, whether while running errands or someplace on vacation, if I passed a store that advertised watches, I had to go in and at least peruse the displays, no matter the brand. By so doing, I started to slowly but surely develop an appreciation of the type of watch that appealed to me.

Assuming Position and Possession

When I cruise watch stores or displays, I usually assume a typical posture with my hands behind my back, clasped, hiding the watch I am wearing. Sadly, in most retail situations, whether in a store specializing in watches or one with only a watch counter, salespeople display little interest in or knowledge about watches besides the ones they are trying to sell. Rarely does a salesperson inquire about the watch I have on my wrist.

In the early days of my collecting journey, I did not wear a watch of any special significance, but as my collection has grown, I might have on something notable and interesting when shopping. If, by chance, the salesperson sees or maybe even inquires about what I have on, it is even less common that they are familiar with what I am wearing, whether a common piece or a rarity. The sales staff typically only knows a bare minimum about the product lines they are trying to sell. It seems to me that, at least in the high-end establishments, the sales staff should want to see what the customer is wearing and have a broader working knowledge about different brands. In this way the salesperson might have an inkling of the degree of the person's interest in watches and be directed to something that might interest him or her. Knowledge would enable the salesperson to create the "story" of a particular brand or watch that might make the buying experience a more memorable one. I am not an expert in the retail business. This just seems logical to me.

To a certain degree, it is a fun sport to interact with sales staff who have no idea about watches, even the ones that they are trying to sell, though at other times it can be quite scary. This ignorance, or at least lack of experience, has led to some interesting interactions. During a trip to Bangkok, I, of course, found several watch stores to visit in a particular mall. In one of the stores, I saw a beautiful Glashütte Original Senator with a Meissen dial. It is a piece that I admired then and to this day. I knew that the watch had a hand-wound movement. The salesperson, however, insisted that it was wound by wearing it. She proceeded to shake the watch mercilessly in demonstration. I had to walk away. If someone was going to mishandle the watch in front of me, there was no way I could consider purchasing the piece no matter the price.

There have been times when I had to point out to salespeople that the watch in their case was not working properly. This occurred when I tested an alarm watch that did not alarm and a watch with a date that read 32. Despite these challenges, over time I was able to identify who of the sales staff in the various watch outlets that I frequented had a good understanding about watches and could, unknowingly, contribute to my education.

Twenty-plus years ago, the internet was not the force that it is today. Influencers did not exist, and the number of websites dedicated to watches was limited. Eventually, I discovered several sites that contained content focused on the watch-collecting community, and in short order, I began to make daily pilgrimages to those sites. They were good sources of information, especially those that were independently managed as opposed to those that were supported by, and therefore biased toward, certain brands. Some sites were used more for show-and-tell by the participants, but there were others that had scholarly postings, which I found interesting and useful contributors to my journey. Early on, I rarely posted because I did not feel that I knew enough to contribute to the community. Yes, I admit that I was a stalker of those sites.

Over time, I continued to collect books that deal with watches past and present, watch brands, watchmakers, and watchmaking. I still refer to them for reference as well as for the simple pleasure of exploring horology. I tend to shy away from the technical aspects of watch movements that are covered in these books but rather focus on the history and the novelty of particular watches. I have a number of books that describe how to build a watch from the ground up, but that remains an intimidating concept for me.

Visiting stores became a regular feature of my Saturdays. Rarely did a Saturday go by that I did not visit at least one or two. Even on the weekends when I had to work, I would usually get to a store at the end of the day. My wife never had to worry about where I was. She knew where she could find me and how to reach me.

On a visit to the Watch Connection in the later part of 2001, when speaking with the owner and one of the salesmen, Chad, they mentioned a brand that they carried, Ulysse Nardin, and told me that company was going to release a revolutionary watch. They then offered me an opportunity to order one of the first pieces to be sent to the US.

Since then, Chad and I have become good friends, but at that time it was a significant leap of faith for me to trust someone enough to make such a significant financial commitment. I was still new to the world of watches and truthfully did not fully understand what I was ordering. We agreed that although I reserved an allocation, I was not obligated to buy the watch when it arrived. That gave me some comfort, and they figured that should I not take the watch, it would be easy for them to sell it to someone else. What I did not appreciate at the time was that this mysterious watch with a weird name, the Freak, would be a revolutionary piece of horology and would start my long relationship with the Ulysse Nardin brand.

The Freak was released to the public in 2001, and true to their word, the watch was revolutionary. It was the first watch put into production with a movement composed of silicium components. Odder still, it did not have a **crown**. The **bezel** on the front was used to set the time, and the **bezel** on the back was used to wind the visible **mainspring** to its maximum seven-day **power reserve**. The hour and minute hands were formed by the movement. There had never been anything like it in the history of watchmaking. The material used for the components was called silicium and not referred to as silicone at the insistence of Rolf Schnyder, the owner of Ulysse Nardin. He insisted that silicone was for body implants, and silicium was for watch parts (stated in a somewhat more colorful way). Over time, there has been an interchangeable use of the terms silicium and silicone within the watch industry and by the public; however, purists continue to refer to the material used in watch movements as silicium.

I was subsequently told by Rolf that, historically, the first watch movement that contained silicium components was built by Rolex years earlier; however, they never produced the watch commercially. I suppose that, at the time, the cost to industrialize the silicium movement was prohibitive, even for the giant Rolex. Since the introduction of the Freak, most major brands, including those considered to be in the top echelon of brands, have incorporated silicium components into at least some of their movements. The advantages of silicium are improved performance and durability and the decreased need for lubrication. As a result of the incorporation of silicium into the movement construction, the service intervals have increased significantly. The counterargument to the increased use of silicium, in the opinion of some watchmakers I have spoken to, is the concern regarding the availability of replacement parts in the future or the ability of watchmakers to service these movements.

It is my opinion that Ulysse Nardin and the Freak have not received the historical credit that they deserve for the introduction of silicium. Many of the brands that use silicium parts are supplied by a company called Sigatec, now an affiliate of Ulysse Nardin. All this thanks to the work done by Ulysse Nardin under the visionary leadership of Rolf Schnyder.

When the Watch Connection delivered the Freak to me, it was one of the first produced, and at the time, only a handful had been delivered to the US. I was smitten by the piece. The combination of a dark-blue dial and strap with the rose gold case and movement was stunning. I was fascinated by the movement's workings. In the span of an hour, the movement, as part of the minute hand, circled the dial once. The fact that the movement rotates, albeit in the course of an hour, has led some people to call this a **tourbillon**; however, Rolf always insisted that the movement should be referred to as a **carousel**, though both terms are similar in function and design. Both types of movements involve the 360-degree rotation of the **escapement** over the course of a unit of time (typically a minute but in the case of the Freak, an hour) to defeat the deleterious effects of gravity on the accuracy of timekeeping, a modification much more important in pocket watches, where the watch is kept in a vertical orientation.

The joy of the Freak was lost when it stopped working within a day. The watch was dead. There was nothing that Chad or I could do to resuscitate it. With no other option, it was sent back to Ulysse Nardin in Switzerland. Various explanations were given for the glitch, and a couple of months later, the watch was returned to me. Again, it stopped working within days. All told, the watch had to go back to Switzerland four times over the span of many months until they could get it right and get the watch to work. It was only later that I found out the reason the watch had problems initially. The watchmakers did not understand that working with silicium was different than working with traditional metal components. Even the smallest defect in a silicium wheel, one that was within tolerance when dealing with the usual brass wheels, could have significant consequences and freeze the movement. I have been told that the specific problem had to do with the shape of the teeth on the **escape wheel** that did not allow for free release of the pallet fork **jewel**.

Freak by Ulysse Nardin

The Meaning of Time

The Freak introduced me to several realities with regards to watch collecting. Obtaining a "first of its kind" piece is exciting. It is an ego boost, to be sure, to be able to claim ownership of the first of anything or to see the serial number 1 on the case. It is fun to be on the cutting edge. However, with the good comes the challenge; there is sometimes a difference between the workbench and the rigors of daily wear on a watch. When one is on the cutting edge and is an early adopter of a technological advancement, there is a conceivable expectation that the owner is, in a sense, a field tester for the watch. There may need to be adjustments or refinements once the watch is put through its paces in real-world scenarios.

The whole experience of receiving the Freak, many months after being ordered, and the time required for each repair to be attempted, taught me a valuable lesson that has been repeatedly reinforced since then. As I have explained to many others, when dealing with fine watches, one learns the true meaning of time. The production time for new or for the servicing or repair of one's current watches can be measured in months, if not longer. One must exercise patience, remembering that everything seems to take more time than expected, and then celebrate when the watch finally is delivered or returned.

Despite all the travails that I experienced with the Freak, it remains a very special watch and a prized possession. From the time that I brought it home until the present, it has been the watch that I wear on special family occasions. Birthdays, anniversaries, weddings, graduations, and holidays are all celebrated with the family and the Freak.

The most incredible celebration was on my sixtieth birthday. My wife orchestrated an incredible day of fun and then a surprise party for me at a nearby gallery in the evening. Of course, given the celebratory nature of the day with my family and friends, I chose to wear the Freak. After the party, we returned to our house for dessert, and there on the dining room table was a sheet cake topped with a replica of the Freak. It was a perfect rendition of the watch. The dial, the movement, and the case were perfect in design, color, and detail. Even the straps had the scaling of typical alligator straps. It was amazing fondant workmanship by the baker. All that and the cake tasted great.

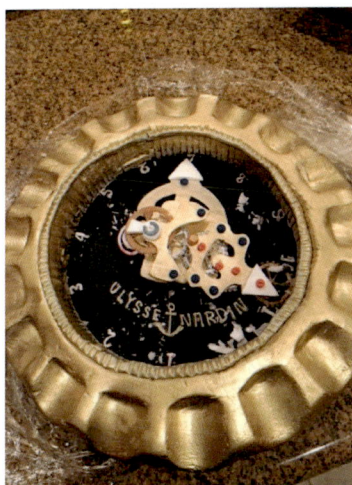

Freak birthday cake

Chapter 4
Friends and Community

After graduate school, I had very few friends, though I had many acquaintances. My time and energy were consumed by my professional career, and I did not have the bandwidth or ability to develop friendships. That was, until watches became my obsession.

Since entering the world of watches, I have developed a number of friends locally and across the world. Not only have other collectors and enthusiasts become friends but also members of the watchmaking community, whether they be independent watchmakers or employees of major brands. In the morning, I might be communicating with someone in London or Switzerland. In the early evening, I might be sitting on my couch in California texting with someone on the East Coast of the US or in Saudi Arabia or Hong Kong. All these friendships started by way of a common interest in watches but, over time, have matured into relationships far deeper and more diverse. These friends have been resources that I have tapped into for garnering education, whether about information in general or a specific watch. Meeting friends, socializing, and developing a community based on a mutual interest has been invaluable for the growth of my fund of knowledge. This community has been a great resource that brings watches to my attention, some that I did not know about or others that I did not fully appreciate. My friends and the social events that I have attended have served as significant contributors to the growth of my collection.

Early in my journey, when I discovered websites dedicated to watches, I happened upon the Purists, whose site I regularly visited. In time, there was a post announcing an upcoming gathering in Los Angeles. As it turned out, the founder and many of those involved with managing the site lived in or around that city.

When I attended my first Purists get-together, I was warmly accepted by the group. That first dinner meeting led to many more. A number of the people I met at those first few events remain my friends today. Although the activity of the greater group has significantly diminished as time has passed, an off-shoot group has been meeting quarterly for at least eighteen years, albeit under different names. The "Under the Radar Gang" was our initial identity, and more recently it was changed to the "Alphabet Soup Gang." The names of the groups are derived from our collective desire to remain anonymous when pictures of our get-togethers are posted online. When one of our watches is pictured, the owner is identified only by a letter. Over time, some members of the online community have been able to identify at least some members of the group, but for the majority of visitors to the site, we remain anonymous.

When I joined the Purists, the watch community world opened up to me, and opportunities began to arise that I would never have had otherwise. At some events, just a small number of us met, which frequently meant the tabletop would rapidly fill with watches of all kinds brought to share with one another. Eventually, the reputation of the website, and particularly our group, grew with representatives of the industry. Then our gatherings periodically became formal dinners sponsored by watch brands. Typically, a sales representative, company executive, or watchmaker attended those dinners. Naturally, the presentations at those dinners were directed toward their particular brand, but invariably the conversation around the table would include discussions of other watches brands, families, friends, restaurants, and travel.

In the early years, I mostly kept my mouth shut and listened. At any get-together there are always people with different levels of knowledge regarding watches, be it technical details, design particulars, or even industrial happenings. It is fun to participate in the discussion of inside information regarding different brands and watchmakers. True, it might be considered gossip, but if kept private, it does provide some perspective about the industry that produces the objects of our desire. Crucial to those discussions is the understanding that when something is told in confidence, that request should be honored.

An advantage to being part of a group discussion is that there are always questions asked that I have not thought about. With the passage of time, I began to feel comfortable sharing information and actively participating in discussions, although I remain more interested in what others have to say. I know what I know, and I want to learn what information others have to share.

Over time, I became aware of other groups of like-minded watch collectors. Brought together by the common interest in all things horology, these groups are composed of people from all walks of life. Whether it be driving an hour or two after work or on a weekend, I am willing to travel anywhere for the chance of meeting with other collectors and having another opportunity to meet new people and learn new things. The time it takes to get to these get-togethers is valuable and well worth the effort. These are also opportunities to find new watches to lust after. Some groups have come and gone while others are growing in attendance, attracting collectors new and old. Whether talking to a person who has collected for decades or someone who has yet to purchase their first watch, there is always an opportunity for sharing information and knowledge, benefiting both.

Some groups I have joined have long since ceased to exist while others continue to thrive and grow. The common thread in all the groups I have joined in the course of my journey has been the sense of community created by a common interest in timepieces. Whether they be current models or vintage, inexpensive or costly, big-brand products or independently created, it is all about the watches. People of all stripes meet and share the interest, and from those meetings lasting friendships spawn and grow.

To this day, the gatherings are male dominated, but it is gratifying, especially for my wife, who will often accompany me at my request, to see an ever-expanding number of women joining the groups and contributing to the experience.

Meeting Industry Leaders

At a number of dinners, I've had the opportunity to meet notable people in the industry. One dinner I attended early on featured two young watchmakers who were unknown to me. Their presentation described the work they were engaged in to build their watches, work that revolved around **tourbillons** set at an angle to improve the accuracy of their movements. In great detail, they provided evidence of the consistency of their movements with regards to **amplitude** of the **escapement** and timekeeping over the whole range of the movement's **power reserve**. They had improved the accuracy of their timepieces by a number of seconds per day compared with the standard movements on the market. Since then, Robert Greubel and Stephen Forsey have gone on to develop one of the most respected brands in the industry.

At another dinner, I had the privilege of sitting next to Jérôme Lambert who, at the time, was CEO of Jaeger-LeCoultre. He came to Los Angeles to unveil two new watches, the first of which was the Gyrotourbillon 2, a rather large, difficult to wear Reverso. The model featured the gyrotourbillon, a three-dimensional **tourbillon** that is a marvel to look at in and of itself. He also brought the Duomètre Chronographe. To say the least, at first glance I was smitten with the Duomètre Chronographe. The watch was constructed with a new concept for the brand. The concept behind the creation of the movement was a "dual wing." The dual wing contained two separate power supplies for the components of the watch. One powered the time indication on the left side of the movement, and the other power supply was for the **chronograph** displayed on the right side. The **monopusher chronograph** was operated by a **pusher** located at the two o'clock position. With separate power supplies, the accuracy of timekeeping was not deteriorated by the activation of the **chronograph**, a common problem that occurs with other **chronographs**. As an added attraction, the movement, visible through the exhibition back, was beautifully finished to a degree much finer than anything that the brand had done to date.

At his presentation, Mr. Lambert wore the Duomètre Chronographe in a pink gold case but spent most of the time talking about the Gyrotourbillon 2 that was subsequently passed around the table. Jérôme presented the Duomètre Chronographe and passed it around as well. When the Duomètre Chronographe came to me, I had no one else to pass it to, but I did not give it back to Jérôme. Throughout the presentation of the Gyro 2 and then the ensuing dinner, the Duomètre Chronographe sat in front of me. I could not take my eyes off it. Maybe I was a bit rude to those around me at the dinner table. I participated in polite conversations but would not surrender the Duomètre Chronographe and kept inspecting the watch front and back. I cannot remember what food was served that evening, but I do clearly remember the Duomètre Chronographe sitting on the table in front of me. There was no doubt in my mind, from first sighting, I was going to acquire that watch.

When the Duomètre Chronographe was released for sale, it was produced as a limited-edition model in a yellow gold case and a production model in a pink gold case. I elected to pursue the yellow gold-cased model. It came with a beautiful antique white dial that I had not seen previously. I thought that the dial color, unique to the limited edition, was an appropriate choice as many gold vintage watches were housed in yellow gold cases with off-white dials. The combination was beautiful. In comparison, the pink gold version had a dial that was a bit too stark white for me and was a less appealing combination compared to the yellow gold version.

The attraction of obtaining one of a limited edition was not lost on me either. There is a definite appeal to limited editions. The watch industry is well aware of the allure of the commercial advantage of limited editions when dealing with collectors. In fact, there are some watch brands that market most of their releases as limited editions. They make minuscule changes each time, whether by altering the color of the dial or **bezel** or some other decorative component, and declare it another limited edition. Definitely a marketing ploy. Some companies market as limited edition a model series of five thousand pieces. Not my concept of a limited edition.

In this case, although the movement was the same as the production piece, the limited edition was distinct enough and more attractive to me. There were three hundred numbered pieces in this limited series, and I received number 94.

The promised accuracy of timekeeping has borne out for the whole Duomètre line. The theory of the dual-wing design is to separate the power given to timekeeping and that supplied to the other **complication**s of the watch and has ensured excellent accuracy in all the examples within the model line.

Duomètre Chronographe by Jaeger-LeCoultre

With the Duomètre Chronographe in my possession, I was completely enamored with the Duomètre concept and the product line. The next model to be released was the Duomètre Quantieme Lunaire, which shows the time on the right side of the dial and the moon phase on the left. There is a **foudroyante** on a **sub-dial** at six o'clock that divides one second into six segments, and the hand spins around the **sub-dial** once every second. Now that seems to be a useless **complication**; however, it was important when it was developed in the late nineteenth century for timing horse races. On several occasions after I acquired the watch, I was asked by a casual observer if my watch was broken because what was perceived as the second hand was racing around the dial so fast.

One power source for this model is for the time, and the other power source is for the moon phase indicator and the **foudroyante**. As with the Chronographe, it was released as a limited edition of three hundred also in a yellow gold case and a regular production model in a pink gold case. The limited edition once again came with the same antique white dial, and the moon phase indicator had a beautiful maroon sky that was quite unique, while the pink gold model had a more typical blue sky. I saw the watch in both iterations at a Jaeger-LeCoultre boutique. Immediately I knew that I wanted the yellow gold edition.

About Face

A year prior to the release of the Quantieme Lunaire, but after I already had the Duomètre Chronographe in my possession, I visited the Jaeger-LeCoultre Manufacture in Switzerland with a group of Purists. One evening, Jérôme Lambert joined us for dinner, and once again I had the good fortune to sit next to him. This time I was better behaved and did not monopolize the watch he was wearing.

In the course of conversation, I mentioned to Jérôme that I had one criticism of the Duomètre Chronographe. It was my opinion that the layout of the dial was not user friendly. The **sub-dial** for the time display was on the left side of the dial, at the nine o'clock position. When worn on the left wrist, as most people do, a long-sleeved shirt or jacket must be, inconveniently, pushed up to read the time. I suggested to Jérôme that it would be preferable to have the time indication on the right side of the dial, in the three o'clock position. That way the time could be read with much less effort.

I am not saying that I had any influence, but it is interesting that when the Duomètre Quantieme Lunaire was released the following year, and for all the subsequent Duomètre models created since then, the time indication has been on the right side of the dial. Coincidence, or was it my feedback that was an impetus to change the dial layout? I will never know.

A. Lange & Söhne and Glashütte Original both have models that continue with the time display on the left side of the dial, which remains a small annoyance to me, though they do make fine watches. Throughout the years, Lange & Söhne has always been highly regarded. Well-constructed and nicely finished, many collectors consider the brand to be among one of the top in the market.

After studying the brand and seeing several of their watches on the wrists of friends, I thought that a Lange would be a nice addition to my burgeoning collection. After discussions with friends and telephone calls with a couple of dealers, I decided I wanted the iconic representative of the brand, a Lange 1. Once I made that decision, I vacillated between the original model and the one with the moon phase. I knew that whichever I chose, it would be in a pink gold case, as that, at the time, was the precious metal I preferred. Ultimately, I decided that the presence of the moon phase indicator added some contrast to the dial and made it more interesting to me. Once I made the decision to get the Lange 1 Moon Phase, it took me a while to finally come into possession of one. That happened only after I had obtained a watch by Jaquet Droz, which I ultimately returned, and I used those funds to make the purchase.

I had attended a dinner hosted by the brand when the president of Jaquet Droz gave a presentation. Eighteenth-century clockmakers Jaquet Droz and his son were known for their timepieces and for their construction of automata: programmable dolls using a system of cams. In a sense these marvels were the first types of computers. The most famous ones are The Musician, The Writer, and The Draughtsman. Several of their automata are housed in the Musée d'Art et d'Histoire in Neuchâtel, Switzerland.

As a result of the contacts I made during that dinner with representatives from the brand, they generously arranged for me to have a private showing of the three automata when I was next in Switzerland. I received what truly was a behind-the-scenes demonstration of the workings of the automata with a detailed explanation about their design and function from the gentleman who was responsible for their upkeep.

After that dinner I was so impressed with the brand that I decided that I wanted to acquire one of their watches. I subsequently purchased one that had a **grand feu** enamel dial. The watch was beautiful but sadly had problems. The minute hand seemed to catch on the hour hand such that it could not move around the dial. Back it went to Switzerland for repair, but after it was returned, it still did not function properly. Compounding the mechanical problems, as it turned out, the watch did not sit comfortably on my wrist. I could have adapted to the fit had the watch worked properly. In this situation, I decided to return it to the retailer and traded it for the exact model of the Lange 1 Moon Phase that I wanted. In the end, I was satisfied, and I got to see some amazing eighteenth-century computers.

Lange 1 Moon Phase by A. Lange & Söhne

When I ordered the Duomètre Quantieme Lunaire limited edition, I asked if I could get number 94. Once again, there were to be three hundred numbered pieces of the limited edition produced. Luckily, I received the watch with case number 94/300. There is no significance to the number 94 for me. Nothing. I just thought that it would be fun to have the same number as my Duomètre Chronographe. More Duomètre were in my future, and when possible, they, too, would be number 94.

Quantieme Lunaire by Jaeger-LeCoultre

Big Bang Theory

Jean-Claude Biver is a true celebrity in the watch world. Trained as a watchmaker, he made his name in marketing and corporate development, where he had many significant accomplishments over the course of his career. He purchased the rights to the Blancpain name, a company that had long since gone out of business, and successfully rebuilt the brand in conjunction with Jacques Piguet. After the sale of Blancpain to the Swatch group, he remained as CEO until he was asked to move to Omega. There he was able to resuscitate that brand and set it on its ever-escalating course by concentrating on product development and marketing. He accepted his next challenge by joining Hublot as CEO.

Hublot had been wallowing under the original ownership and he, once again, transformed the company into a huge success. The success he achieved was based on product development and his keen sense of marketing, which drove the company to strong profitability. Under his leadership, the Big Bang was introduced. Numerous iterations of the Big Bang were released, many of which were marketed as limited editions defined by a change in the dial or **bezel** and given attractive names. Hublot developed new and novel materials for their cases and, at times, the movements. Different alloys and combinations of gold, sapphire, carbon, and ceramic were created, optimizing the benefits of the different elements for strength, scratch resistance, color, and appearance.

The first time I met Jean-Claude was at a dinner sponsored by Hublot in a local restaurant. It was an honor and pleasure to meet him. He was affable and truly a showman, but the star of that evening was the watch he was wearing. He graciously handed me the watch, and with it came a surprise. It was a Big Bang that, at 44.5 millimeters in diameter, was bulky. But holding the watch and then, with permission, strapping it on, I found it to be as light as a feather. It truly felt like I was wearing a Lego toy. The case was composed of a magnesium alloy that Jean-Claude called "Hublonium." The watch was called the Mag Bang. The alloy was said to be very sturdy and scratch resistant, much better than any other metal routinely used in the construction of cases. In addition, the movement, a Valjoux 7750, had all the **bridges** replaced with magnesium and titanium components, thus contributing to its minimal weight. I was smitten.

Jean-Claude's Mag Bang was not yet commercially available, nor would it be for a while. So I made sure the brand representative knew that once it was available, I wanted one. When it was released as a limited production run of two hundred fifty, I did get one. I subsequently was told that because the case and movement **bridge** were so difficult to produce that it is very possible that not all of the two hundred fifty pieces were built. A second model run was produced called the Mag Bang WALLY, which had a similar Hublonium case, but the movement **bridges** were standard issue and not like those in the first iteration of the Mag Bang.

Years later, I was at another dinner event with Jean-Claude as part of a tour of the Hublot Manufacture. In honor of the visit, I wore my Mag Bang. When he spied my watch, Jean-Claude took note of it and said that I was wearing a collectible piece. Unfortunately, I did not think to ask him about the production numbers of the Mag Bang. No one else has been able to confirm the exact number produced.

Mag Bang by Hublot

Vintage Pieces

The topics of conversation at get-togethers with friends is always very diverse, but when watches are shared, they become the centerpiece of our discourse: the different facets of watches, the watch industry, and other aligned subjects.

Over time, I have branched out and joined other groups of collectors for get-togethers where I've had the opportunity to interact with collectors of vintage or preowned watches. Learning about the world of vintage watches is an essential component to understanding current offerings. So far, I am not a collector of vintage watches. I have identified several vintage pieces that I might consider adding to my collection someday, but I remain wary.

To collect vintage or preowned watches, one needs to have an extra level of knowledge, about not only the watch itself but the movement and the iterations of particular models. Understanding the provenance of a watch is also very important. There is a constant concern of whether the watch has all original parts. Dials, hands, or other components of the movement may have been replaced at some time in the past. The collector or a trusted adviser needs to be able to inspect the watch to look for evidence of tampering or underskilled servicing or repair. There may be many watchmakers in the community, but not all have the skill or talent to work on all watches. Even the brands themselves might have tampered with the movement of a watch when they "upgraded the movement" thus altering the piece from its original state, potentially without the owner's knowledge. More basic is the need to be able to distinguish a knock-off from the real thing. Some fakes of vintage pieces are obvious, but others are so exacting that even some very knowledgeable collectors have been fooled.

In 1999, Omega launched the Omega De Ville Co-Axial Limited Edition series. The series was the inaugural release of watches with a newly created movement. Developed by George Daniels, it was the first time in more than two hundred years that a new movement had been created much less put into production. Early in my journey with watches, I was offered one of these watches in yellow gold. At the time I was not aware of George Daniels or of the significance of the watch, and I turned down the offer. As it turned out, of the initial production run of watches, a number of them had problems with the movement and needed to be sent back for repair. An adjustment and possibly different lubricating oils were required to ensure the excellent function and performance expected from the co-axial movement. The original movement was caliber 2500A. I was told that some of the De Villes had the movement replaced with caliber 2500B.

Recently, I decided to take my chances in the vintage marketplace. I sought the advice of a friend, Art, who is very learned about the Omega brand. He recommended that I get a watch with the original 2500A movement and not the 2500B. Intimidated by the task of finding the "right" one, I asked for his help. Art contacted me several times when he came upon a watch for sale. When I contacted the sellers, I followed my instructions and asked about the movement. The sellers either did not respond or did not know specific details of the movement. The model has a closed back, and the sellers were not keen to open the watches. If they did, they probably would not know what to look for how to differentiate between the A and the B movements (nor would I). Wanting to do right, I did not pursue any of those watches. Ultimately, Art alerted me to another De Ville Co-Axial Limited Edition for sale. The watch was said to be "new old stock," never worn and never serviced. I contacted the seller who lives in London. Not only did Antony and I come to an agreement and the watch was added to my collection, but I gained another friend. As promised, the watch functions perfectly and keeps time accurately. Neither of us knows what the movement is, but given that it came with all the original packaging and showed no evidence of ever being worn, I assume that it has the 2500A movement. I am happy in my ignorance.

Successful as that acquisition was, I remain wary of the vintage market and will only dip my toe in it again if there is specific model that tempts me. I will be sure that I have obtained sufficient information, education, and advice before proceeding with any such purchase. I have been advised by friends that the key to success when shopping in the vintage marketplace is to buy the seller, not the watch. So true.

De Ville Co-Axial Limited Edition by Omega

How to Choose

As watch forums on the internet grew in number and popularity, I read many posts asking for advice regarding which watch to purchase.

Sometimes the posts included technical questions, posed to assist with the decision-making process. For the most part that was not the case. It was a simple matter of one versus another. I never liked those posts. There are so many variables that go into buying a watch; the only person who can answer the question is the person himself or herself. In the end, the person struggling with the decision is the one who will be wearing the watch, so who cares what anyone else might think?

Some people feel that they need the reassurance that they are buying the "right" watch, but what is "right" for me is not necessarily "right" for anyone else. It is necessary to understand why the watch is being purchased. Is it for personal enjoyment, as a statement of success, for investment purposes, or for some other reason? The struggle to make a decision typically comes from a lack of confidence in understanding one's personal aesthetic. To gain that confidence, it is important to see many watches. As I said earlier, I believe you have to kiss a lot of frogs to find the prince. Also, one needs to get educated about the subject. While websites, periodicals, and other collectors or enthusiasts can help provide necessary information, groups of watch collectors are probably the best resource for education and a way to avoid possible missteps. To this day, I continue to rely on my friends and fellow collectors to fill the gaps the still exist in my knowledge.

Our Alphabet Soup Gang meets regularly. Over time, we have learned about the preferences and interests of the different attendees. Table-side conversations can range from an obscure vintage model to a modern brand and its latest release.

One December, our group got together for dinner to celebrate the holiday season. One of the attendees, Mark, was wearing a watch that immediately caught my eye. Mark and I enjoyed similar aesthetics with regards to watches. We preferred contemporary over vintage watches. Mark was wearing a Master Ultra Thin Jubilee, a watch I again spent a meal admiring.

The Master Ultra Thin Jubilee was released to celebrate 180 years of watchmaking by the brand. At the time of its release, it was the thinnest watch on the market. In general, I am not a fan of thin watches. I once tried on a Piaget 9P watch, which was just slightly thicker than the Jaeger-

LeCoultre Ultra Thin (the Piaget movement was 2 mm in height while the Ultra-Thin Jubilee was 1.85 mm in height). The 9P felt like a wafer that would snap easily. It did not feel good on my wrist. My preference is for a certain degree of heft on the wrist. I prefer the feeling of weight to match the concept that I am wearing something of value. The Mag Bang, though very light, still had a bulk that gave me the feeling that I sought.

When, with permission, I put on his Master Ultra Thin, all my previous biases vanished. It was thin but still felt substantial as the case was made from platinum, which is heavier than gold or steel. I wanted the watch. By that time, I was working with someone at the Jaeger-LeCoultre boutique. I was concerned, since the model had been released several years earlier, that there would not be a watch available in the company's inventory, and I did not want to take chances in the secondary market. Fortunately, Jaeger-LeCoultre had one available. I was told that it was the last piece available from the manufacture. Truth or not, I did not care. Even if it was a marketing ploy, I still wanted the watch. It would look great under the sleeve of the tuxedo that I have never owned.

Master Ultra Thin Jubilee by Jaeger-LeCoultre

At a different gathering, Mark mentioned a particular watch that sparked my interest. By then he knew of my interest in the Jaeger-LeCoultre brand. He told me about a particular model, the Reverso 101.

When the conversation turned to other topics, I searched for information about the Reverso 101. I still cannot decide whether a smart phone is a handy device to have or if it is a very dangerous piece of equipment. Regardless, in very little time, I found what I needed. Nowadays there are very few mysteries thanks to the internet and Google. Yet getting information so easily does not help someone with roaring watch ADHD and can put a tax on one's wallet.

Jaeger-LeCoultre is famous for the Calibre 101, the smallest mechanical movement ever created. First constructed in 1929, it is usually incorporated into a bejeweled bracelet. Queen Elizabeth II wore one during her coronation. To build the Reverso 101, Jaeger-LeCoultre embedded the baguette movement in a clear sapphire case so that the complete movement is visible front and back. The movement itself is hand engraved, an exceptional feat given its size. The art deco styling is reflected in the design of the case.

Three different models were created. The cases of two models were heavily decorated with diamonds, and the third iteration did not have diamonds but had mother-of-pearl stripes on the inner surface of the case. Only five pieces in that configuration were produced, a total of eleven watches in all. The **crown** that was fixed in the usual three o-clock position did nothing. The **crown** had to be unscrewed and attached to the stem on the back of the case, where it attached to the movement, for the watch to be wound and set. Once done, the **crown** had to be detached and screwed back onto the stem on the side of the case. I was struck by the appearance and rarity of the watch.

As the lunch gathering continued, I texted my contact at the Jaeger-LeCoultre boutique and sent her a picture of the version that piqued my interest. I have several watches with mother-of-pearl highlights and felt that I could wear that model, but not one that came with diamonds. My contact got back to me quickly and told me that she would investigate. Once again, the watch had been released several years earlier, so she could not be sure of availability. I held out little hope that she would find one for me.

Two weeks later, I received a call from the boutique and was told that not only had they found the model I was looking for, but of the five pieces produced, this one was number 1. In limited editions, certain case numbers hold special significance for watch collectors. Certain members of the watch community give some extra value to production numbers such as 6, 8, and 9. The last number in the series is also considered by some as desirable. There are also numbers that some collectors try to avoid, such as the number 4 because of its association with bad luck in certain cultures. But a number 1 is the most sought-after number. To be offered the number 1 of such a rare piece was truly icing on the cake.

The watch was shipped to the boutique from Switzerland. The original intent of the Reverso 101, especially the model encrusted with diamonds, was for it to be a women's watch. I am sure that the model that I was looking at was also conceived to be worn by a woman, but I am secure of my self-identity and purchased it.

It is a bulky watch, but I can still wear it comfortably. I still question how it would be conceived as being the correct size and easily worn by most women. Over the years, when I have worn the Reverso 101, no one has ever questioned whether it was a women's watch, at least not out loud.

Reverso 101 by Jaeger-LeCoultre

The Powers of a Host

Not only did I regularly attend Purists meetings, but I started to develop a list of watch collectors that expanded past the Los Angeles area into the surrounding communities in Southern California. I decided to volunteer to host a gathering, both for a change in venue and to be able to invite others besides Purists. I had heard about a watch aficionado who lived in the San Francisco area by the name of Jeff Kingston. Jeff had published numerous articles about watches and served as a moderator of the Blancpain forum on the website Timezone.

Jeff made a yearly pilgrimage to the Basel Watch Fair, where, because of his reputation and credentials, he was afforded access to different brands and was able to preview many of the new releases. The Basel Watch Fair was an annual event in Switzerland where many manufactures and even some independent watchmakers presented their latest releases. Because it was a trade show targeted toward the industry, members of the public who attended the event might have difficulty getting into the booths to see the newest models. Doing so required an appointment with each brand, and those were usually reserved for retailers, journalists, and VIPs like Jeff.

The year prior to the event that I planned to host, I learned that Jeff had presented a review with pictures and commentary of the Basel show to his local group of collectors. The talk was well received, and I thought that it would be interesting for him to give a similar presentation of the recently concluded Basel Fair to our group. Jeff graciously accepted my invitation and agreed to fly down to spend the day with us. The event venue was arranged, and I sent email invites to my list of watch friends. It was also advertised on the Purists website. Forty-five people attended the luncheon at a local restaurant. It was a huge success. Jeff talked for well over an hour, presenting pictures and inside stories about the different brands and their new releases.

Jeff also told me that around the time of my event, he met with the management of *WatchTime* magazine and pitched the concept of giving a yearly Basel review lecture sponsored by the magazine. It is my assumption that the success of his trial run with us helped him make his case. The magazine agreed to an arrangement, and Jeff went on to give an annual Basel Review lecture that attracted large audiences in Los Angeles as well as in other cities across the country. Subsequently, Jeff has further partnered with *WatchTime* magazine to develop a watch show with exhibits by multiple brands along with lectures and social gatherings. All of this came to fruition, at least in part, as a result of that Saturday afternoon event in Southern California that I organized.

During that Saturday lecture, Jeff spoke about a relative newcomer to the market who had developed a unique watch based on a clock built in the 1800s that had two dials powered by two separate movements. The two time displays were synchronized by the resonance of the two separate **escapements**. After studying the clock, François-Paul Journe designed and built his Chronomètre à Résonance and subsequently became the first person to master the resonance challenge within the confines of a wristwatch. The two movements were mounted in such a manner that the **escape wheels** were in such close proximity that the movement of one affected the movement of the other, creating a precision in timekeeping that has been hard to match. The pictures Jeff showed revealed a beautiful watch design, one I had not seen before. Given that plus the description of such unique technology, my appetite for the watch was whetted. Over the course of the next several days, I sought out as much information as I could find about the brand and the watch, all of which fueled my desire for the watch.

Attending the luncheon was someone I had met at several other events. His name is Steven Rostovsky, and he was in the process of developing his business model to sell watches. When we got to talking about F.P. Journe and the Chronomètre à Résonance, he told me that he happened to have a new Résonance for sale. A week later I visited Steven's office in Los Angeles and purchased the Résonance. Initially all the watches produced by F.P. Journe had brass movements. In 2004 he started building his movements out of gold instead of brass. Mine, a very early model, contains a brass movement. Over time, I have considered trading my Résonance for one with a gold movement or for a different model, but I did not. A correct decision, as it turned out. I believe that I have the iconic

F.P. Journe watch in my collection.

Résonance by F.P. Journe

On a trip to the Vallée de Joux, the region of Switzerland that is the home of many watchmakers, watch companies, and watch factories, I met Christian Pfeiffer-Belli. A well-respected journalist, author, and watch collector, Christian Pfeiffer-Belli has published a number of books about watches. When we met, he gave each of us in the group a copy of his latest publication, *365 klassische Armbanduhren*. It features pictures of 365 classic watches with descriptions and technical details, one watch for every day of the year. Some of the pictured watches are modern, but most are vintage. My birthday is November 23. As it happens, the watch pictured for November 23 is the F.P. Journe Chronomètre à Résonance. An irony not lost on me.

After the success of the Jeff Kingston luncheon, I have periodically hosted other get-togethers at restaurants or my home. It has been fun to host events, particularly the ones at my house. At a number of those get-togethers, I have hosted watchmakers and invited collectors and enthusiasts. Whether the attendees have enjoyed and collected watches for years or are newbies to the field, it has always been an honor and fun to promote the appreciation and understanding of fine timepieces. The newbies can be those who are still teetering on the precipice of the rabbit hole or have taken their first tentative steps into it. Like I was at the start of my journey, newbies are sponges, looking for any and all information and direction. The more seasoned collectors serve to expand the fund of communal knowledge and engage in discussions about the most minute details of a watch.

The opportunity to share watches and the knowledge that I have garnered with others is truly one of the most significant joys of collecting. I absolutely enjoy the treasures that I have. I am quite fortunate to own what I do, and the ability to share them with others adds a whole different level of pleasure to the experience of collecting. Even though I have studied my watches closely, it is not unusual that someone will point out a feature about one of my watches that I had not appreciated. Seeing art through someone else's eyes is always a mind-expanding experience. Sharing my collection is not a matter of having my ego stroked but rather a matter of spreading the enthusiasm and passion that I have for watches to others, regardless of their depth of involvement in the field.

Aside from my own hosted events, I have, on occasion, been asked by retailers and watch companies to help organize groups of collectors for particular events. I happily comply with the requests, once again out of the sheer pleasure of providing friends and acquaintances with opportunities to see and learn more about watches. Sometimes I am more successful than others. The number of attendees at a particular event is less important to me than the shared enthusiasm of the group; that is what gives me ultimate joy.

Introducing My Wife

During the early stages of my journey, I typically went to the watch get-togethers alone. Whether it was for an informal Purists meetup, a collector dinner, or a hosted dinner, my wife had little interest in the world of watches and preferred to stay home. Of course, if the event was at our house or if it was one that I was hosting, she would willingly participate, but I thought that she was doing it more to be kind rather than out of any interest in watches. On a rare occasion, she did join me at other events. In time, she began to develop friendships with some of the other participants, usually talking with the wives of fellow collectors. My wife described herself as a "watch widow" and would seek the company of those who believed themselves to be in a similar position. More recently, as her knowledge about watches has grown, she has been more participatory in the get-togethers with me and my friends. I continue to get a thrill every time she speaks about a features or characteristics of a watch, discusses a watch brand, or mentions a watchmaker.

One of the first watch dinners that my wife attended was the dinner sponsored by Jaquet Droz. There were at least twenty-five people in attendance, many of whom I knew. As an icebreaker, we were asked to identify ourselves, tell what watch we were wearing, and relate one thing about ourselves. Dutifully the participants around the table contributed as instructed. When it was my wife's turn, she introduced herself and stated that she was wearing a Victorinox quartz watch. It was a mass-produced quartz watch that I bought her for daily wear. It was certainly not something to pique the interest of those around the table.

The watch aside, what she next said was something that chilled my heart. She stated that she did not know anything about watches and did not really have any interest in them. For a passionate watch collector, it was traumatic to hear my life partner's words so honestly spoken. Graciously, none of the attendees, including friends, made any note of her statement. So traumatic was the admission that the memory of that moment remains burned into my memory banks.

After that traumatic episode, I started my campaign to have my wife accept a "nice watch." Until that time, she steadfastly refused to accept any watch I suggested. She saw no need for such an expense. Many of the watches marketed to women contain diamonds. Take any watch and add diamonds to the **bezel** or to a pink or pastel dial, and then it is called a lady's watch. I know my wife's tastes, and those are not colors that she enjoys, nor would she want a watch with bling. She would absolutely refuse to wear a flashy watch where she worked, an extravagance totally inappropriate in her mind.

Victorinox Quartz

Finally, after I presented multiple options to her, she relented and accepted a Jaeger-LeCoultre Reverso Duoface. The model she accepted did have diamonds on both sides, but she was okay with them being subtle and certainly not in the category of bling. As an added incentive, the gift included different colored straps. I had a buckle mounted on each strap so that she could easily change the strap to match her outfit or mood. She gratefully accepted the present, an ultimate victory for her watch-collecting husband.

Reverso Lady Ultra Thin Duetto Duo by Jaeger-LeCoultre

Over time, my wife has acquired several other watches, and although the Duoface is her daily wear, she does seem to enjoy wearing others. We even purchased one watch together with the intent to share its use. We came upon a Zenith Pilot 20 Extra Special with a bronze case.

Pilot 20 Extra Special by Zenith

Talking to the salesperson, we were told that since the case was bronze, over time with exposure to sweat, it might develop a patina. Even though the case is big at 45 mm (after all, it is a Pilot watch), we discovered that we could both wear it. We agreed that it would be fun if we both contributed to the patina over time, which we have. I have given her a couple of watches from my collection that I do not wear any longer, but the Zenith is the only one that we share.

Have Watch? Will Travel.

Not only did the Purists help me develop a local social network, but they also provided me with unique travel opportunities, and I was fortunate to be able to tour a number of factories. Over the course of time, we were hosted by Audemars Piguet, Chopard, Piaget, Jaeger-LeCoultre, Zenith, and Hublot. On the different tours, we were granted access to all of the different departments within the manufactures. We went from the design department to where parts were manufactured to the watch benches where the finest pieces of the brand were assembled; we saw it all. When necessary, the tours included visits to the brands' subsidiaries that provided necessary specialty components or skills not available in the main plant. The only department that was restricted to visitors was the product development section. If we did gain access to the "skunk works," the staff was quite secretive, careful to not reveal plans for future projects. Computer screens were blacked out, paper drawings turned over, and discussions limited to vagueness at most.

Visiting a watch manufacture is an experience that any watch collector would absolutely enjoy. It is fascinating to learn what it takes to build a watch, whether it is a basic, entry-level model or a highly complicated piece. When brands produce modern watches, they typically use the most advanced modern technology. Computers and computer-assisted design (CAD) with multidimensional programs are used to assess the function of every component of the watch movement and create the templates that are used to program the various machines in the factory. Huge computer numerical control (CNC) machines produce the parts, both large and very small, needed for the creation of a watch movement. The mass of technology defies the concept of the lone watchmaker hunched over a bench creating a horological masterpiece. Even the independent watchmaker, working alone in his or her atelier, relies on technology, though to a much lesser extent, to build a watch. All the technology aside, ultimately, the mechanical watch does require the touch of the human hand for the final assembly and regulation.

The first tour that I was invited to attend was to the Jaeger-LeCoultre factory. I arrived in Geneva on a Sunday, the day before the tour was scheduled to begin. I was to meet the group on Monday for our two-and-a-half-day trip to the Vallée de Joux and the Hôtel des Horlogers in Le Sentier. Sundays are very quiet in Geneva. Most businesses and museums are closed. It seemed that the thing to do was to go for a stroll around Lake Geneva. Although I was tired from the overnight flight, I forced myself to stay awake. Trying to combat jet lag, I joined the locals and went for a long walk around the lake. On Monday I joined the group, and after a one-hour ride, we arrived in the Vallée de Joux. This was not my only visit to the valley, but the first time was certainly magical and awe-inspiring.

The Vallée de Joux, a valley in the Jura mountains, is the heart of the watchmaking industry in Switzerland. The area was settled centuries ago by French Huguenot farmers who had escaped religious persecution in nearby France. The farmers tilled the land during the summer. During the winter, unable to work the land, they spent their days working in their attics, manufacturing watch parts for sale to watchmakers or even building complete watches, all for supplementary income. There the Swiss watch industry was born. The valley is known as the land of the **complication** because it is where many of the most complicated wristwatches are constructed.

The town of Le Sentier is small and magnificently peaceful. Before our introductory lunch was served, I took the opportunity to stroll around the tiny town. Across the street from the hotel, cows grazed on beautiful grass-covered hills. Around the neck of each cow was a bell that clanged as it moved, a sound that added to the archetypical Swiss scene. After lunch we had some free time. It so happens that next door to the hotel is the Audemars Piguet Manufacture. With nothing organized before a welcome dinner, several of us took the opportunity to see if we could get into the Audemars Piguet building. One member of our group had an ongoing relationship with the brand and was able to arrange for an impromptu tour of the building. As it was my first tour of a watch factory; everything was new and exciting. The tour guide was quite accommodating, and our visit lasted a couple of hours. We were shown all facets of the production process. Most impressive was the haute horology department. There, several master watchmakers were working on **grand complication** watches. Most people at the manufacture were friendly, but I may have gotten a bit too close to the back of one of the masters in the haute horology department. At one point, he turned around and scowled at me. No words were necessary. I do not think he spoke English, but certainly his stare was all that was needed, and I rapidly backed away.

We spent the next two days touring the Jaeger-LeCoultre factory, where we saw all facets of their creative and production process. At one point in the factory, each of us took a turn working the machine that created the **perlage** pattern on movement plates. I was getting the hang of it and was able to create the correct pattern until I was distracted, and then all was lost. Creating a proper finish on any part of a watch movement requires absolute concentration.

We were driven around the Lac de Joux, the lake in the valley, to visit several buildings that Jaeger-LeCoultre owned that housed various specialty departments that had not yet been incorporated into the main building. As we traveled, we passed numerous houses with characteristic large windows set below the eaves. Those windows were placed to let the winter's light into the attic where the farmer-turned-watchmaker honed his craft in times gone by. In stark contrast to the bucolic surroundings were ultra-modern buildings that seemed to have sprouted out of the fields. Some buildings carried the names of famous Swiss watch brands, while other buildings had names I did not recognize. Most of those buildings were occupied by companies that supported the watch industry.

Across the lake from the factory, we stopped at the building that housed the gem-setting department where, we were given the opportunity to attempt to place a diamond chip in a setting. I was able to set the diamond chip, but it did not give me the confidence to consider changing careers. In a different building was the engraving and enameling department, where we saw beautiful workmanship but were not given an opportunity to try our hand at anything that creative.

At the time of our visit, Jaeger-LeCoultre was preparing to release the first watch with a gyrotourbillon. As the name suggests, the gyrotourbillon is a multi-axis **tourbillon** built to defeat the effects of gravity on the watch movement when it is worn on the wrist. With our understanding that the curtain of secrecy was being pulled back for us, the watchmaker in charge of the development of the gyrotourbillon brought out a prototype movement secured within a plastic case. The movement was fully functional. When it was my turn to look at the movement through a microscope, it was as if I was looking at a beating heart. It was incredible. When it was time for me to return the prototype to the watchmaker, as I handed it back, I dropped the plastic case. After a moment of absolute horror and embarrassment, I realized that the movement was securely fixed, and the anti-shock system worked. The gyrotourbillon continued to pulse, to my great relief. I do not believe that I hazarded a look at the watchmaker for fear of what his expression might reveal.

During the afternoon of the second day, we were invited to participate in what they called a "master class." The purpose of this class was to give us a window into the world of a watchmaker. Under the tutelage of a master watchmaker, we were tasked to disassemble and then reassemble a watch movement. Over time, Jaeger-LeCoultre has held these master classes all over the world, but at the time of our visit, the class was in the development stage and was only available at the manufacture in Le Sentier. Dutifully, I was able to disassemble the movement, being sure to lay out the parts in order so that reassembly would not be such a challenge. The parts of a watch movement are of variable sizes. The screws are so tiny that a magnifying loupe is needed to manipulate them. The quiet of the class would be interrupted periodically by an expletive, socially acceptable or not, when someone sent a screw flying off their bench. There were plenty of spare screws available for those in need; the launching of screws was clearly expected to occur given the reserves that were readily at hand. I, on the other hand, carefully controlled my screws.

When it came to the process of reassembly, I started off well but when replacing a **bridge**, I had difficulty with the alignment onto a pinion. When I was applying a bit of force with my tweezers, a **jewel** popped out of the **bridge** and went flying to the floor, never to be seen again. Synthetic rubies are used in watch movements to limit the friction at contact points between watch parts. Rubies vary in size and tend to be between 0.5 mm and 2 mm in diameter. Faced with the loss of the **jewel**, I had no option but to go to the front of the class, where the master watchmaker sat. I meekly reported, through a translator, what I had done. Needless to say, he was extraordinarily displeased and gave me a look that would wilt a rose. With a specifically designed tool, he replaced the missing **jewel** into the empty hole in the **bridge**, and totally cowed, I returned to my bench. I was able to rebuild the watch, but it was not in working order. Even in the face of my epic failure, at the end of the course I received my "Diplôme" for having successfully completed "le cours de formation horlogerè" and I received a text book, *The Theory of Horolgy* autographed by the master watchmaker.

Despite the memory of that look from the watchmaker, I am proud that of all the people who have taken the master class from Jaeger-LeCoultre, I am the only one, I believe, to have popped a **jewel**. This is one of the many reasons that I am not destined to be a watchmaker.

The trips to Switzerland were designed for clients to learn about particular brands. Of course, for the brands, this served as a tool for publicity and a marketing device. I believe that another benefit for the brand is to get insight into the thoughts of the consumer. For me, it was also an opportunity to meet like-minded people from around the world, some of whom have since become friends.

Fortunately, I had the opportunity to go on several of the Purists trips. There was a core group of us who were able to join up. With familiarity came collegiality. Although we spent much of the daylight hours learning about the watches produced by the sponsoring brands, during meals, social hours, and certainly late into the night, we discussed watches, watch collecting, and the industry in general. Many a late night found us sitting in the hotel bar discussing minutia that only a watch geek might care about or some upheaval in the watch industry or tiff between different watch-related websites. •

Most of the attendees on the tours had traveled to Switzerland from the States or from Asia. As a result, some of us took the opportunity of our time in Switzerland to broaden our watch experience beyond that scheduled by our host. On the trip to Jaeger-LeCoultre, I met Philippe Dufour for the first time when one of the members of the group had a watch made by Philippe that needed servicing. Several of us ducked out of a lunch provided by Jaeger-LeCoultre and drove over to Dufour's workshop, which was only a few minutes' drive from the manufacture. The contrast between the Jaeger-LeCoultre factory and Dufour's atelier was remarkable. It was as if we'd traveled back in time. In the Jaeger-LeCoultre Manufacture, white coats, hair nets, and booties were the required dress. The assembly rooms had negative air flow, forcing the air out of the room, along with potential contaminants. Walking into these "sterile" environments, we had to walk on sticky mats that were supposed to remove dirt from our booties. The environment was strictly controlled to prevent foreign particles, no matter how small, from getting into the movements, an absolute hazard for a watch movement.

When we met Philippe Dufour, we crowded into his workshop. He was smoking his pipe. The windows over the workbenches were open to allow fresh air in as he puffed. The floor was wood and the space cluttered with old machines, exhibit cases, books, and magazines. Here, one of the most respected watchmakers in the world, someone who has produced some of the highest-quality watches, worked in an environment that was diametrically opposite to the sterile workshops in a modern factory just down the road. The difference was stunning. Our time there was short, as we needed to return to the group, but despite the limited interaction with Dufour, it was one of the highlights of that trip. It was an honor to be in the presence of and listen to this luminary.

Another year, Audemars Piguet invited the Purists to attend a sponsored trip. This invitation was unrelated to our previous spontaneous visit. Once again, we were invited to stay at the adjacent Hôtel des Horlogers. The cows were still grazing on the grass across the street, and the area remained serene and pastural. This time our tour was led by Martin Wehrli, who, at the time, had the distinction of having the most years of service in the company. He had been a watchmaker but then transitioned to the role of curator of their museum, historian, and public face of the brand. In addition, he authored several comprehensive books about the brand, including one dedicated exclusively to the Royal Oak. The tour of the Manufacture and their museum was once again quite comprehensive. This time I was not met with a scowl from a watchmaker when we visited the haute horology department. Maybe I stood sufficiently at a distance so as not to incur the wrath.

As part of the Audemars experience, we were taken to Renaud & Papi to see where some of the most complicated pieces are assembled. Although Audemars has a controlling interest in Renaud & Papi, the company produces complicated watches for other brands as well. Over time it has served as the training ground for many of today's finest watchmakers. Our tour guide for that facility was Giulio Papi. Upon our arrival, we were told that Giulio was running a bit late. When he rushed into the lobby, he gave us a quick hello before excusing himself for several minutes. I noticed that when he came to say hello, he was wearing a Tissot T-Touch, apparently a very popular watch among watchmakers at the time. Here was someone who was responsible for some of the most complicated mechanical watches presently made, yet he was wearing a T-Touch, a quartz watch. I also have one, and since it was good enough for Giulio Papi and other watchmakers to wear, it is good enough for me to continue to wear it.

T Touch by Tissot

When he came back to start our tour, he had not changed clothes but did change watches, such that he was wearing an Audemars Piguet **tourbillon** in a rectangular case, not bad for something to throw on in a pinch.

The main workroom was filled with rows of workbenches and watchmakers. Off to the side, mounted on a wall, I saw a chart that detailed all the complicated watches that Renaud & Papi had produced, including those for other brands. While we walked around the workshop, at some of the benches along the back row, several watchmakers were assembling Richard Mille watches using movements from the Vaucher Manufacture, a subsidiary of Parmigiani.

We also had the opportunity to visit the case manufacture owned by Audemars Piguet. When we were met by our guide, he requested that we not take pictures, as there were cases being produced for other brands. Of course, we respected the request; however, immediately in front of us in the reception room was a poster for A. Lange & Söhne watches. This was just another example of the interdependency of watch brands despite their insistence to the contrary. The concept that watch companies make all the parts that go into their watches is frequently nothing more than marketing hype.

Prior to this visit, I acquired a Royal Oak Offshore Polaris. At the time, Audemars had a sponsorship arrangement with the Alinghi sailing team. AP produced several models with the Alinghi logo, starting with the City of Sails. The Polaris was one such model. It came with a twenty-minute-countdown feature necessary in yacht racing. I wore the watch proudly on the tour. It is always nice to sport a watch built by the sponsor of the attended event. On this tour it was quite fortuitous that I wore it. After acquiring the watch, I asked for a short strap given my small wrist size. Chad, at the Watch Connection, had all sorts of problems obtaining the proper one. With the standard strap, the watch was wearable, but the extra length of the strap was annoying. During the tour, we met with the AP CEO. At lunch, I mentioned to the CEO how I was having trouble getting a short strap. Almost miraculously, the next day, I was presented with a short strap. It helps to have the right connections.

At one point during the tour, we met with the head of design for Audemars. He, again, swore us to secrecy and revealed that the company planned to release an industry first. It was to be a limited edition Royal Oak Offshore with Alinghi branding, but what was novel was that watch would be housed in a case of forged carbon. At the time, it was a revolutionary concept. When I returned from the trip, I was able to make arrangements to obtain one once it was released, although it required the authorized dealer to promise that he, too, would keep the secret until the watch was announced to the public. When it was eventually released, the Team Alinghi, as it was labeled, was much in demand. Since I was early in the queue, I secured one. It was a big watch and wore bigger than its 44 mm case, yet it was incredibly light. It was an interesting match to the Hublot Mag Bang. Two big, bulky watches that did not weigh down the wrist. Two featherweights from different companies.

In time other watches have been produced with forged carbon or carbon fiber cases, but no watch has been built using Hublonium since the Mag Bang. Despite the novelty of the case, the Team Alinghi was still a big watch. Wearing it did not give me pleasure, and even though it was an industry first and a limited watch much in demand, I ultimately sold it because if it does not give joy when it is worn, then what is the point of owning it?

Polaris by Audemars Piguet

When watch collectors get together, in no time, watches are taken off wrists and passed around for others to examine. At one point during the tour, when we were on the bus, I took off my watch at the request of the person sitting next to me. After the typical complementary comments, my neighbor pointed out that one of the screws securing the case back was missing. It was not a small screw, and I cannot imagine how or when it fell out or how I had not noticed that it was missing. Once again, good fortune shined down on me. When I pointed out the problem to our tour guide, he took the watch, and at lunch the watch was returned to me, screw replaced and all others tightened. This was total luck. Had the screw fallen out at any other time, I would have had to send the watch in for servicing, and it could have taken weeks to months for the watch to be returned.

I was not the only one in the group to have a flaw discovered. Others on the tour wore their Audemars Piguet watches. On the bus, another lucky soul passed around his Royal Oak Offshore for all to see. Passed from hand to hand, someone noticed that the **bezel** with the tachymeter was set upside down. The **bezel** was rotated 180 degrees. It was fascinating that the owner, as well others who had inspected the watch, people very familiar with watches, had missed the error. The owner told us that he had just recently purchased the watch, and this was exactly how the watch came from the manufacture. Some of us campaigned loudly for him to leave the watch as is since it could be considered a one-off. There was speculation whether this watch could be considered like the "Inverted Jenny" in stamp collecting. In 1918 the US Postal Service printed a single sheet of twenty-four-cent airmail stamps with the picture of a Curtis JN-4 airplane mistakenly printed upside down. The one sheet was put into circulation before the error was realized, and all other sheets were destroyed. It is one of the most famous errors in the world of stamp collecting. Only one hundred stamps exist, each extremely valuable.

Sadly, I do not know the end of the story. The **bezel** could easily have been rotated the 180 degrees, but I do hope that the owner left it alone just for fun. How often do we use the tachymeter anyway?

When I made plans for my first trip to Switzerland with the Purists, I arranged to add a visit to the Ulysse Nardin Manufacture at the end of my trip. By that time I had several of their watches and was developing a keen interest in the brand. I was in Switzerland and had a day to spare, and it never hurt to ask for a tour, so I did, and they graciously invited me to visit. The Ulysse Nardin Manufacture has two locations, one in Le Locle and the other in La Chaux-de-Fonds. The morning after the Purists tour ended, I took the train from Geneva to La Chaux-de-Fonds, where I was met by Susanne Hurni, the director of marketing. The visit lasted the whole day.

The benefit of touring with a group is that others will often ask questions that you may not think of or know enough to ask. I was the sole guest on this tour, and I will admit to some trepidation. It can be stressful trying to hold up one side of the conversation, feeling you're only acting as if you know something. That said, I was able to hold my own, and Susanne was very forthcoming with information. Toward the end of the day, I was ushered into a conference room, where I met the Ulysse Nardin executive team. Among the staff sitting around the table was Pierre Gygax. Ludwig Oechslin was the dreamer, the one who conceptualized many of the Ulysse Nardin innovations, but it was Pierre, I was told, who made sure that they worked. He also developed the material science that helped to make Ulysse Nardin such a leader in innovation. Soon after our meeting started, in walked Rolf Schnyder. I was stunned that the leadership of Ulysse Nardin should take time out of their day to meet with me, a relative nobody.

It seemed that Rolf and his team were truly interested in what I had to say. During our conversation, they were surprised to learn that they had produced a GMT +/- with a yellow dial. I informed them that, indeed, they produced the one that I owned, one with a big date, but also they had made an earlier version with a small date. I never did find out how they could produce a watch that their design team and leadership had no idea about. We discussed my concerns about quality control. I cited problems that I had encountered with several of my purchases and what I uncovered with several other Ulysse Nardin watches at several retailers. Rolf and the team took this very seriously. We discussed where the gaps might be, whether it was on the company side or if it reflected a problem with the retailers. Rolf insisted that it was incumbent on the retailer to examine each watch received to be sure that it was in working order prior to putting it in the display case.

Subsequent to that meeting, I cannot say exactly when, there seemed to be an improvement in the quality control of the brand's watches. Was it the result of that meeting? I would not be so pretentious as to say so, but I would like to believe that it helped them be more aware of a problem that existed, at least in my experience. Nonetheless, I appreciate that the team did have interest in what someone early in his career of collecting, and certainly no one of note, might have to say about their products. It spoke well of the leadership of the brand at that time.

On another Purists trip, several of us added on a trip to see Paul Gerber in Zurich. It was the first time that I met Paul in person. By that time, I already owned a watch built by him that Michel Schmutz, Paul's representative in the US, had helped me acquire.

Paul's workshop, as is true of many independent watchmakers, was in the converted garage of his house. Entering his workshop, there was a small anteroom that was filled with pictures of his work. Mounted among them on the wall was a tiny clock made by Paul. All the components of the clock, including the movement, were made of wood. It was an excellent example of Paul's skill and inventiveness and his ability to work with miniaturization.

Paul's abilities were previously put to the test when he was asked to work on what was, in 1995, the most complicated watch in the world, a fact that was certified by *Guinness World Records.* The watch was based off a base caliber made by Louis-Elysée Piguet, which was then modified by Franck Muller. Paul was asked to add a flying **tourbillon** and a split-second **chronograph** to the already completed watch. Paul succeeded where many would have failed.

Paul shared a desk with his wife, Ruth, who handled correspondence and the business side of the brand. A small computer was on the desk. Paul spoke about how the computer gave him the ability to rapidly make corrections to a component of a movement when necessary. In so doing, he could then reprogram his simple CNC machine. The result was that he had the ability to rapidly correct a detected problem in a very short time frame, when in the past such corrections might take days if not longer.

It gave me insight into the modern-day creative process as opposed to that faced by watchmakers in the past. Some collectors and historians might be tempted to look askance at the use of modern technology in the design and creation of watches. The concept of a watchmaker designing all the parts of a watch with a pencil and paper and using hand-built tools from yesteryear to create them is romantic but not reality in modern times. On several occasions, watchmakers have said to me that there is little doubt that had Breguet, Mudge, or other historically significant watchmakers of the past had the equipment available today, they would surely be using it. Romance aside, the goal is to produce watches to sell, and whatever technology is available at the time that might expedite the process would certainly be used.

On one of the benches sat a row of MIH watches in the process of assembly. Paul told us of his disagreement with Ludwig regarding the production of the MIH. Ludwig, not a believer of fine finishing of watch movements, proposed that the movement not be finished but rather left in its raw state. Firmly, Paul refused and told Ludwig that he was not going to allow any unfinished watch to leave his workshop. Ultimately, Ludwig relented, and the movement was finished to Paul's satisfaction, even though the watch back is closed.

The Retro Twin created by Paul is another example of his inventiveness. He took a hand-wound Peseux 7001 movement and highly modified it such that it contains two (twin) rotators, thus transforming it into an automatic movement. The watch also features a first-of-its-kind **retrograde** second hand. **Retrograde indicators** for hours and minutes had been done but not for the second hand until Paul built his watch.

The Retro Twin that I own has the added feature of a dynamic **power reserve** indicator. When the watch is wound, the **sub-dial** rotates, and the **power reserve** is read by way of a stationary hand, which then moves while the **sub-dial** is stationary as the **power reserve** runs down over the course of time. It is a small watch at 35.6 mm but a true mechanical marvel. Only twenty Retro Twin Power Reserve watches were produced, and I am proud to have one.

Retrograde Power Reserve by Paul Gerber

Subsequent to that first meeting, Paul and I met on several other occasions. During a different trip to Switzerland, I arranged to meet Michel Schmutz in Zurich, and together we went to visit Paul at his house. After spending some time in Paul's workshop, Paul, with his wife, Ruth, drove the four us to Bern. There we toured the downtown shopping area. We walked into one store that had antique timepieces, watches, and clocks. Paul examined several of the pieces and had a very animated conversation about them with the staff. Unfortunately, the discussion was in German, so I wandered around the store on my own. When the sales staff realized who Paul was, their demeanor changed, and they became very deferential. Paul, a very humble and unassuming person, was treated like a celebrity. I knew that he was a renowned watchmaker within the watch community, but it was remarkable to see how respected he was by the public.

After walking in and out of shops for an hour, we drove into the hills above Bern. There we went to a restaurant in what seemed like an old barn. Lines of tables faced a stage where a group of local musicians were playing what I was told was traditional folk music. Michel joined the band and played the accordion while we ate and had a grand time. Everything was in Swiss German, but it was fun and clearly a local hangout that Michel and Paul visited on a regular basis.

In Bern, there are a number of statues and fountains in the main streets that date back five hundred years. Knowing that I worked with children, as a memento of our time spent together, Paul sent me an 8 x 11 inch photograph of the famous Bern statue the *Kindlifresser*. When I received the picture in the mail, at first I was taken aback. When I realized the intent of the gift, I was very honored to be the recipient.

The *Kindlifresser*

What Happened in Vegas

The next time that I crossed paths with Paul was not in Switzerland but rather in Las Vegas. To celebrate the tenth anniversary of the Purists, the management team arranged a four-day event that brought together Purists from all over the world, representatives of several brands, and independent watchmakers. The event was titled IGOTT 2: International Gathering of the Tribes—number two because there had been a smaller event previously held in Asia.

I am not a fan of Las Vegas. I will spend a ridiculous amount of money on a watch, but I do not enjoy the casinos. For me, gambling is not fun. I do not like to lose, and at the tables it is possible to lose quickly. Regardless of the outcome, at the table there is no story associated with the losing or winning when gambling, unlike those associated with most of my watch purchases. Over the course of those four days, I ended up ten cents ahead: I found a dime on the floor of a casino.

The event was attended by approximately two hundred people. It included presentations by representatives of the brands and independent watchmakers. Attendees included representatives of Audemars Piguet,

Bulgari, and DeWitt (now defunct) and even Chopard's co-CEO Karl-Friedrich Scheufele. Independent watchmakers were also well represented by Peter Speake-Marin, Bart and Tim Grönefeld, Kari Voutilainen, Ludovic Ballouard, Max Büsser, and Paul Gerber. Not only were the formal talks fascinating and illuminating, but the informal social events were great. Whether during a planned event, a meal, or a late night at the bar, collectors and watchmakers had the opportunity to mingle. I was able to renew friendships with people I met during tours or people I only knew via the website. It was great to be able to put faces to names. Meeting watchmakers at such an event, examining watches with them and socializing in a bar, often with some alcohol-assisted lubrication, provided me with invaluable education as well as a window into their personalities.

As with any artistic endeavor, a watchmaker's product is in part a reflection of the creator's persona. The memories of those interactions have become part of the story for several of my acquisitions. It was at IGOTT that I spent more time with Paul. Michel was there as well, and he served as Paul's translator when it was Paul's turn to speak.

When he came to Las Vegas, one of Paul's desires was to visit the desert. It seems that many watchmakers from Europe have a special interest in the desert when they come to Southern California as well. One day Paul, Ruth, and Michel left the event and drove to the desert to visit a ghost town. On their return, Paul presented me with a sheriff's badge that he purchased. I wore the badge proudly for the rest of the event and have treasured it ever since.

Abroad Again

In Switzerland with the Purists for another tour, the group's first-night dinner occurred in the Old Town section of Geneva. About twenty of us were seated around the table. I sat next to an American ex-pat living in Switzerland, Don Corson, who was a moderator of the Independent Watch Forum on the Purists website and was very active in the watch community. An engineer by education and profession, Don proclaimed two passions: music and watches. As the evening progressed, Don told me more about his interest in watches. He mentioned he'd read George Daniels's book, *Watchmaking,* three times and decided that he wanted to build a watch. Since he knew a number of independent watchmakers, he was able to spend time with several of them in their ateliers to gain needed technical knowledge, use their equipment, and get advice regarding the movement and finishing. His first and second attempts were not successful. On the third attempt, he was able to build a watch that worked, and he presented it to his wife. He then went on to build his fourth watch, something completely different from the others, which he named the Dresdner 3. The idea for the name came from a pocket watch Don saw in a museum in Dresden.

At the dinner he was wearing the watch. As any watch collector would do, I asked to see the watch and, of course, put it on. It was unique in its styling. He said that it was not completely finished and he felt that the watch still needed some last touches before he could be happy with it and consider it completed and ready to sell. We spent the dinner talking about how he made the watch and the challenges that he faced during the process. His story seemed familiar to me.

In the late 1990s, I wrote a novel. It was a murder and spy novel, the kind of story that I like to read. I never thought of myself as a writer, as it always was a struggle for me to do any type of creative writing. The fact that I was able to write a book of five hundred twenty-five pages that contained a beginning, middle, and end and have it make sense (according to my wife) was an incredible accomplishment that, to this day, I am very proud of. After doing my best to edit the book, I sent copies to several people with the hope of getting it published. Ultimately, I realized that to get it published, I was going to have to devote time to it. I feared that it would turn into work, and I already had a job. I wrote the book for fun, and that I achieved. I left it in my computer, and it sits there today.

As I inspected the Dresdner 3, it was clear to me that the movement was not built from a preexisting base movement but rather constructed from the ground up. The dial was unique, something I had not seen before. I was attracted to the watch not only because it was so unique but also because of what the watch represented to me on a personal level. To me, it was analogous to my experience writing my book. It was a project taken on by Don for the satisfaction of seeing it through to a successful conclusion without concern about its final disposition. That was how I approached writing my book. I decided that I wanted the watch for its uniqueness but also to support Don's passion to build interesting watches. If I could not get support for writing my book, I could at least support Don. I tentatively explored the possibility of purchasing the watch, to which he was very receptive. I was surprised by how easy it was for Don to agree to part with his creation. Don explained that for him it was the creative process that he enjoyed. He did not have any emotional connection to the watch. *Sell it and move on to the next project* was his thought process. In fact, he was already thinking about his next watch, a uniquely presented **tourbillon**.

By the end of dinner, we agreed that I would purchase the watch. However, Don did not give it to me and was not sure when it would be ready for sale. Over the next few months, we had further discussions to clarify the design of the case and the **crown**. We decided that the case should be made from white gold and that the **crown** should have a design element similar to that of the second hand. Don pointed out that on the back of the movement's base plate, he tried to add a **power reserve** indicator but could not make it fit. The indicator was too tall for the allotted space. As a result, there was a circular cutout in the back of the base plate. Don offered to cover the cutout. I said absolutely not. I wanted it visible because, for me, it showed that the watch was hand done. Clearly it was not perfect, yet its idiosyncrasies made the piece even more special to me.

When it came time for Don to deliver the watch, the question was how. Sending a watch through any international delivery service carries with it a certain level of risk. Since Don was not a jeweler or a watch company, he did not carry any insurance policy that would cover the transportation of the watch. We agreed that hand delivery would be best. By chance, he was going to be in New York City visiting his son at the same time that I was going to be at a family event in Washington, DC. We agreed to meet at a midpoint, Philadelphia. I picked a restaurant for our meetup.

Dresdner 3 front and reverse by Don Corson

Early in the morning on the appointed day, I set out, accompanied by one of my sons. The three of us arrived at the restaurant almost at the same time. It was an Italian restaurant with the decor straight out of the '70s, but the food was excellent. It so happened that we were the only ones in the restaurant at the time. We were able to talk freely, and when Don presented the watch to me, my son memorialized the moment photographically. The drive back to DC was fun. My son and I chatted nonstop as I drove, but I do admit to being distracted periodically by the watch on my wrist.

When I received the Dresdener 3, contained within the presentation box was a book filled with photographs that documented the step-by-step production of the watch. The pictures, as it turned out, were also on Don's website, but it was special to have this book memorialize the complete creative process, start to finish. Since then, I have recommended to a number of watchmakers that they consider doing something similar. For a collector, a pictorial record of the creation of their watch adds another dimension of personalization. Unfortunately, I have not seen something similar from any other watchmaker.

###

After the completion of one of the Purists trips, I traveled to La Chaux-de-Fonds with several others from the tour to visit the Musée International d'Horologie. The visit was a sheer delight. The museum is dedicated to all aspects of timekeeping, from the science of time to the construction of clocks and watches to the exhibit of special or historically significant timepieces. Included in their permanent display is the Ulysse Nardin Trilogy of Time, the sight of which set my heart aflutter. The Victorian clock that was being restored from the funds raised by the sale of MIH watches was also on display. It was nice to see what I was supporting.

I have met many people in the watch industry, including some of the most significant watchmakers of modern time. One person that I have yet to meet is Ludwig Oechslin. It would be fair to say that it would be special to spend time with such a brilliant person, the one responsible for the Trilogy and other horological innovations. At the time of our visit to the MIH, Ludwig was serving as director of the museum. When we arrived at the museum, I tried to convince my friends to ask the staff if Ludwig was on site and if we could meet him. The others balked at my suggestion, and we proceeded to the exhibits. As we were leaving, I asked one of the staff if Ludwig was on the premises. She told me that he had been there but had just left for the day. To say the least, it was a disappointment for us all.

Chapter 5:
Fanboy

I do not buy watches for investment purposes. I acquire those that interest me. What interests me might be a technological innovation, historical significance, classical lines, or sheer beauty. The bottom line is that the watch must mean something to me. If the impetus for collecting watches was financial, then I have not spent my money wisely. But fortunately, I have purchased wisely because my acquisitions have given me joy, and that is priceless.

After purchasing the Freak, I started to learn more about Ulysse Nardin. When I met Rolf, experienced his enthusiasm, and learned about his association with Ludwig Oechslin, I realized that it was his intent to lead the brand to the forefront of horological innovation. I rapidly became a fan and supporter of the brand.

The GMT +/-

Saturdays were not complete if I did not stop by the Watch Connection and spend time looking at their inventory and talking watches with Chad. In a showcase, perched on its own stand, sat a watch that kept drawing my attention. It was cased in rose gold with a copper-colored dial. I became enamored with the GMT +/- Perpetual. As it turns out, it was another one of Ludwig's creations, a **perpetual calendar** that was very user-friendly. When setting the date in most watches, the user is required to advance the date forward until the correct date is displayed. If the proper number is passed, then the user must cycle through all the numbers again and stop at the right number. With this watch, the date can be set forward or backward by way of the **crown**. This would seem to be merely a convenience factor; however, in most **perpetual calendars**, if the user passes the correct date when setting the date, the watch needs to be "put to sleep" by pulling out the **crown** to stop the watch until the displayed date matches the calendar. The only other way to reset the errant date would be to send the watch to the service center, an absolute inconvenience for a simple problem that Ludwig solved.

This ability to set the date forward or backward, more significantly, will come into play in the year 2100. Due to the vagaries of the earth's orbit around the sun, the year 2100 will not be a leap year. Virtually all **perpetual calendar** watches are built to know the leap year correction, but they do not know of this exception to the rule and will have to be sent back to the manufacture to have the date reset, otherwise the date **indicators** will be off by a day. The ability to set this watch forward or backward eliminates this problem, and I will be happily wearing it as others struggle with their **perpetual calendar** watches (of course I will still be walking the planet—there are watches that I must check to be sure that they fulfill their promises in the future).

The GMT function included as part of this watch is simple to use by pressing one of the **pushers** on either side of the case to move the hour hand forward or backward. A separate indicator reads the hour at home in a twenty-four-hour scale to indicate whether it is day or night at home. Like other watches produced by Ulysse Nardin that have the same GMT function, the date corresponds to the time zone that the traveler is in and not at home. Another small but important feature. Unlike most **perpetual calendars**, it does not have a moon phase, but it displays the day of the week, a very useful and, at times necessary, piece of information. When traveling, it is easy to lose track of the day of the week, which is often more important than knowing the date or the moon phase. Not having a moon phase indicator is not a worry at all. I cannot remember ever panicking because I did not know the phase of the moon.

I decided to purchase the watch but had to pay for it in installments over the course of several months, during which time I visited "the baby" whenever I stopped at the Watch Connection. The day that I finally got to bring it home was exciting. After making the final payment, I strapped the watch to my wrist and proudly wore it out of the store. Shortly after getting home, I realized that the watch was not telling the correct time. It was reading several minutes ahead of the actual time. It was not the first time that I'd set a watch incorrectly, so I reset the watch and thought nothing more about the error. However, within the hour, I realized that the watch was again not reading the correct time. The watch was racing, gaining about eight minutes within the span of an hour. On the dial of the watch is inscribed *chronometer*, which means that it is certified to function within certain strict parameters with regards to how many seconds it will gain or lose over the course of a twenty-four hour period. Gaining eight minutes per hour is way out of compliance, to say the least.

GMT +/- Perpetual by Ulysse Nardin

That same day I returned to the Watch Connection and handed the watch to them. I told them I wished my son ran track meets as fast as the watch was running. Having already had experiences with the Freak, I figured that the watch needed to be returned to Ulysse Nardin, and I assumed it would take a fair amount of time for it to be repaired. In fact, the watch was returned in proper working order within two weeks and has been working fine ever since.

When one gets to a certain age, it becomes necessary to periodically undergo certain screening tests. A colonoscopy is done to screen for early signs of colon cancer. My time had come, and it was necessary to undergo the procedure. A procedure of that nature is not a fun experience, but it is made tolerable by the use of anesthesia. Fast asleep, I underwent the procedure without an issue. Upon awakening, the after-effects of the sedation were very pleasant. I found myself relaxed and felt uninhibited; this sensation lasted for several hours after I was discharged from the procedure center.

I do not like to shop. Cruising around a shopping mall is not my idea of fun. I do not enjoy the crowds or the process of shopping—that is, unless I am looking at watches. After my first colonoscopy, I asked my wife to take me to a local shopping mall, and we spent several hours going in and out of every men's store, floating from one store to the next. My wife had to beg me to take a break so that she could sit down for a few moments and get a soda. Ultimately, I bought a sweater that became known as my Versed (the name of one of the medicines used for sedation during the colonoscopy) sweater.

Several years later, after my next colonoscopy, I was again floating on a cloud of medication-induced uninhibited relaxation. This time, my wife guided me away from the shopping mall but acceded to my request to go to the Watch Connection. In the haze of post-sedation bliss, I wound up buying a Ulysse Nardin GMT +/- with a yellow dial in a steel case, the one that the leadership team at Ulysse Nardin did not remember they made. I debated between the Ulysse Nardin and a Chronoswiss Timemaster. The Ulysse Nardin prevailed. It was a spur-of-the-moment purchase that has given me years of service and fun. Once again, the GMT +/- feature, the same as in the what is in the Perpetual GMT +/- that I owned, was a Ludwig innovation. Similarly, the hour hand can be changed forward or backward as time zones are traversed by way of the **pushers**. The time at home is shown in a window on the dial by the nine o'clock position. It reads the time on a twenty-four-hour scale so that the traveler always knows if it is day or night at home, a very useful piece of information, especially if one wants to call home and not wake up the recipient. In my opinion, it was and still is the most user-friendly **GMT watch** available in the market.

The yellow dial is certainly not subtle and not common. I have only seen one other GMT +/- with a yellow dial and big date. It was on display in a store window in Rome near the Spanish Steps.

Because of the yellow dial, the GMT +/- watch has been christened by my family as the "goofy watch." It has become my constant travel companion, especially when I am going to be crossing time zones. Even with the yellow dial, it is not a watch that I ever thought would attract much attention, something I try to avoid whenever possible. When I travel, I might pack another watch to wear on nicer occasions, but when I am in transit, it is usually the goofy watch that is on my wrist. Because it is in a steel case and on a steel bracelet, I am less worried about accidental trauma. It has proven to be a robust watch, able to withstand the rigors of travel.

This watch has traveled with me to disparate places in the world. I have taken it across the United States and to Central and South America, Europe, Asia, and Africa. On a trip to Uganda, my son and I had our picture taken, me with the goofy watch and him with his IWC Mark XV while on safari. We submitted the photo to *WatchTime*, and it was published in the "FaceTime Gallery" section. On that trip, the watch and I, along with my family, had the experience of a lifetime. We visited the Kidepo Valley National Park in the northeastern corner of Uganda next to South Sudan. The adventure was highlighted when we met an alcoholic elephant and had a lion roaring under the window of our cabin one night. On the flight back from the park to Kampala in a six-seater plane, the pilot asked us if we wanted to touch a cloud. We, of course, said yes. He reached behind and opened the window and we proceeded to stick our hands out the window as he flew through a cloud. Asked if we wanted to do it again, we again said yes, and we did it again. With the Ulysse Nardin GMT+/- yellow dial watch on my wrist, I touched a cloud. The cloud was cold and wet, but more importantly, it was a very magical moment that I have never forgotten. We look at clouds every day. We fantasize about them and try to imagine what it might be like to touch or even stand on a cloud. We touched a cloud, so we know.

This watch continues to be a traveling companion without any concern about security, except on one trip. My son spent a semester abroad in Rio de Janeiro. Because of his admonitions regarding personal and property safety and security, we were very thoughtful about what valuables we brought with us. That was the first and only trip of any kind where I did not bring any of my watches. Before leaving for Rio, I bought a cheap quartz watch specifically for the trip. The watch told the time but did not give me any joy when I put it on. In fact, the watch barely made it through the two-week trip. At some point during the second week, the strap broke, and the watch finished the trip in my pocket.

During my travels, I only once had a watch I was wearing commented upon by a random person. We were traveling to Venice, Italy. I was, of course, wearing the goofy watch, which was in full view since I was wearing a t-shirt. Leaving the train station, we went to get a water taxi. A taxi driver, leaning against a railing at the taxi stand, pointed to my watch and yelled, "Ulysse Nardin GMT." A water taxi driver who clearly knew watches! And this one in particular. What were the chances.

GMT +/- by Ulysse Nardin

Years later, I was discussing with one of my sons what might happen to my collection should anything happen to me. It is a topic one does not like to consider but needs to be given serious thought nonetheless at some point in time. He was very definitive. He did not have an interest in the majority of my watches but did want it known that he wanted the goofy watch. When asked why, of all the watches I own, it would be the one he wanted, he said because that was the watch I always wore when we traveled, and he associated it with wonderful memories of those trips. So very sweet.

Rolf

Ulysse Nardin has been in continuous operation since 1846. The company specialized in the production of marine **chronometers**. By the 1980s, the company had only two employees. In 1983, the company was purchased by Rolf Schnyder. Soon after acquiring the company, Rolf hired Ludwig Oechslin, a true Renaissance man. Ludwig studied archeology, theoretical physics, and astronomy and earned a PhD in philosophy while studying to become a watchmaker. Together Rolf and Ludwig conceived, designed, and built some of the most innovative watches in modern times. It was their vision that ultimately led to the production of the Freak.

I had the pleasure of meeting Rolf on several occasions. The first time was when I visited the company in Switzerland. The next time was when he came to Los Angeles to introduce Ulysse Nardin's Sonata, a watch that featured an alarm that could be set to ring at any time within a twenty-four hour period or after a countdown of up to twenty-four hours. The Sonata also had their patented GMT function. As an added innovation, the setting for the alarm adjusted when changing time zones. This way the traveler would not have to reset the alarm when changing time zones and would not miss a meeting or an event. As is true with other Ulysse Nardin models, the large date could be moved forward or backward. Even more remarkable was that the chime of the alarm was created by the striking of a hammer on a gong. The gong was the same as that used for a **minute repeater**. The alarm was guaranteed to ring for a minimum of sixty seconds in a beautiful sonorous tone. The Sonata was and remains a remarkable feat of engineering. The complexity of its design and function is illustrated by the fact that the movement has 105 **jewels**, more than twice what is found in a typical movement, meaning there are that many contact points that need to be accounted for during its construction. Once again, I was allowed to examine the watch that had been on the wrist of the CEO.

The Sonata was produced in several versions. When I ordered mine, I wanted the version Rolf was wearing: gray dial and rose gold case. The original Sonata I ordered came with a closed back, and the alarm was somewhat muffled. Not long after the release of that Sonata, Ulysse Nardin created an updated version. In the new version, the Sonata Cathedral, there was a display back with a sapphire crystal, and the sound of the alarm was substantially louder. Fortunately, Ulysse Nardin allowed me to exchange the first edition for the Cathedral model, and I have been very happy with the piece ever since. In my opinion, it is a perfect travel watch and the most versatile alarm watch on the market. The alarm is beautifully melodious and will wake me from a deep sleep.

Sonata by Ulysse Nardin

By happenstance, the Sonata I received was number 56. It was a number that carried some degree of significance for me. When my older son was in elementary school and learning multiplication, he had what seemed to be a mental block about what seven times eight equaled. He could not remember 56. We went around and around about what seven times eight equaled. It has remained a joke between the two of us to this day. When I got the watch with its number, I told my son that it would be his watch because of the 56. His response was a patented roll of the eyes. Unfortunately, when my Sonata was upgraded, I lost out on that case number and had to settle for number 37, another number that is of particular interest to me. It is a prime number I like even though it does not carry the same significance as does 56.

On a different visit, Rolf came to California with the idea of combining business with pleasure. Another get-together was organized with Rolf, to be followed by a visit to retailers in the region the following day. He came with his family and intended to take a drive up the California coast for a brief vacation. I attended the dinner event and then met him the next day at the Watch Connection. That was the first time that I faced failure in my watch-collecting journey. According to what Rolf told me, when the family was planning their trip, Ludwig asked to come along. He volunteered to be the family's chauffeur, offering to drive the RV they planned to rent. The family did not accept Ludwig's offer despite his protestations.

Despite the rejection, when Rolf was preparing to leave for the US, Ludwig handed him a watch that he'd just assembled, requesting that it be worn and field tested. In a beat-up bronze case with an unremarkable dial and hands, it was strapped to the wrist by way of a piece of fraying cloth. Despite its appearance, the watch was another revolutionary creation by Ludwig. The watch represented a first of its kind. It was the first watch ever constructed to feature an **annual calendar** function with a linear display. Indications of the day, month, and date were horizontally laid out at the three o'clock position on the dial. Ludwig had adapted a standard ETA movement to achieve the feat.

Rolf wore the watch dutifully. Seeing it, I recognized that what Rolf was wearing was something new and revolutionary. I tried to convince him to sell it to me. After all, it was not attractive, and who would ever wear that piece? No go. Maybe I got a smile from Rolf, but there was no way he would part with the watch. Even after Rolf left, I tried working through the brand representative, but to no avail, even with a bit of a whine added to my plea. My philosophy is you cannot get arrested for asking. Although I have failed to wrestle a watch off the wrist of a CEO or a brand president at times, on other occasions I have succeeded. No doubt I will keep trying to pry special watches off the wrists of brand executives when the opportunities arise. As long as I plead with respect, appropriate politeness, and a smile, I might be rebuffed, but at least it is seen as good fun. To date I do not think that I have damaged any relationships by my requests.

Ludwig

Ludwig demonstrated his ingenuity by creating that movement, but Ulysse Nardin did not produce a watch with that **complication**. Instead, Ludwig used that concept to create the first MIH watch. By adding nine parts to a very commonly used Valjoux 7750 movement, Ludwig was able to turn the standard **chronograph** movement into a unique **chronograph** with a **monopusher**. He moved the minute counter to the underside of the movement and added an **annual calendar** function with the linear display to the front. The day of the week, month, and date display was the same as was present in the watch that I tried to get from Rolf. It all started with that thrown-together watch in the beaten-up brass case worn on a threadbare cloth strap.

When Ludwig became director of the Musée International d'Horlogerie (the MIH) in La Chaux-de-Fonds he used his innovation to create a watch called the MIH watch. As mentioned earlier, the proceeds from the sale of the watch were targeted to fund restoration projects at the museum. Working with Ludwig were the designer Christian Gafner and Beat Weinmann of Embassy, who handled the marketing. The watch was produced by Paul Gerber in his Zurich atelier, a.k.a. his home. It had to be ordered through Embassy or purchased directly by visiting the museum. The waiting list was long, and successful fulfillment of an order was not assured. Fortunately, another friend helped me.

Knowing that Paul Gerber was producing the MIH watch, I reached out to Michel Schmutz to help me obtain the elusive watch. With his assistance, I was able to obtain an allocation. Eventually, the watch arrived wrapped, as advertised, not in a presentation box but rather in a recent copy of the Swiss newspaper *Neue Zurcher Zeitung*.

The MIH

In the world of horology, it is said that the two **complications** that demonstrate the skill of a watchmaker are the **tourbillon** and the **minute repeater**. Ulysse Nardin produces watches that chime and have automata that move in synchrony with the chiming. One such watch is the Hourstriker. It chimes the number of the hour on the hour and chimes once on the half-hour. It can chime automatically (en passant) or on demand. When it chimes, the figure crafted on the dial "strikes" the bell. The figure and bell are in homage to the bell strikers on the campanile in St. Mark's Square in Venice. A watchmaker I know who assembles such complicated **minute repeaters** with automata for Ulysse Nardin told me he has been asked on a number of occasions whether the chiming in these watches comes from the automata "striking" an object, a bell, or an anvil (in a model called the Forgerons). Really?

As a consideration for the tribulations I experienced with the Freak, I was offered an Hourstriker at a very attractive price. It was an opportunity of a lifetime, and I jumped at the chance. It is a beautiful piece cased in rose gold with rose gold automata and numerals. The dial is mother-of-pearl. Not sure of what the future had in store for me (this was before the release of the Sonata), I saw it as potentially my one chance to obtain a chiming watch. The Sonata and repeaters are constructed and function differently from the Sonata event, though both utilize the same type of gong.

Hourstriker by Ulysse Nardin

Lessons Learned

Besides being a beautiful watch and a pleasure to wear, the Hourstriker taught me a valuable lesson about the watch industry and watch collectors. Many watch collectors prefer watches with in-house movements. There are watch movements built for the industry by companies that specialize in building movements, and these **ebauches** (the basic movement) can be found in a number of watch models from different companies. In-house movements are those built by the watchmaker or watch company supposedly from the ground up, though even that is not always the case.

Many watch collectors believe that a watch with an in-house

movement is superior to and more valuable than one with an off-the-shelf movement. Knowing this, many watch companies often advertise their movements with their own designations, implying that the movement is unique to them, when, in fact, the movement is based on a commercially available one with minimal, if any, modifications. Even some of the most prominent and well-known brands have employed movements developed by outside entities, making the advertisement "we make every part" of dubious validity. That said, there are an ever-increasing number of truly in-house movements being brought to the market by the brands and independent watchmakers.

The movement of the Hourstriker is a combination of an ETA 2892 movement (a very common and readily available movement built by the movement specialty company ETA) and a module built by Ulysse Nardin for the striking and the automata function. I asked Rolf Schnyder why the ETA 2982 caliber was used to run the Hourstriker. He told me that they tried different movements but found they did not have the necessary power generation and reliability of the ETA 2982. I asked about the general perception that a watch with an ETA off-the-shelf movement was somehow of lesser significance. His response was simple and clear: "Get over it!"

It is rare that a watch company makes all the components for a watch. There are a few brands that are vertically integrated such that all components required to build a watch come from their subsidiaries. Most brands, however, do not have the capability to manufacture every component and turn to suppliers for specific parts such as **mainsprings**, **jewels**, sapphire crystals, and hair springs. I saw evidence of that during my visits to Switzerland. I saw cases being made by an Audemars Piguet-owned company for another brand. On a tour of the Zenith Manufacture, we were shown how they made dials. When we watched the stamping machinery, there, right in front of us, were Panerai dials being made. Some independent watchmakers supplement their income by providing services to or making specific components for major companies. When we toured his workshop, Romain Gauthier showed us machines busily producing specialized components for several companies, but he would not tell us for whom. Donzé Cadrans, a highly respected enamel dial maker owned by Ulysse Nardin, is well known to make dials for quite a few other brands.

Equally, not every watch is assembled under the roof of the Manufacture, despite claims to the contrary. Renaud & Papi is a perfect example. On my visit to Renaud & Papi, on the poster listing all the watches they had produced was the Ulysse Nardin Hourstriker. In fact, I was shown the bench where my watch had been constructed. I am told that more recently, Ulysse Nardin has brought the production of the Hourstriker under their roof.

The dependency of watch companies large and small on the expertise of outside services is an almost universal fact with few exceptions.

Ahmad

For a number of years, my wife and I did trail-running with a group known as the Hash House Harriers. It consisted of a group of crazies who referred to themselves as a drinking club with a running problem. The Hash House Harriers is an international entity with Hashes (chapters) in most major cities around the world. Typically, the trails were four to six miles in length and the runners pre-lubricated with beer. My local Hash ran on Saturdays, even though in my area there were hashes (runs) most days of the week. Saturday was also the day that I would visit the Watch Connection and possibly other watch establishments. It was not uncommon that after the run, I would go straight to the watch stores sweaty, dusty, dirty, and, at times, bloodied to talk about or try on fine watches.

When I ran the trail, I typically wore a Bell & Ross Military. Its ceramic case is virtually indestructible and the dial easy to read, especially when I was tired and my glasses were dirty and sweat stained. Because of its Velcro strap, I was not concerned about dirt or water damage. Although I have not done trail runs over the last several years, I still use the watch when I anticipate traveling along rough terrain or unusual activity that might otherwise jeopardize a watch.

Bell & Ross Military

On one such Saturday, I stopped by the Watch Connection immediately after a run. I was suitably attired with a sweat-stained ball cap, sweaty t-shirt, dirty shorts, scraped legs, and dusty sneakers. At the same time, the sales representative for Ulysse Nardin, Ahmad, was paying a visit to the store. It was my first time to meet Ahmad face to face, although he knew about me from Chad, as I had already purchased several Ulysse Nardin watches. Ahmad and I connected immediately. Besides being a brand representative, he has an interest in watches that long predates his employment in the watch business. We often speak frankly and honestly about various watch brands and their products. He has since left Ulysse Nardin to become US brand president for Breguet, and we remain good friends to this day. Although it has been years since we first met, he still likes to relate the story of our first meeting and the way I presented myself.

Connecting with Ahmad gave me access to some amazing products from the brand. Ulysse Nardin numbers the cases of each different series of their watches whether they are limited editions or not. Like the situation with the Duomètre where my number was 94, with Ulysse Nardin I became number 6 for no particular reason.

As time passed and additional watches were released, my appreciation for the technical prowess of Ulysse Nardin continued to grow. When the Basel Watch Fair was still in operation, it was the highlight of the year for most collectors. Before the fair opened, information regarding new releases was a closely guarded secret. Strict embargoes were employed by the companies. Even though the information was not to be released, I would ask Ahmad for a hint of what was to come. Sometimes he would divulge some small tidbit of information about a new product, but only in the vaguest of terms. We agreed that if he thought there was a piece that fit my collection, he would automatically reserve the number 6 for me, pending my approval, of course.

I obtained several watches by this method. One was a musical watch called the Stranger. It is a watch that functions much like a music box, with pins on a rotating disc that strike mounted tines, all visible under the sapphire crystal. When activated on demand or, if selected, on the hour, the disc spins, and the pins hit the tines to ring out the tune "Strangers in the Night," hence the name. It functions like the Hourstriker, but the movements, I was told, are completely different. The Stranger is not a modified ETA movement but rather an in-house one. There have been very few wristwatches created that contain a functional music box. Rarer still, is it possible to see the turning disc that holds the pins as the music plays.

An additional interesting feature was introduced in this watch: the owner does not have to pull out the **crown** to set the time or the date. Rather, when the **crown** is pushed its function changes as indicated by the "T, D, W" on the indicator at the four o'clock position. The **crown** can be used for winding or setting of time or date. I was told that this feature was developed by Ulysse Nardin at the request of Rolf Schnyder because his wife did not want to have to pull out the **crown** to set her watch, something that risked damaging her nails. The Stranger was the first Ulysse Nardin watch to include this feature, although it was incorporated into other models subsequently, especially some women's models. The concept is also available in watches from several other brands. I do not know who was first to introduce this type of winding mechanism, although I'm sure every company will say they were first.

Ahmad was correct when he told me about the Stranger. I did want that watch and had him proceed with my order. When the watch, number 6, came to the store, I needed several months in order to complete payment for it. Of course, when I went to the store to make a payment, I exercised my visitation privileges. On each visit, I dutifully wound it and activated the music either by pushing the appropriate **pusher** or advancing the minute hand past the hour. It was a thrill to see the turning wheel and hear "Strangers in the Night."

Stranger by Ulysse Nardin

On the day I made the final payment, to say the least, I was excited. My credit card was swiped and the presentation box packed up and made ready to go. I set the correct time and strapped the watch on my wrist. I then started to chat with Chad about it and other related topics. Fifteen minutes passed, and I noticed that the watch was reading five minutes slow. I figured that I had made a mistake when I originally set the watch, once again not the first time this has happened. I quietly set the watch to the correct time, made sure that it was properly wound, and then put it back on my wrist while I continued to talk with Chad. Another fifteen minutes elapsed, and again the watch was slow by five minutes. I knew that I did not make a mistake this time. Now concerned, I showed the watch to Chad and told him of my observation. Together we reset the watch and waited. In time we confirmed that the watch was indeed not running correctly. We agreed that there was no way I should accept it in its current state. The presentation box was removed from the shopping bag, the watch returned to Chad's keeping, and the credit card transaction canceled. Chad immediately called Ahmad to relay the sad news. He was appropriately upset and promised that the watch would receive immediate attention once it was shipped back to Ulysse Nardin. Every time that I visited the watch, I was sure to check the music feature but never thought to check how it kept time.

Typically, when a watch is sent back to the Manufacture for repair or servicing, it can take, at a minimum, several months to be returned. The Stranger was returned to me in a matter of several weeks in perfect working order. About a year later, my wife and I visited the Ulysse Nardin Manufacture. When we visited the haute horology department, the section responsible for building the most complex watches, I mentioned my challenges with my Stranger. In most manufactures, complex watches are assembled by a single watchmaker from start to finish. The watchmakers tend to remember the pieces that they build. I am told that in the case of musical or chiming watches, the sound produced by each watch is distinctive to the particular watchmaker. In the Ulysse Nardin haute horology department, the watchmaker we were talking with immediately remembered my watch and its problem with timekeeping. He instantaneously blushed, clearly very embarrassed. As it turned out he was not the one who built my Stranger. That person had already left for the day. Nonetheless, everyone in the department took ownership of the problem. I tried my best to reassure them that I knew that things happened and that now I was very happy with the watch. I assured them that it was functioning perfectly, which it still is.

Two years later, Ahmad told me that he'd again reserved a watch for me, number 6 of course, but he said nothing else about what the watch was. From the beginning of my interest in Ulysse Nardin, I was captivated by Ludwig Oechslin's creation the Trilogy. As the name suggests, it consists of three watches, each created to display different astronomical indications. They were so complex that they are registered with *Guinness World Records* and are on display at the Musée International d'Horlogerie in La Chaux-de-Fonds. The Trilogy was my grail. However, I was not sure if I would ever be able to acquire the Trilogy.

Meanwhile, the watch that Ahmad reserved for me was called the Moonstruck. The Moonstruck was another watch with astronomical indications conceived by Ludwig. It showed the moon phase, date, position of the sun and moon, and timing of the tides. It is also a travel watch since the hour can be changed by way of **pushers** like other Ulysse Nardin watches. It does not have a home time display but does display the Greenwich Mean Time.

The watch industry is very secretive in many ways. They certainly do not release any information about projects in the pipeline. When I saw the Moonstruck, I had no way of knowing what was planned for the future but felt that this was my opportunity to build my Trilogy set based on the assumption that other astronomically related watches would be forthcoming eventually. It is a big watch at 46 mm in diameter. Some watches are built big for style or effect, but the Moonstruck is so big because of the requirements of the movement and the associated **complications**. Even though it is a substantial watch and I have a thin wrist, I am able to wear it comfortably. Ahmad was correct in his assumption, and I did bring it home. Besides, I am still a Ludwig fan (or is it a man crush?).

When I studied the Moonstruck, I realized that the piece had another incredible feature. There are many watches on the market that have a moon phase indicator, a **complication** of somewhat questionable utility. When someone like me has tendencies toward a mild obsessive-compulsive personality, having a moon phase indicator can be quite challenging. If the watch runs out of power, it often takes some time and patience to set the moon to its correct position. Watches with moon phase displays can be correct for a variable amount of time. Some watch companies advertise that their moon phase indicator will not need adjustment for twenty-eight years. In other words, if kept in continuous operation, the moon phase indicated will be in incorrect by one day every twenty-eight years. Other, more accurate moon phase displays claim an accuracy of one hundred twenty years. Due to the brilliance of Ludwig, the Moonstruck's moon phase display is said to be accurate for more than one thousand years. I have decided that it is my duty to the world to be sure that Ludwig's calculations are correct. Therefore, I believe that it is the Moonstruck that will keep me alive for a millennium. That way I can ensure the accuracy of the moon indicator as claimed by Ulysse Nardin. While monitoring the moon phase for accuracy, the watch will also keep me informed as to the status of the tides, useful, I am sure, because I live near the ocean.

Moonstruck by Ulysse Nardin

With the approval of Patrik Hoffmann, the CEO of Ulysse Nardin at the time, Ahmad and I had a "boys' weekend" in New York City. Our stated purpose in going was to attend the finals of the US Open that pitted Rafael Nadal (wearing his Richard Mille on his nondominant hand) against Novak Djokovic. During the adventure, we spent almost no time talking about watches, except for a detour into the Audemars Piguet Boutique in Manhattan, at Ahmad's suggestion. I did not kid myself: the trip had everything to do with watches. It was about maintaining our relationship and a thank you for my support of the brand. Boys being boys, on our first evening in the city, we headed for a late-night Italian dinner. We found a nearby restaurant where we were served by a young woman who made excellent recommendations even though she was Romanian and had only been working at the restaurant for one day. Of course we flirted. What else should two guys on the town do? She took it as it was intended, all for fun, and a great time was had by all.

Besides the tennis match, it was a highly educational trip. Ahmad taught me about the benefits of a finely constructed pair of shoes, purchased for an ungodly sum of money, and about an app called Uber. The finals themselves were incredible. The match was long and exciting. It was amazing to watch the two athletes compete for four grueling hours. Amazingly, at the conclusion of the match, when interviewed, the players seemed to be fully recovered, as if they'd just finished a walk in the park.

The Tourbillon

The **tourbillon** was created by Abraham-Louis Breguet to defeat the negative effects of gravity on the oscillating **escapement** in pocket watches. A pocket watch is typically stored in a vertical orientation. As the **escapement** of the pocket watch vibrates back and forth, gravity causes the gradual deterioration in the **amplitude** of the swing of the **escape wheel**. This change in **amplitude** affects the accuracy of timekeeping. The **tourbillon** has a cage within which the **escapement** is located. The **tourbillon** rotates the **escapement** 360 degrees once every minute, in most cases. Because the **escapement** is rotating continuously, the deleterious effects of gravity are abated, and timekeeping is improved. Breguet created the **tourbillon** in 1795 and patented it in 1801. From that time until 1945, very few **tourbillons** were built—an estimated six hundred to nine hundred in total. Since the early 1990s, there has been a proliferation in the number of **tourbillons** produced. The ability to build a **tourbillon** is still considered a test of a watchmaker's skill, but the question is whether it has a functional value in a wristwatch. When the watch is worn on the wrist, it is not kept in a single orientation. The effects of gravity are much less of a negative factor on the **amplitude** of the **escapement** swing, thus making the need for a rotating **escapement** of questionable benefit.

Accuracy of timekeeping has always been the goal of most of the innovations in watchmaking. The **tourbillon** improved the accuracy of the pocket watch. A single-axis **tourbillon**, one that rotates 360 degrees per minute in a single plane, is of minimal value in a wristwatch. However, since the creation of double- and triple-axis **tourbillons,** there have been some improvements, at least theoretically, in the accuracy of timekeeping of a wristwatch. Arguably, modern-day technology and material science have contributed more to the accuracy of the present-day watch than has the **tourbillon**. That said, the **tourbillon** is a beautiful mechanical heartbeat that is fascinating to behold.

John McGonigle, a very well-respected watchmaker now living in Ireland, is capable of constructing **tourbillons** and **minute repeaters**. For quite some time, he built the most complex watches for Ulysse Nardin, such as the Genghis Khan, a **minute repeater** with **tourbillon** and automata. He told me that he preferred a **tourbillon** to a **minute repeater**. The repeater, he reasoned, was a useful feature in the days of the pocket watch because when the ambient light was low, which it typically was once the sun set, the watch could not be easily read. The **minute repeater** function permitted the wearer to know the time by counting the number of hours, quarter hours, and minute gongs when activated. In modern times, thanks to the light bulb and the use of luminescence on the hands, numbers, and indices, a watch can be easily read day or night, making the repeater less of a necessity and more of a novelty. Although also a novelty, John preferred the **tourbillon** because it was always doing what it was intended to do, usually in clear sight of the owner, and could be appreciated all the time. It is constantly functioning and is beautiful functional art.

I understood what John meant and agreed with him, to a point. Both are, to this day, considered to be the pinnacle of watchmaking, the collector in me is not always swayed by practicality but rather by the concept of functional beauty and, of course, I wanted to own examples of both, if possible.

The first **tourbillon** I bought was purchased in early 2003. It was the Chronoswiss Régulateur Tourbillon. The base movement for the model was the Progress 6361, a **tourbillon** movement produced in large quantities in order to be affordable. It was labeled "the people's **tourbillon**," and indeed it was for the short period of time that the movement was in production. The Chronoswiss watch fulfilled its mission in that it was quite affordable compared to other **tourbillon**-containing watches on the market at the time. I was excited to be able to own a **tourbillon**, even one with an off-the-shelf movement. Whereas other Chronoswiss watches have come and gone from my collection, I continue to enjoy this piece. It is well built, and its finishing is much better than expected given its price point. One feature that stands out is loudness of the **tourbillon** movement. It is fun to be in a quiet place and hear the ticking of the movement.

The **régulateur** feature was an interesting additional **complication**. **Régulateur** clocks were first invented in the eighteenth century to allow for better timekeeping. The hour indicator was not accurate to the minute, but with an oversized minute hand, the accuracy of the clock was improved, and the minutes were easier to read. With a **régulateur**, there is a short period of adaptation when it comes to reading the time, as the time display is different from a standard watch or clock.

Régulateur Tourbillon by Chronoswiss

Since it was invented by Breguet, the basic concept and function of the **tourbillon** has remained the same. Over time there have been a number of modifications to improve function: changes of materials used to construct the **escapement** or cage, an increase in the number of axes that the **tourbillon** rotates, the angle at which the **tourbillon** is mounted in the movement, and even the number of **tourbillons** included in a single watch, to name a few.

Once again, Ulysse Nardin was at the forefront of innovative change of the tourbillon. Prior to another Basel Fair, Ahmad decided to reserve another watch for me. All he told me was that I was going to like it and it was going to be produced as a limited series of one hundred. Pending my approval, number 6 was mine. The watch was the Skeleton Tourbillon Manufacture. The brand already marketed several models with tourbillons in the past, but this was the first one made completely in-house. Built from the ground up as a skeleton watch (not a skeletonized version of another movement), it had a 170-hour power reserve. Most significantly, the tourbillon was constructed out of silicium, the first of its kind. It can be argued that the Freak was the first tourbillon watch to utilize silicium components; however, it is still debated if the Freak movement is a tourbillon or, as Rolf referred to it, a carousel.

Skeleton Tourbillon Manufacture by Ulysse Nardin

Ahmad, once again, was right. Without reservation, it is as beautifully executed and technologically advanced as I had come to expect from

Ulysse Nardin. I believe that the watch-collecting public underappreciates what this watch represents and how innovative it is to create an escapement made completely out of silicium. With such a movement, it is lighter than the standard tourbillon, thus requiring less energy, which, in turn, allows for better performance and a longer power reserve. The research and development that went into the creation of this tourbillon set the stage for further developments in the construction of the tourbillon by Ulysse Nardin.

Patrick

In 2011 Rolf Schnyder died unexpectedly. It was a terrible shock to all the members of the Ulysse Nardin family, staff, and the watch community in general. Patrik Hoffmann was appointed CEO in place of Rolf. Prior to his appointment, I knew Patrik when he served as the Ulysse Nardin brand president in the Americas. We met on a number of occasions, during his visits to local retailers, at hosted dinners, and during late-night sessions at bars, typically with Ahmad. After the change in leadership, I visited the Ulysse Nardin Manufacture a second time, on this occasion accompanied by my wife. In the evening after the tour, we were invited to have dinner with Patrik and Susanne Hurni, the marketing director. It was a lovely dinner, and we spent a very pleasant evening with them in La Chaux-de-Fonds.

At dinner, I spied something unusual on Patrik's wrist: a watch I had never seen. When I asked about it, once again, I first had to promise to keep secret what I was about to see. Of course, having been in similar situations in the past, I agreed. The watch Patrik handed me was a prototype of the revolutionary anchor **escapement tourbillon** that Ulysse Nardin was preparing to launch. Patrik told me that there were only two such prototypes in existence. Sheepishly, he admitted that he could not find his and was, instead, wearing Pierre Gygax's.

Instead of the typical Swiss pallet fork construction, something used for centuries by watchmakers, the "arms" of the anchor **escapement** that held the pallet **jewels** were silicium blades that flexed under tension.

Made completely from silicium, the goal was to reduce friction and eliminate the need for lubrication. The prototype was in a platinum case and had a very simple dial with stamped indices. It was actually a Skeleton Tourbillon Manufacture watch where the silicium **tourbillon** was exchanged for the prototype new anchor **escapement tourbillon**. Looking under the rudimentary dial, I could tell that the movement was the **skeletonized** one. I wondered if the limited edition of the platinum Skeleton Tourbillon Manufacture was decreased by two.

Anchor Escapement by Ulysse Nardin

As opposed to my failure to pry from Rolf's wrist the **annual calendar** assembled by Ludwig, I eventually succeeded with Patrik. When I returned home from Switzerland, I contacted Ahmad and asked about the possibility of obtaining one of the prototypes of the anchor **escapement**. Once again, I applied the principle that one cannot get arrested for asking. Ahmad was able to work his magic, and I received the approval I sought. I was asked what engraving I wanted on the back of the watch. The back of the prototype had a blank plate covering the **skeletonized** movement without a cutout for the **tourbillon**. I requested that the back plate be engraved, "Prototype," simple and to the point. One of only two in existence. Not bad.

Ulysse Nardin continues to use the anchor **escapement** in some of their **tourbillon**-containing pieces. I am told that the anchor **escapement** is not used in all the models with **tourbillons** due to the higher cost of production.

The Grail

The search for the grail is something that consumes collectors. Regardless of what is being collected, often there is something in that genre that is held to the highest esteem. Typically, the grail achieves such a label by a collector due its unique artistry, historical significance, rarity, or cost. The grail may not be an object but rather a concept that is the basis for a system of beliefs or a personal goal. The grail may be defined by a collective or by the individual.

The concept of the grail traces its origin to the Templars of medieval times and their search for the Holy Grail. When watch collectors assemble, the discussion will often include opinions regarding the grail watch. The variables that are factored into the definition of the grail can be many. As there are so many watches to choose from, there are many different opinions. Usually there is not universal agreement, but rather it is typically a very personal opinion. Sometimes the designation of the grail might change over time (I am not the only one with watch ADHD). More typically, the grail is a long-standing obsession, one that is dreamed about but with no clear path toward acquisition. Unless, of course, the tooth fairy or a leprechaun can pave the way.

Over the course of my collecting journey, there has always been a thrill associated with the acquisition of a new watch. The joy may emanate from the conclusion of the hunt or the excitement of finding a watch thought to be unattainable. For whatever reason, most acquisitions are not spur-of-the-moment purchases but occur with some degree of planning, anticipation, and time. For sure there is an ego boost when I bring home a new piece, especially a rare one, but the thrill I gain is very personal and is not determined by others' opinions. My goals and my search are mine and mine alone.

Early in my journey, IWC released a limited edition of the Portugieser.

Someone I knew had one in steel and raved about the watch. It was early in my journey, but I was inexplicably attracted to the rose gold version. At the time it was a limited edition and was difficult to find. Compared to what I'd previously spent on a watch, the Portugieser was expensive, but it continued to occupy my thoughts. When, eventually, I acquired a rose gold Portugieser, I was giddy with excitement. As my wife drove me home from the store, I could not take my eyes off of the watch. That night we went out to dinner and, when I saw someone at the next table staring at my watch, I will admit to experiencing a definite thrill. Despite what others thought about the watch, it was more the fact that I now owned the piece that gave me joy. I could admire it, hold it, wear it, and wind it whenever I chose. This is the joy and the emotional rush of collecting. Of course, the enjoyment of the new watch does not replace the pleasure I still get from the watches I own regardless of how long they have been with me; it is an additive process. It is that feeling of joy that keeps me going back to the well for the next watch. These feelings, addictive as they may be, pale in comparison to the ultimate joy and excitement experienced if one is fortunate to obtain the grail.

For me, from the earliest phase of my watch-collecting journey, I knew about the Trilogy of Time, the marvel created by Ludwig Oechslin for Ulysse Nardin. The Trilogy is composed of three watches that each display astronomical indications from different perspectives in the cosmos. The more I learned about the complexity of each watch, the more they became my grail. Nothing matched them in beauty and technology. Should I be lucky to own a set, they would be the pinnacle of my collection.

The Tellurium Johannes Kepler takes the view of the earth from the perspective of the North Pole. It shows the sun and moon positions, timing of sunset and sunrise, rotation of the moon, and eclipses of the sun and moon, as well has having a **perpetual calendar**. The center of the dial is a disk with an enamel representation of the earth.

The Planetarium Copernicus demonstrates the solar system from the perspective of the sun. It shows the positions of the first six planets of the solar system in relationship to the sun with the inclusion of the position of the moon circling the earth. It, too, is a **perpetual calendar**.

The last and most complicated of the three is the Astrolabium Galileo

Galilei. It was designed by Ludwig based on his own personal astrolabe clock. Upon its first release in 1985, it was crowned the most complicated watch ever made by *Guinness World Records*. The amount of astrological information delivered by the watch is amazing. Positions of stars, moon, and sun; moon phase; astrological information; sunrise and sunset; and month, day, and date are all displayed.

The movement of each watch is highly engraved. Although Ulysse Nardin has given the movement a specific model number, it is a modified ETA 2892. Yes, it started life as an off-the-shelf movement, but to repeat Rolf's comment, "Get over it." It was necessary to have a very reliable movement that could provide the needed power for the various **complications** of the watches.

The Trilogy has been released in several series, but my grail was the last version. Housed in updated platinum cases, the set was incredibly beautiful and something dreams are made of, at least for a watch collector.

Sometimes a simple question can set a ball rolling that ends with an unexpected result. Both Chad and Ahmad knew my grail. During casual conversations, we talked about it a number of times. At a moment of weakness, or inspiration, during one of Ahmad's visits to the Watch Connection, I asked whether any of the Trilogy sets were still available. Ahmad said that he would investigate. Within several days he got back to me with the information that there were only two sets left. In the world of collecting, when a collector hears about something that is very difficult to get, limited in production, or not available, it is like waving a red cape in front of a bull. Sales hype or not, I felt that my relationship with Ahmad was such that I had confidence that I was being told the truth.

I usually am able to come to a decision regarding the purchase of a watch, or a piece of art, for that matter, relatively quickly. It is the matter of accumulating the funds to complete the transaction that takes the majority of time. In this situation, the possibility of obtaining the Trilogy of Time was not something I could decide at the drop of a hat. Ahmad let me know that number 6 was not available, but number 65 and another number were the only ones left. A six in the case number was an attraction but was not going to seal any deal. Back-and-forth negotiations proceeded. As the discussions continued, again applying the principle of you can always ask, I asked Ahmad if there was something special that he could do to set my Trilogy apart from any other. Once again it took several days for him to get back to me. When he called me, he relayed that Ulysse Nardin agreed to have Ludwig Oechslin's signature appear on the sapphire crystal on the back of each of the watches, something never done before. The deal was just about sealed, except for one person I had to convince.

I have always been open and honest with my wife. She knows about every watch I have purchased and every dollar I have spent on watches. Even after I convinced her to get her first mechanical watch, she did not share my interest but continued to tolerate my insatiable appetite for the next watch. Not uncommonly, as I descended deeper into the rabbit hole, I had to talk her off the ledge a number of times when she heard about the prices of the objects of my desire. I knew that I needed to get her agreement to this particular purchase before I could commit to such insanity.

If one acquires one's grail, does that mean that the motivation for further collecting will abate? That was a topic for discussion with my wife. In the course of conversation, I might have said to her that should I acquire the Trilogy, I would dampen my collecting urges and set my sights much lower. At the time I meant it. Seriously I did. How was I to know what opportunities lay ahead? I did not promise to avoid temptation again. I am not sure that she ever truly believed me. Eventually my wife agreed, although how many nightmares she had about the purchase along the way I will never know.

I can properly set all the indications on most watches without difficulty. If a watch, no matter the complexity, goes to sleep for a period of time, I can reset the time, date, moon phase, etc. I freely admit that I am intimidated to set the correct time, date, moon phase and other **indicators** on any of the watches in the Trilogy. There is a very good reason the set comes with a winder for all three watches. That way they never go to sleep, and besides minimal adjustment of the minutes, the owner will not be faced with the complex task of setting the watch whenever it is to be worn.

When my set arrived at the Ulysse Nardin office in Florida, I asked to go there to inspect and approve the watches before making the final commitment to the acquisition. It was a major purchase, after all. I also wanted to have an in-person lesson about each watch to better understand the information displayed by each. More importantly, I wanted to be shown how to set each piece appropriately. I flew to Florida and visited the office that serves as the US headquarters and service center for Ulysse Nardin. There I met the staff and was introduced to the service director, Kris Endress. With little fanfare, the Trilogy set was presented to me. Aside from pictures, it was the first time, outside of a museum, I saw the set. I was speechless. They were incredible. As promised, each watch had what I am told is Ludwig Oechslin's signature on the rear sapphire glass. I immediately approved the watches. What else could I do? The watch set that I was inspecting was truly one of a kind. No other Trilogy set had Ludwig's signature. The pleasure of having something unique is like a drug to the collector.

The Trilogy was everything I hoped for. There they were, the grail, laid out in front of me, then in my hand, and then on my wrist. A watchmaker himself, Kris gave me a lesson that took well over an hour and a half about the watches and how to set each piece. He made it look and sound so easy. What he showed me at the time made sense; however, over time I did not retain all the facts and instructions. Once again, I am intimidated by the watches.

When I went to bring the grail home, my wife accompanied me to the Watch Connection, and Ahmad arranged to be there as well. A small celebration was held—no balloons or confetti, just hugs and a bottle of cold water. Already aware of the finances for some months, I guess my wife had accepted the grim reality of the situation and was beautifully supportive. She occupied herself mostly talking to the staff of the store while Chad, Ahmad, and I drooled over the set.

There was a several months between the time that I went to Florida and had the watches set by Kris and when I made the final payment and was thus able to bring the watches home. Sadly, in that period of time, the watches were not kept on the winder, so I was faced with the necessity of setting each of the three watches.

I admit to having some obsessive-compulsive tendencies certainly when it comes to my watches. I try to set the watch to the correct second by coordinating the second hand with that displayed on a clock in my bathroom. That clock is my most precise timepiece. It is in radio communication with the atomic clock and cost $10 from Radio Shack. The moon phase needs to be set properly after checking the calendar on the computer. Other functions need to be appropriately set because why else have the watch? It needs to do what it is built to do.

Because the watches had been asleep for a number of months, I needed to reset each watch. I faced the choice of trying to muscle through and figure out how to set each watch or suffer the ignominy of calling Kris for a refresher course. The third option was to use the crown and wind my way through the five months since they were set to get to the current day and time. I chose the last option. It took a couple of days to set all three watches. I did not count on the fact that the **crown** for each watch was comparatively small and required extra effort to wind the minute hand through so many days. I was eventually successful but at the expense of blisters on my fingers. In the end, however, it was absolutely worth the effort. Ever since then, whenever any of the Trilogy watches are not worn, they are kept on the winder. I am very careful to periodically check the batteries in the winder to be sure it does not run out of power.

Once the Trilogy was home, I owned my grail. What now? If one is successful and obtains one's grail, does that mean that the passion has been satiated and the hunt is over? The collecting is over? I know what I told my wife, and I was truthful at the time, but temptation continued to be thrust at me. Besides, does the mountain climber, after scaling Mount Everest, not want to climb other mountains? If a swimmer crosses the English Channel, is there no more swimming to be done? My collecting was not done, grail or not. Sorry, honey.

The Trilogy by Ulysse Nardin

In 2017 the America's Cup was held in Bermuda. One of the teams competing was the Artemis boat from Sweden. Ulysse Nardin was one of their sponsors, and Ahmad invited my wife and I to attend the event. We had never seen a sailing competition before. I had the Polaris, a watch built for yacht racing, but had never been on a yacht, seen a race, or understood the meaning of the countdown indicator. Going to such a premier sailing event was an incredible and unique opportunity. We spent four days in

Bermuda and had a great time. We were a small group, and Ulysse Nardin arranged for us to watch the race from a boat that was positioned next to the racecourse. Watching those yachts up close was amazing. Lifted out of the water on foils, the boats literally flew. Not only did we get to see the boats in action, but we had the pleasure of meeting several members of the crew.

Ulysse Nardin supplied each of the sailors with a special edition Marine Diver that they wore when they were on shore, not during the competition. Shaking the hands of the team members was like shaking bricks. They were kind not to squeeze my hand; they would have easily broken multiple bones with little more than the slightest effort. These men were in incredible physical condition; working those boats took maximum physical effort. These were not archetypical weekend sailors but rather athletes in top condition. The team members have to wind "grinders" that are responsible for producing the pressure within the hydraulic system that, in turn, allows the boom to move and the sails to be trimmed. Our group was given an opportunity to try our hand on a practice grinder. No one lasted more than a couple of minutes, whereas the team members must grind at maximum effort for at least thirty minutes during a race.

Much like in the watch industry, the racing teams are very secretive about any innovations for their boats and, of course, race strategies. We were ferried to the Artemis team's base and were asked not to take pictures and to keep anything that we saw or heard strictly confidential. How many times have I heard that when I visited watchmakers or manufactures?

One day there were no races scheduled. Several of us decided to have our own experience with speed. While the Artemis team trained and prepared their boat for their next race, we rented jet skis. For some, driving a speeding car or boat is a passion. Being on the open water in a jet ski is an exhilarating experience for the thrill-seekers in our group. For others it is nothing less than frightening. While the others jetted across waves and left caution way behind us, I was reminded I had no need for speed. I puttered along and was very happy to pull into the dock when our time was up.

The event space for the America's Cup was composed of a large area set aside for festivities with vendors, a concert stage, and food stalls. Ulysse Nardin had a private reception area for their guests located above the fray. A large television screen was present to watch the race if desired. There was little chance to see the race live from the reception area, hence the boat. Center stage in the reception area was a display case with several of their latest releases in the Marine collection. The Marine **Annual Calendar** called my name. Under the display lights, the dial was beautiful. It had a blue enamel dial with a sunburst **guilloché** pattern. Ahmad and I agreed that the watch was a great piece, and the price point made it even more attractive. It had an in-house **annual calendar** movement, that was obvious, but what was even more impressive was the fact that it included Ulysse Nardin's patented DIAMonSil **escapement**. The silicium **escapement** was coated with a thin layer of diamond powder that served to improve durability and avoided the need for lubrication. I was told that number 6 could be mine.

Prior to going to the America's Cup, I saw the Marine Chronometer 1846 150th Anniversary piece at the Watch Connection. Since I was building a representative collection of Ulysse Nardin watches, it stood to reason, at least to me, Chad, and Ahmad, that I should have a piece from the brand's Marine collection. This anniversary piece was very simple, yet again, there was more to it than met superficial inspection. The dial was enamel without **guilloché**. The purity of a white enamel is hard to compare with other white dials. The Roman numerals grabbed me. Sometimes, it is hard to express why a certain watch is so alluring. This was one of those occasions. The inner workings were, once again, very special. This watch has the DIAMonSIL **escapement**, and it met chronometric specifications to be labeled "**chronometer**," which spoke for its timekeeping accuracy.

Returning from the trip to the America's Cup, I found myself in a conundrum. Which watch to get, the anniversary **chronometer** or the **annual calendar**? Both were great pieces and were excellent representatives of their respective model lines. I was torn because I truly liked them both, and like easily translates into want. I was informed that the number 6 for the anniversary piece was not available. Nonetheless, I did something that I had not done before or since: I purchased two watches at the same time. When they arrived, the **annual calendar** was, as promised number 6 and the anniversary **chronometer** was number 33.

Marine Chronograph Annual Calendar by Ulysse Nardin

1846 150th Anniversary by Ulysse Nardin

As advertised, the watches with the DIAMonSIL **escapement** have performed with flawless chronometric accuracy.

Revisiting the Freak

At one Basel Fair, Ulysse Nardin unveiled an incredible piece of innovation. It was a prototype Freak, which served as a platform for the designers and watchmakers to incorporate ten revolutionary innovations. The watch was called the InnoVision 1. Over time, many of the developments introduced in the prototype were incorporated into production pieces. Ten years later, the InnoVision 2 was introduced at the Basel Fair. It also presented another ten new and unique developments to the watchmaking universe. Shortly after the release of the InnoVision 2, I emailed Patrik Hoffmann, the CEO of Ulysse Nardin, and asked about its availability for purchase. It was a very special piece, and I learned that it would not be produced commercially. It certainly would be a great complement to my Ulysse Nardin collection. In short course, Patrik responded and said I could have the watch. It is always good to have friends in high places. The watch was mine as long as I covered the price tag, over one million dollars. I am comfortable discussing, without batting an eyelid or choking, a watch, piece of art, jewelry, or anything of interest that is priced well into the seven figure range. Comfort discussing something priced in the "ridiculous to consider" category does not translate into a purchase. My bank account does not permit anything more than a conversation, certainly not if I want to stay married or able to afford anything more than peanut butter to eat.

I had a similar experience years later with the current Ulysse Nardin CEO, Patrick Pruniaux. I spent time with Patrick in Cannes (see chapter 12), and he was wearing another Freak prototype called the Freak NeXt. Its major innovation, only one this time, involved the **escapement**, which was constructed in a multilayer format consisting of silicium blades that vibrate at 12 Hz. It has the anchor **escapement** and the grinder winding system, a new development within the realm of watch winding developed as part of the InnoVision 2 project. Seeing the watch, I was immediately interested; however, it was in a white case with a white dial and strap. I am absolutely not a white watch guy. Too flashy for my tastes.

I was allowed to wear it for a while, which led to several conversations about the possibility of acquiring the watch. The sales team discussed how they might tone down the white for me. Their first suggestion was changing the white strap to a black one. That was easy. They even discussed the possibility of constructing a black case for the movement. However, when the topic of price was discussed, my enthusiasm rapidly waned. The price point for such a prototype was too rich for my blood. Subsequently, I was told that there were performance concerns for the watch, and I have seen no evidence that the movement ever went past the prototype stage. It probably was for the best that I passed on the watch.

Since the release of the original Freak model, Ulysse Nardin has produced a number of different model variations. The developers in the company used the Freak platform to test innovative developments that were subsequently incorporated into other model lines, such as the use of silicium in the **escapement**, the DIAMonSIL **escapement**, and the grinder winding system. Despite the changes that were made, the basic design of the Freak was the same or very close to the original; therefore, I was able to resist the temptation to obtain another.

That changed when the prototype InnoVision 2 was unveiled. When I was in discussion about the InnoVision 2, I was told that Ulysse Nardin would be incorporating some of the novel features from the prototype into the next rendition of the Freak. When it was released as the Freak Vision, it was significantly different from the original. The basic features of the watch were true to the concept of the Freak; however, the design was modernized into a sleeker version. The structure of the case is different. The movement was updated to include the **balance wheel** with silicium micro-blades. The anchor **escapement** replaced the standard pallet fork, and the grinder self-winding system was totally new, since all previous models were hand-wound. It is a large watch, but because of the construction of the case and the combination of titanium with platinum, it is much lighter than expected and wears very comfortably. Of course I did get number 6.

The Freak has always been honest to the name. A singular piece of horological art and design, for years it remained true to its original design concepts. Sadly, the brand decided to produce a less expensive version of the Freak, called the Freak X. At first glance, it might be mistaken for a Freak because the dial appears to be like other Freaks, but on second glance, the presence of a **crown** destroys the image of the original concept, in my opinion. The Freak X is composed of a standard movement with a Freak-like module placed on top. I understand why it was created. It was a marketing decision, one targeted at those not able or willing to spend what it takes to buy a true horological marvel, the Freak. As someone who has followed the brand for so long and admired how they pushed the envelope technologically and in design, I am saddened to see such a commercialized decision. I can only imagine what Rolf might have said and what Ludwig thinks.

The Freak Vision by Ulysse Nardin

Chapter 6
A Second Career

My wife believes that everyone should, at some time, work in retail and food service. She reasons that we interact with people employed in those service industries on a very regular basis, and we should have an appreciation for what they do for us. They deserve, she preaches, for us to treat them with kindness and respect. My wife and sons have worked in both arenas.

I tended to be lagging there. Being a waiter in a summer camp, I am sure, does not qualify as working in food service. A friend of our family who was a McDonald's franchisee, invited me to participate in Founder's Day, an annual celebration of Ray Kroc's birthday. On that day, the administrative personnel work in the stores preparing food and serving customers for several hours. That was my one day working in food service. The scattered, minimal work that I did when I was younger at stamp and coin shows was so long ago that I cannot suggest that it counts as working retail.

Professionally, my typical work week encompassed sixty to seventy hours at a minimum, very rarely less. My work was stressful and exhausting. At one point, I knew I needed a break and scheduled myself for a week's vacation. My wife was not able to take the time away from her job, so I was faced with a week with nothing planned. At first, I considered applying for a job at McDonald's; as it was after my tour of duty on Founder's Day, I considered myself a veteran employee. However, I realized that applying for a job at the Golden Arches required a lot of creativity. I would have to create a résumé that would explain what I had been doing over the recent decades and why I wanted to work there. After giving further consideration (meaning on the spur of the moment), I asked Chad if I could work at the Watch Connection for the week. To his credit, Chad did not immediately break into hysterical laughter. We talked about it, and we agreed that he would discuss the idea with the owner of the store, Robert. I knew Robert from my numerous visits, and he was the one who sold me my first Hublot. As a regular at the store, I periodically had animated conversations with him about a range of topics. I guess those discussions served as my employment interview.

Robert did question others in the store as to why I would ever want to work there. It was pointed out to him that if he was offered the opportunity to be the bat boy for the Angels during spring training, he would do it in a heartbeat, as he was a huge Los Angeles Angels baseball fan. That analogy gave him enough clarity to agree to my request. Without a formal application process or even a handshake, we agreed to the arrangement, and on the first day of my vacation, a Saturday, I reported for work. I did not require any orientation since I was quite familiar with the store, the staff, and the inventory. Previously, I'd helped to put out the watches in the morning and clear the display cases in the evening, so I was familiar with store procedures too. The store hours were Tuesday through Saturday, and I worked each day of my vacation when the store was open.

My reason to work at the Watch Connection truly was unrelated to my wife's philosophy about working retail, although it was a good excuse. Rather, I saw it as an opportunity to learn more about watches, have interesting discussions with like-minded customers, and perhaps impart the some of the knowledge I possessed to the interested public. I certainly wanted to share my enthusiasm for watches and contribute to the growth of a community of watch enthusiasts and collectors.

The week was a success. It was a different world than I was used to professionally. I had interesting interactions with several customers and was even able to make a few sales. More so, I enjoyed the camaraderie with the other employees. My presence was accepted without question. The highlight, however, was that during lulls in the business, I was able to examine the watches on display. I had favorites and would do my best not to drool over them.

When the store was closing on the second Saturday of my vacation, Robert presented me with a gift as recompense for my service. I then approached him with the proposal that I continue to work there, even after I resumed my regular job responsibilities.

To my surprise, he agreed. I was not to get paid but would receive consideration for the time I put in behind the counter and the sales that I made. This consideration would be applied toward the purchase of a watch. Professionally, I worked five days per week, although I periodically worked a stretch of twelve days in a row, including the weekend. When I worked the twelve days, I then had a three-day weekend as compensation. I arranged to come to the store on Saturdays, the occasional Fridays, and any other days that I had off. On the rare occasion my workday ended early on other days, I would go to the store as well.

Much to the dismay of my wife, this went on for about eight months. I enjoyed the experience, for the most part. It was something I had never done before, and certainly it was a challenge, as being successful at selling luxury goods requires skill. I received some education about the art of salesmanship—Robert gave me a sheaf of papers outlining his philosophy of selling that I read multiple times, but even though I tried to apply the lessons, I never became great at selling.

There are different types of customers who enter a luxury goods store. Many approach watches primarily as a fashion accessory. They're looking for something nice to look at. Some are more focused on a brand or a category of watch. There are those who are on the hunt for the latest and "hottest" piece or otherwise the "right" watch. Still others having found what they are looking for and are comparison shopping. Some are browsers with no intent to buy; they may be looking out of interest or may have some free time to waste. Maybe they brought a watch in for a repair or a battery change and are "just looking." And yet others are on a mission to find a present for someone.

The salesperson of luxury goods tries to entice the potential customer to purchase something that he or she may or may not want and usually does not truly need. It is the skill of the salesperson that creates passion and desire within the customer by presenting a story about the item that caught his or her eye. One technique that I learned, though did not practice well, was to start the conversation with the customer by asking to see what watch they were wearing. I understood that it was a tactic used as an icebreaker, a way to start a conversation with the customer. Why most salespeople in other watch stores do not do this I cannot understand. Seeing what the customer was wearing on the wrist could give the salesperson an idea of the level of interest and guide a sales presentation.

Regardless of what is on the customer's wrist, the salesperson is always complimentary in order to boost the customer's ego and imply that they have good taste. Bolstering their ego makes the customer feel good about themselves and makes them more receptive about what the salesperson has to say next. I found it difficult to be complimentary about a watch that was a cheap quartz toy or some kind of knock-off. If the salesperson is successful, whether it is a planned or a spur-of-the-moment purchase, the customer not only buys a watch but also receives a treasured memory. Of course, the sale is not done at that point. There is always the possibility of the purchase being returned for whatever reason.

Follow-up after the watch is delivered, when it is brought back for the bracelet to be sized or the strap to be changed, is important. The salesperson continues to be very complimentary about the newly purchased item in order to continue the good vibes and solidify the sale and perhaps a future relationship with the customer. Since I was not in the store often enough, I did not have the opportunity to do the follow-up contacts when I was able to make a sale, but I am sure others in the store did.

During my time working at the Watch Connection, I faced an unexpected conundrum. When I worked at the store, I thought that I should wear a watch that, at a minimum, was from a brand the store carried. Better yet, it would be best to wear a watch that was either in the display case or available by order. I thought of it as acting as a wrist model, trying to subtly create interest in a watch by letting the customer see it on the wrist. The problem was that, as a collector, I was building my collection with pieces that were limited in production or models no longer available or from brands that the Watch Connection either no longer carried or never had. To add to the challenge, since I was working on my days off, I wanted to wear one of my special, weekend watches. If I did not wear a special watch then, my opportunities to wear one would be even more limited than they already were. To make matters even more complicated, if I did wear a non-work watch, something unique or unusual, I had the additional concern of accidentally damaging the watch while accessing the display cases. This was a debate that I faced every time I prepared for work at the store. As it turned out, I did not make a sale influenced by what I had on my wrist, nor did I damage any watch of mine. Yet the struggle was real: choosing the right watch to wear to meet the requirements or needs of the occasion is a burden that all collectors must face on a daily basis. Yes, it was truly a first-world problem but still presented a challenge I had not anticipated when I started working there.

Over time, it became apparent that the vast majority of customers shopping for a watch choose one solely based on appearance. They did not have even a basic understanding or interest in how it worked or what mechanical features separated one from another. The purchase was primarily based on, "That's pretty." Occasionally, I assisted someone who had a smattering of knowledge or was familiar with a specific brand or watch they were considering purchasing, if the price was right. In time I became a bit disheartened as the goal of my interaction with the person on the other side of the display case became more transactional rather than educational.

Perhaps to balance out the disheartening nature of some of my interactions with customers, there were some who I found curiously amusing. While I truly have small wrists, what I found fascinating was that it seemed that every customer, no matter their body size, claimed to have small wrists. A guy could be six foot three inches tall and weigh two hundred fifty pounds and yet insist that his wrists were small. To this day, I have no idea why people cannot face reality. If they looked in the mirror, would they not realize that their body habitus would not go along with small wrists? If you are a big person, there is no shame or embarrassment in admitting to having large wrists.

Sometimes the sales were enjoyable, like when I sold a Chronoswiss Régulateur Rectangulaire. That was a fun sale because I liked the watch as much as the customer and his wife. The watch utilized a movement from 1932 made by a company called Fabrique d'Horlogerie Fontainemelon.

The owner of Chronoswiss, Gerd Lang, had bought all the available vintage movements and was able have the movements restored, modified to his specifications, engraved, and then cased. Six hundred fifty watches were released between 1992 and 1998. The particular watch in the display case was offered to the customer as new old stock (an older watch that had never been sold).

The customer had to return to the store several times to look at the watch and try it on before he finally committed to its purchase. Like me, he really did have small wrists, and the proportions of this watch fit him and me perfectly. This watch serves as an example of one that is underappreciated by the general watch-collecting community yet is a quality product. Many watches do not get the attention that they deserve because they do not have the "correct" brand name, are not fashionable, do not have celebrity endorsement, or do not have the latest technological advancements.

I did such a great job selling that watch to that customer that I sold it to myself. Fortunately, Chad was able to secure another one for me.

Régulateur Rectangulaire by Chronoswiss

Under Pressure

Sometimes making a sale was easy. A customer might come into the store, survey the display cases, select a watch, and then throw down a credit card. Other times it required a lot of work to first create interest in a particular watch and then negotiate the deal. Some days I would talk to people but make no sales. I thought of those days as "casting bread upon the water." Hopefully I laid a foundation of interest that would culminate in a future sale. Unfortunately, there was a difference in opinion. Robert believed anyone who entered the store, and certainly those who expressed any interest in a particular watch, should be a buyer. Over time, that difference of opinion created stress for me when facing a potential customer. Toward the end of my stint working there, I started to become more interested in making the sale than imparting information. In my mind, I would be chanting, "Just buy the damn watch, please."

I am not capable of high-pressure sales and did not attempt to cajole anyone into making a decision. I have been the recipient of that approach. It is an immediate turn-off to be told that the piece I am looking at is the last one available or that the price is sure to go up or the model is to be discontinued very soon and this is my last chance to secure the watch. I found myself in such a situation in a store in Los Angeles. I was very interested in a particular watch the store had in stock. Even though it wore large on my wrist, the movement was quite innovative, and I was sorely tempted; however, the price was not insignificant. The salesperson gave me the line that it was the last one available in the world, and furthermore, another salesperson in the store had a customer for the watch. I needed to decide as soon as possible otherwise I might lose my chance to get this incredible piece. The piece was certainly desirable, that was true, but the salesperson agitated me. I walked out of the store and immediately emailed the founder and owner of the company, who I knew. I asked about whether the model in question was still available. He responded that the model was quite limited in number but there were several pieces still available and, by the way, the watch was going to be released in different case materials and color combinations in the future, so there was no urgency to decide whether to purchase the piece.

The salesperson called me several times over the next several days but with the benefit of caller ID, I chose not to answer. I enjoyed listening to her messages as they got increasingly urgent. The moral of the story is that salespeople have no idea who is standing across the counter from them. They have no clue who the customer might know and to what information he or she might have access. Sales staff should assume the customer knows everything and be honest in their sales approach. I understand the economics of the situation. The salesperson is there to sell. It is in their financial interest to make the sale, but I believe that they should take their foot off the gas pedal and build interest and desire for the watch. If they do their part well, the sale will be more likely to occur, and everyone will be happy. Even if the sale does not happen at that moment, the good feelings engendered, and the creation of an ongoing relationship, can result in one or more sales in the future. I have visited that store several times since that encounter, but I have never bought a watch from that retailer.

Friends with Watches

One day, early in my stint at the Watch Connection, I saw someone I knew professionally approaching the store. I was aware that he owned a small collection of watches. We had discussed our mutual interest at work as well as in the store when we happened to be there at the same time. I was not willing to reveal my "secret" life to him, so I hurried into the back office to hide behind the two-way mirror. I remained there until he conducted his business and left.

As time went by, I became more comfortable being behind the counter and willingly greeted customers I knew to be regular visitors to the store. Very aware that I was not going to sell them anything, as they typically worked with a particular salesperson, I was still happy to engage them in conversation. Initially they were surprised and maybe even a bit taken aback to see me acting as a salesman. Eventually they seemed to understand my situation and accepted me as part of the store's team. They probably found it humorous, and maybe they were a bit jealous?

Possibly the most challenging sales that I made were the ones to friends. Never did I try to "sell them" on a watch nor try to upsell them. I am not that skilled of a salesman anyway. I have witnessed several situations where a salesman sold a watch to a customer who had not intended to buy one when they entered the store. It is a marvelous ability to make something out of nothing. That was not me. I certainly was not going to do anything but help my friends purchase the watches that they wanted at the best prices possible. If they were not quite sure what they wanted, or even whether they wanted a watch at all, my tact was to first ask about their price range. After that we discussed why they wanted the watch or for whom they were shopping. Occasionally, they were either looking for a particular watch brand the store did not carry, or they had a price point in mind that did not match the inventory of the store. That was fine, and I told them where to look for the particular watch they sought or what brands to consider that were in their price range. When someone is buying something from a friend, though, frequently the buyer hopes to get the "friends and family" price. However, when I sold a watch to a friend, I believed that the price that I offered was the best one possible. I was not the one to set the final price; I deferred that decision to someone else in the store.

When selling a fine mechanical machine, there is always a chance of there being a problem with the watch. I certainly have had a number of such experiences. When I made a sale to a friend, I always hoped that wouldn't occur. I did not want my friend to think I had sold him or her a lemon. Fortunately, I never heard any grumbling from any of my "customers" about the price or any mechanical problems. Certainly nothing that I was held responsible for, anyway.

A Member of the Crew

Working at the Watch Connection gave me a better understanding of the business aspects of the watch industry. I was able to learn information that is not generally accessible to most collectors, and the insights that I gained gave me a perspective of the challenges retailers have when dealing with the brands when it came to them obtaining stock and managing financial relationships. This knowledge translated into making me a better customer.

Despite the oddness of my situation, a customer and then a coworker while still being a customer, I was warmly accepted by the staff. Even though I worked limited hours, I was able to meet sales representatives and was accepted by them as an employee. I am sure at some juncture they were told of my unique situation. The store was a high producer for the Baume & Mercier brand. In thanks, the brand offered each employee the opportunity to be gifted a watch of their choice. Not one to look a gift horse in the mouth, I selected and was given a Capeland S Chronograph in steel and titanium. This was an appreciated and unexpected present, and one that I enjoyed. In time, I no longer felt the need for this watch and passed it to one of my sons, who still wears it intermittently to this day. Certainly, a nice benefit for me and my son.

Capeland S Chronograph by Baume and Mercier

In addition to the Watch Connection, Robert owned a store, Roman Times, in Las Vegas in the Forum Shops of Caesars Palace. Typically, the staff at the Watch Connection went to Roman Times to help with the annual inventory, which happened during my stint at Watch Connection, and I was invited to join the crew. Since the Watch Connection is closed on Sundays and Mondays, the plan was to drive to Las Vegas Saturday after work and return Monday evening. The inventory had to be done at night when the store was closed, as that store was open for business every day of the week. This meant that we ate a late dinner, stayed up most of the night, and had the daylight hours to relax.

With my wife's laughing agreement, I accepted the invitation, but I told them I could not stay until Monday evening because I had to be at my regular job that morning. We agreed I would catch a flight back early Monday morning, and off I went.

The store in Las Vegas had the same brands as did the Watch Connection, but that store catered to a different clientele. As a result, there were different models in stock. The inventory was geared more toward people with money to burn before or after they hit the tables, and there were considerably more diamond-encrusted pieces than at the Watch Connection. I helped as best as I could but found adequate time to examine and handle some pretty unique pieces. I am not one to favor diamond-encrusted watches, but there were enough fun watches to entertain me. Most notable was a Franck Muller Revolution. The watch had a **tourbillon** that, at the press of a button on the case, rose above the dial to almost touch the underside of the sapphire crystal. It was fun to play with. Of course, was it necessary, or did it improve the timekeeping of the watch? Almost assuredly no. But it was fun to see, as it allowed for a multidimensional view of the **tourbillon**. Sometimes a **complication** is done just for the sheer beauty of it or to prove that the watchmaker has the skill to create it and not because it is needed or beneficial to the function of the timepiece. Watches are about microtechnology and art as well as function.

When not working in the store, I had the opportunity to relax by the pool, but the highlight was the expansive dinners that Robert hosted. Mounds of food and glasses of fine drink were served in what seemed limitless quantities. The irreverent banter was nonstop. The time in Las Vegas was as much about bonding as it was about taking inventory.

Early Monday morning, I took a flight out of Las Vegas so that I could get to work by eight o'clock. Taking an early morning flight from Las Vegas is a fascinating experience. It was by far the quietest passenger cabin I have ever experienced. The passengers were asleep, too hungover to care, or just bleary-eyed from partying or gambling to the early hours of the morning. Fortunately, not being a gambler or a partier, I managed to get some sleep the previous night and was able to go from the airport to my job without anyone being aware of my jet-setter lifestyle. I was able to get through the day without issue but went to sleep early that night.

After eight months of working at the Watch Connection, for the first and only time in my life, I was dismissed from a job. One Saturday afternoon, Robert walked up to me in the middle of the sales floor and, with a smile, told me that I was fired. No preamble or comment was offered. In fact, I knew he was in the process of hiring a new salesperson, and I am sure he did not want me to interfere with the new person's ability to make a sale. Joe, the incoming salesperson, was not only a watch enthusiast and collector but also a certified watchmaker. I completely understood and was actually glad for the dismissal. Working on my days off was exhausting. When I informed my wife of the change in my circumstance, she was exuberant and did a happy dance. I was done as an employee of the Watch Connection but not as a customer. Years later, we still laugh about my stint there.

As it turned out, Joe did not work at the Watch Connection for very long. He realized that he much preferred working with his father at the bench as a watchmaker. Joe and I have remained friends since. He has repaired some of my watches, and we continue to share the love of watches.

After he left the employ of the Watch Connection, I did not ask for my job back. But I still consider the time I spent there as invaluable. I solidified friendships, developed better relationships with brand representatives, and had the opportunity to be exposed to watch brands I had not previously considered. I still spend time at the Watch Connection on a regular basis. I visit and talk about watches, the watch business, and life in general with everyone in the store. I still buy watches from them as well.

Chad and I continue to have fun hunting for certain watches that strike my fancy or ones he thinks might fit my collection.

Chapter 7
Technology and Art

Before I bought my first mechanical watch, I thought that I wanted a TAG Heuer watch. I cannot say why I had that on my mind or why it became a mantra of mine, but there it was. Despite the idea of a TAG Heuer, I ended up selecting the Maurice Lacroix. At the time there was nothing in the TAG Heuer showcase that appealed to me. Eventually that changed.

For a period of time, TAG Heuer had a team of engineers and designers who pushed the limits of horological science, technology, and art. The result of their efforts truly intrigued me. The group, led by Guy Sémon, a former fighter pilot with a PhD in physics, developed a series of watches that, to this day, have not been matched in innovation and technologically.

The first watch designed by Guy Sémon and his team that drew my attention was the Monaco V4. When Chad learned about this watch, he thought of me immediately. The watch was built to replicate a V4 engine block. Unlike any other mechanical timepiece ever built, the V4 was designed to transfer energy in a unique fashion. The power to run the V4, stored in the **mainspring** within each of four **barrel**s, is transferred to the **escapement** not through a series of gears, usually made of brass, but by way of steel-reinforced rubber belts, as found in a standard combustion car engine. It has an automatic movement that is wound by the motion of the wrist. The **mainsprings** are wound by the vertical movement of a mass in the center of the back of the movement rather than employing a circular **rotor** found in virtually all other automatic movements. It was a technological novelty. The first iteration of the watch was housed in a platinum case and produced in a limited edition. The store was allotted

135

several pieces to sell. Sight unseen, I agreed to have Chad reserve one for me.

Monaco V4 by TAG Heyer

When the V4 arrived, it was not a small watch, and it weighed heavily on my wrist. Whether to acquire the V4 was an easy decision to make. To this day, I still enjoy watching the movement at work, with the belts turning the gearing, and feeling the clunk of the weight winding the **barrel**s as I rotate my wrist. It is definitely a watch that draws attention, which is why, when worn, it sits snuggly under a long sleeve shirt or sweater.

Chad and I agreed it was unique and quirky yet a fun piece. When I bought it, the caveat to the purchase was that TAG Heuer requested that the watch be sent back to them once a year for two years for them to inspect the watch. I do not know if all purchases of the initial series of one hundred fifty pieces came with the same request. It was my assumption that the team at TAG did not know how well the belts would last over the course of time. As agreed, I sent the piece back, and they kept it for about six weeks each time. I can only assume they were testing it. The flaw in their plan was that it was not a watch that I wore on a daily basis. I do not tend to wear the same watch more than one or at most two days in a row, and it may be a month or more between times that it is on my wrist. I am sure the movement did not experience enough wear and tear to give the technician at TAG valuable information, but I am a team player, and an agreement is just that, an agreement. To date, it has functioned well, and the belts continue to work as designed.

Another Trilogy

The next series of creations by Sémon's team that attracted me was the Mikro chronograph series. Several years after the release of the V4, TAG Heuer announced the creation of the Mikrograph, Mikrotimer, and Mikrogirder, **chronographs** that measured time in fractions of a microsecond. I read that the Mikrograph would be released in a limited edition, and the production of the Mikrotimer and the Mikrogirder were to follow but in very limited numbers. Chad and I discussed the three, and we agreed that the concept of owning all three was a challenge, one that stoked my desire and, yes, my ego. To be the only or one of a very few collectors in the world to possess the three Mikro models would be a significant feather in my cap. That said, it was the industry-first technological features that were the true driving force behind the hunt.

The first model released was the Mikrograph. The **chronograph** measures time to 1/100 of a second. The watch has two separate **escapements**, the same principle as the Jaeger-LeCoultre dual-wing movement in the Duomètre line, so activating the **chronograph** does not deteriorate the timekeeping function of the watch. The **escapement** for timekeeping beats at 28,800 vibrations per hour. The second **escapement**, the one that powers the **chronograph**, beats at 360,000 vibrations per hour. When the **chronograph** is activated, there is a distinct audible hum as the blue central hand spins around the dial, making one revolution per second. The **sub-dial** at six o'clock counts the seconds, and the **sub-dial** at three o'clock reads the elapsed minutes. On the reverse side of the movement, the **escapement** for the timekeeping is seen to beat as in any other watch movement; however, due to the **vibration frequency**, the **escapement** disappears from sight when the **chronograph** is activated. Because of the power required, the

chronograph has a **power reserve** of only ninety minutes.

The Mikrograph was initially released in a rose gold case in a limited edition of one hundred fifty pieces. Once I successfully brought home the Mikrograph, the next step was obvious.

Mikrograph by TAG Heuer

There are other watches that measure time in one-hundredths of a second (I am not aware if these other watches have two separate **escapements** as the Mikrograph does), and that alone might not have attracted me, but once I acquired the Mikrograph, I moved on to the hunt for the next in the series, the Mikrotimer. The Mikrotimer was built to measure time to 1/1000 of a second, a first for a purely mechanical watch. As in the Mikrograph, it also had two independent **escapements**. As in its predecessor, the timekeeping **escapement** beats at 28,800 vibrations per hour, but this time, when activated, the **chronograph**'s **escapement** beats at an incredible 3.6 million vibrations per hour. It is the fastest beating mechanical watch with a **hairspring**-containing **escapement** that has ever been built.

The Mikrotimer is considered a concept watch. It was submitted for consideration by the Grand Prix d'Horlogerie de Genève in 2011. In the watch world, the Grand Prix d'Horlogerie de Genève is considered to be equivalent to the Academy Awards for the film industry. Every year multiple watches are submitted for consideration in various categories. An independent group of judges selects the winners for each category. To be considered for the competition, the rules require that a minimum of eleven watches of the model must be built. For 2011, the Mikrotimer won as the best sport watch of the year. At the time, many articles were written about the watch and its mechanical firsts, further whetting my desire to acquire it.

Neither Chad nor I had any idea how many Mikrotimers were built. Even the regional TAG representative did not know and could not get any information when he called headquarters in Switzerland. Production details are typically closely guarded secrets. It stood to reason that it would be a significant challenge to find one for us to inspect much less for me to buy. After a number of telephone calls and email exchanges, Chad told me that his TAG representative was unable to find one much less bring one for me to see.

Sirens and flashing lights went off in my brain; telling a collector that the target of interest is not available is like pouring fuel on the fire of desire. What does the consumer want most? That which he cannot get. Unfortunately, there was nothing that we could do to change the situation. Over time I know I have been very fortunate to acquire some rare or unique watches. However, I am not successful 100 percent of the time, and I accepted that this would be one of those situations. I would have to accept defeat. When I was a teenager, when my heart was broken by a girl, my father reassured me that there were many fish in the sea. Remembering the lesson, I moved on.

One year later, out of the blue, Chad called me to tell me about a phone call he'd just received from the TAG Heuer representative. A Mikrotimer had been found. Oh, and by the way, it was number 1. Chad asked if I was still interested. Some time had passed since I'd last thought about the Mikrotimer, and my attention was focused on other watches. Within several heartbeats, I said, "Yes, please. Get it." Arrangements were made, and the watch was delivered to the Watch Connection. Once notified of its arrival, I got there as soon as I could.

The watch and strap were very shopworn. It was obvious that it had been handled quite a bit. The presentation box was in a similarly used condition. As was the case in the Mikrograph, the watch had an automatic movement. On the **rotor** of the Mikrotimer, 01/11 was inscribed. For all Chad and I knew, this was the actual piece that had been in the competition and won the GPHG prize. After winding the watch, I pressed the **pusher** to activate the **chronograph**. The center hand flew around the dial in a yellow blur with an audible buzz. The sound of the spinning hand was only drowned out by our giggles. It was stunning. The **escapement** of the **chronograph** was just a spring without a supporting ring, as is the case for all other **hairsprings**. For the **escapement** to be able to vibrate at the incredible speed of 3.6 million vibrations per hour, its mass had to be minimized. When the **chronograph** was activated, the **hairspring** disappeared from sight. Because the energy needed to run the **chronograph** is so large, the **power reserve** for the **chronograph** is only three and a half minutes. It seems ridiculous to have a **chronograph** that, at best, can only time something for such a short period of time. A rationalization offered to me was that if a race is being timed to a precise one-thousandth of a second, it is probably not a long event. In truth, since the Mikrotimer was a concept watch, its primary purpose was to test the boundaries of technology. Practicality was not the purpose of its creation, nor were there any plans for mass production.

True to the name of the watch, it took microseconds, maybe several spins of the **chronograph**, for me to agree to purchase it. Not because of its beauty but rather the technical novelty—and besides, it was number 1. I was now two-thirds of the way to getting the trilogy of the Mikro series. I was told that before TAG would allow the watch to be sold to me, they wanted to take the watch back to refurbish the movement and case. They would also make a new strap and, with Chad's insistence, build a new presentation box. Off went the watch to the team in Switzerland.

Many months later, Chad called me to say that the watch had been returned and was ready for pickup. When presented to me, it was in pristine condition and functioning properly. It had been fully reconditioned and looked good as new. The strap was replaced with a new one, and they even supplied an extra one, both black with yellow stitching to match the color palette of the dial. Oh, and by the way, I was told each of the numbers on the dial had applied luminescence in case I needed to time something in a situation with low or minimal light. To demonstrate the degree of luminescence, I was given a UV flashlight. When I illuminated the dial, as promised, I saw that all the numbers lit up. Except for the seven. It was unbelievable but true. There was no luminescence on the seven. The credit card went back into my wallet. The watch was packed up and returned to Switzerland for a new dial, as that was the only option.

After another four months, I asked Chad about the status of my Mikrotimer. Sheepishly, he told me that the watch had actually been sent to the TAG US headquarters from Switzerland but was never sent to the Watch Connection. On inspection, a defect was detected in the sapphire crystal on the front of the watch. Back to Switzerland went my watch once again.

Finally, after another few months, the watch made it from Switzerland to the TAG headquarters in New Jersey to the Watch Connection to my house and has stayed with me ever since in fine working order. It is still a thrill to watch the **chronograph** fly, albeit for three and a half minutes at a time.

Mikrotimer by TAG Heuer

I do not know if TAG ever produced all eleven of the Mikrotimers. Several years after I purchased mine, I was talking to salesman in a TAG boutique in Lucerne, Switzerland. He told me they recently sold number 7. I wonder if the seven on that watch had luminescence.

After finally taking delivery of the Mikrotimer, I mentioned to Chad that after such an adventure with the watch, certainly I deserved a reward for my patience and perseverance. Chad agreed and told me, in fact, so did the people at TAG Heuer. I was informed that I was going to receive a special present from them. Several weeks later—not months, as had been the case with the watch—I received a call from Chad notifying me that he had received my gift. I am not sure who at TAG arranged the gift, but it was very thoughtful. The gift consisted of a *WatchTime* article written about Guy Sémon and his creations, including the V4, Mikrograph, and Mikrotimer. The article was mounted in a 36 x 30 inch frame. The highlight of the framed article is the handwritten message from Guy, followed by his signature. The message reads, "Reach for the stars!"

Yes, sir.

TAG! You're It!

Once the epic adventure with the Mikrotimer was completed, I was even more motivated to find the third piece of the Mikro trio, the Mikrogirder. Guy Sémon and his team created this watch to measure time to 5/10,000 of a second. This feat was not accomplished with a **hairspring** but rather utilizing metal "blades" that vibrated at the rate of 7.2 million vibrations per hour. The Mikrogirder was so revolutionary that in the 2012 Grand Prix d'Horlogerie de Genève, it won the Aiguille d'Or Grand Prix, the top prize for the year across all categories. It was the belle of the ball. The hunt was on.

Mimicking its predecessor, the Mikrogirder was nowhere to be found. Multiple phone calls were made to the TAG Heuer team but to no avail. No one seemed to know if any existed for inspection much less for purchase.

Around that time my wife and I were invited to join a Purist tour of Zenith and Hublot. Coinciding with the timing of the tour, we already planned to be in the south of France for a vacation, so we decided to accept the invitation. It was to be the first tour of a watch Manufacture for my wife. Fortunately, she found the tour interesting, more importantly she met another watch widow on the tour with whom she could commiserate throughout, of course all in good fun. One evening, our group had a wonderful, hosted dinner in Neuchâtel. Joining us was Jean-Claude Biver and his wife. As always, it was a delight to be entertained by the showman Jean-Claude. He spoke about watches, of course, and also the cheese and wine that he produced. By that time, Jean-Claude was no longer the head of Hublot watches. He was in charge of the watch division of LVMH, which consisted of Hublot, Zenith, Bulgari, and TAG Heuer.

During the meal, with nothing to lose, I asked M. Biver about the Mikrogirder and whether it was possible for me to obtain one. To my surprise, he did not know much about the watch. He said he would investigate and get back to me. Later that evening, he emailed me to say that he would discuss the watch with Guy Sémon and let me know if one was available. To say the least, I was shocked to receive such a prompt response to my inquiry.

Eventually, as instructed by Guy Sémon, Bertrand Dolci, the TAG Heuer Haute Horlogerie sales development manager, contacted me. He was very open and honest about the Mikrogirder. He told me that the watch was only a prototype and not for general sale. They had previously built two of the prototypes and were willing to build one for me if I so desired. However, since it was a prototype, the reliability of the watch could not be guaranteed. He compared the watch to a Formula One race car, fast but very fragile. Because of the extremely high vibrations of the metal blades, the temperature of the metal increased significantly, and that, in turn, affected the lubricating oil. He stated that after a few hours of function, the **chronograph** most likely would have to be disassembled and some of the wheels and pinions replaced, much like the tires in a race car. Complicating the situation further was the fact that TAG had only two watchmakers capable of working on the movement, raising a real concern about whether there would be someone available in the future with the knowledge and capacity to service the piece. He also said that TAG would not and could not provide a warranty for the watch.

There were significant negatives to acquiring the Mikrogirder, but owning one would give me a chance to own a piece of history. Though significantly high, the price was not the issue (well, of course it was; when someone says it is not about the money, it is). The lack of any warranty, the concern about durability, and the feasibility of getting it serviced gave me great pause. I do not acquire a watch with the expectation that it is going to spend its existence in a safe. I want to wear my watches and use them to their fullest extent, but what would happen if it was in need of repair or service? After much consultation with friends, other collectors, and, of course, my wife, I very sadly gave up my hunt and thanked Bertrand for his efforts.

Not long after my Mikro adventure concluded, Jean-Claude Biver made the decision to refocus the LVMH watch brands, including TAG. I am told that Biver wanted TAG to target the lower end of the marketplace and not be the brand to pursue innovation or develop high-end products. He wanted TAG to focus on **chronographs**, as that was their DNA, and not try to compete in the innovative and higher price-point market. He moved the Haute Horlogerie group out of TAG and into another division under the LVMH umbrella. This put an end to the incredible run of technological innovations under the TAG Heuer banner. When that move was announced, I realized that my concern about someone being able to service the Mikrogirder in the future was well founded. It seems that it was a good decision not to pursue the Mikrogirder after all.

Several years later, Zenith released the Defy 21. Similar to the Mikrograph, the Defy 21 had two **escapements**, one for the timekeeping and one for the **chronograph**. The time function was controlled by Zenith's El Primero movement, vibrating at 36,000 vibrations per hour. The separate **escapement** for the **chronograph** was at 50 Hz or 360,000 vibrations per hour enabling it to measure lapsed time in 1/100 increments. The Defy 21 is similar to the Mikrograph in function; however, the **power reserve** for the **chronograph** is only fifty-five minutes as opposed to ninety minutes in the Mikrograph. I decided to secure one of the first Defy 21s produced to complement the Mikrograph. I hoped that the launch of this new series was the harbinger of further innovations from Sémon and his team now working for the Zenith label.

Defy 21 by Zenith

Defying Time

Moved out of TAG, the Haute Horlogerie group worked on the Defy Lab for Zenith. Its movement was different from the Defy 21, yet it was part of the Defy family due to the same case design. It was another innovative project, this time featuring a high-frequency movement utilizing an oscillator made of silicium rather than a **hairspring** balance. Ten prototype watches were made and sold as part of a much-ballyhooed launch of the model led by Jean-Claude Biver. Despite all the best efforts by Chad and the Zenith representative, Michael, I was not able to obtain one of the prototypes. At the time, I thought that the Defy Lab was taking watchmaking and design in a new, revolutionary direction, mixing traditional horology with modern material science. l saw it advancing the innovative developments introduced by Rolf Schnyder and Ulysse Nardin to the next level. Silicium components of watch movements have become a standard feature in the industry, even in watches produced by some of the most elite brands. Silicium was being used in some **escapements** but this time it would be a totally new and innovative **escapement** completely out of silicium that would vibrate and not rotate as do all other **escapements**. It would be a movement that would function with improved accuracy and require no lubrication and hence minimal maintenance. I admit that at the time I was a bit saddened to not have gotten an allocation and joined the celebration.

After the initial release event, Zenith announced a production version of the Zenith Lab, labeled the Defy Inventor, which contained the same silicium oscillator. It vibrated at 129,600 beats per hour with the expectation that it would provide highly accurate timekeeping. Not able to get one of the ten Defy Labs, I considered this as an acceptable substitute. On my wish list it went.

WatchTime magazine sponsored an event in Los Angeles not long after the release of the Defy Inventor. The event was a two-day affair that included the participation of a number of brands and several independent watchmakers. It was great to see so many brands in one place. I was in seventh heaven making my way from one booth to the next. Visiting many of the brands that I knew was like seeing old friends. Besides the brands, sales staff, and watchmakers I already knew, there were others that were new to me. In addition to the watches, there were lectures, a couple of which I attended.

More important to me were the friends with whom I was able to spend time. I have found that at meetings, whether for professional or social purposes, the scheduled activities are not nearly as important as the contacts and the side conversations that can occur during the events. In the exhibit space, Zenith had a booth staffed by a brand representative I had not previously met. We discussed the Defy Lab and how the lucky recipients of the ten prototypes had been selected by Jean-Claude. I told the representative that I had tried to get one of them but was unsuccessful. I was considering the option, to soften the blow of rejection, of getting the Defy Inventor. He suggested, sotto voce, that I not pursue that model. I was quite taken aback by his forthrightness. Being at the event and by virtue of our conversation, I guess it was obvious to him that I was a serious collector and had some knowledge about the field. He told me that the Defy Inventor was not performing as advertised. The accuracy of timekeeping was a problem. It must have been a significant problem because the Defy Inventor disappeared quickly from the Zenith website and the marketplace, not to be seen or heard about since. I can only wonder what has happened with the prototypes and whether they, too, were recalled.

Once again, I may have dodged a bullet by being fortunate to not have been one of the "chosen ones." It is purely speculative to suggest that again, silicium presented a problem, this time as the oscillator. Might this have been the Freak situation redux?

Four years after the release and then disappearance of the Defy Lab and Inventor, Frederique Constant announced the release of the Slimline Monolithic watch. Frederique Constant is a long-existing brand I have known about, but until this time, I had never been tempted to acquire any of their watches. When I learned about the anticipated release of the Slimline Monolithic, my antennae perked up. I read that it was to have a movement that replaced the standard Swiss lever **escapement**, a system that has been used by the watch industry for the past two hundred-plus years, with a silicium oscillator that vibrated at 288,000 per hour. Unlike in the Defy Inventor debacle, this silicium oscillator was designed to fit within the space where the standard **escapement** is housed.

This innovative movement was not revealed to the public with the same fanfare that Jean-Claude Biver created when the Defy Lab was released. Once again, silicium was being put to the test. The price point was much more palatable than it had been for the Defy Inventor, so I decided to roll the dice and placed an order for one. The possibility of owning a watch with new, innovative technology drew me to the model, not the name or the reputation of the brand.

This time my order was filled. It has proved to have been an interesting piece. Indeed, it is fascinating to watch the vibrating "**escapement**." The second hand courses around the dial very smoothly. It does not have the typical jerking motion of standard movements. It reminds me of the gliding movement of the second hand as seen in Seiko watches with the Spring Drive. On the wrist it keeps time adequately, although not quite as precisely as expected, but off the wrist not so at all. At this time it remains on the manufacture's website. I hope they continue to improve its performance.

147

Slimline Monolithic by Frederique Constant

The Eye of the Beholder

The TAGs, Zenith Defy 21, and Frederique Constant Slimline Monolithic, among others in my collection, reflect my ongoing interest in technological innovation. But by no means is that the only feature that draws my eye to a particular watch. Enjoyment of modern art has given me an appreciation for color and form, and the artistry of a piece plays a significant role in determining the choice of many of the pieces in my collection. The design of the dial, case, hands, and **indicators**, the color palette, and the treatment and finishing of the dial and movement are variables that come into play when appreciating the artistic quality of a watch. Other watches are attractive simply because they are fun.

One of the sales representatives I met at the Watch Connection was Sebastian. He was the representative for Armin Strom. Sebastian is a delightful fellow, always clothed in bright colors with a personality to match. We met on a number of occasions and shared several dinners. On one occasion, he was wearing a very interesting watch called the Chameleon. It had an in-house movement that was **skeletonized**. Armin Strom, the watchmaker, had made his name producing watches with exquisitely **skeletonized** movements. The current owners of Armin Strom, the company, were friends with the man and had purchased the company from him with the promise to produce watches with **skeletonized** moments. Additionally, at the time, Armin Strom had a program that gave customers the opportunity to personalize their watch by selecting one of a number of colors for the movement, hands, and **bezel**. It was a fun concept. The watch that I saw on Sebastian's wrist was multicolored. It matched his penchant for colorful attire and demonstrated to customers the eight different colors that Armin Strom could **electroplate** onto the **bridges** and plates of the movement. Each visible **bridge**, the plate, and the two **barrels** of the Chameleon had a different color. The in-house movement and **skeletonized** movement were nice, but it was the colors and the concept of fun the Chameleon brought that ultimately led me to pursue its acquisition. It is a true one-of-a-kind piece, which, of course, added to its appeal.

Chameleon by Armin Strom

When I made the decision to attempt to pry the Chameleon from Sebastian's wrist, Chad worked as the intermediary. Fortunately, he was amenable to selling it and in fact agreed to an attractive price. As was my experience with other prototypes, the Chameleon had passed through many hands and showcases, so it was sent to the Armin Strom Manufacture to be refurbished before I was allowed to take ownership. It continues to be a fun watch to wear and is particularly suited for times requiring a bit of artistic flare.

Artful Style

Alain Silberstein is a French architect and designer who applies his unique flare for color and design to his brand of watches. His designs include bright colors, modern forms, and humor. I have admired his watches for quite some time. They are powered by standard, off-the-shelf movements, so it is the creativity of the design that is so appealing to me. He seems to have a similar aesthetic to one of my favorite artists, Alexander Calder, though his canvases are much smaller. Calder's paintings and sculptures feature bright, often primary colors and geometric or primitive shapes presented in a fashion that, for me, creates joy.

I came upon a Krono Bauhaus 2 designed by Silberstein and produced in a limited series of eight for a watch dealer, Louis Black. Housed in a black titanium case, it features a **chronograph** with day, date, and moon phase **indicators** and the typical Silberstein aesthetic. The hands for the various **indicators** are creatively designed with an abstract flare in primary colors. A particular highlight is the day of the week indicator. Located at twelve o'clock, the day of the week is indicated by a cartoon facial expression, called "smile day," starting with a very sad face for Monday. As the week progresses, the frown slowly turns into a happy face that is displayed on weekend days. The **crown** and **pushers** are not the typical cylindrical forms but rather geometric shapes topped by primary colors. Winding the watch would be extraordinarily difficult, given the triangular shape of the **crown**, were it not for a tool that is included with the watch. The creations by Silberstein and Calder always bring joy and happiness when I look upon them.

Krono Bauhaus 2 by Alain Silberstein

The artistry of a watch can extend beyond the choice of colors or shapes for the dial or hands. Roger Dubuis was an independent watchmaker who, after working at Patek Philippe, established his own brand in 1980, where he designed unique movements that included multiple **retrograde indicators**. One of his most iconic designs was of the case for his model the Sympathie. Starting as a square, each side of the case incorporates a curve, making for a unique shape. After his company was acquired by the Richemont group, the Sympathie case design continued to be a feature of the brand.

I came upon a watch built by the Dubuis company while Roger was still at the helm. It is a simple time-only three-hand watch with a Lemania movement. What attracted me was the shape of the Sympathie case. There were more complex models housed in a similarly designed case with **retrograde indicator** functions for day and date. There was an eye-popping model with a **perpetual calendar** with three **retrograde sub-dials** and a mother-of-pearl dial in the same Sympathie case. At the time, however, it was not in a price range that was within my reach. Years later, I learned that the complicated models produced by the Dubuis company back then had some significant mechanical and quality control issues. This was confirmed by a watchmaker who told me he had been employed by the company to improve the quality of their products. He spoke of finding strands of hair in watch cases and movements and how so many of the watches with **retrograde** functions did not work. He lasted one year in that position, leaving due to dissatisfaction with the company. His stories of quality issues were corroborated by a retailer who used to carry the brand and who told me that virtually every complicated Dubuis watch that he sold had to be returned to the factory for repair. However, I am now told by reliable sources that the quality issues are a thing of the past and no longer of concern. Selecting the time-only model turned out to be a good decision. My watch has functioned flawlessly for almost two decades.

There have been two times that I felt the need to cull the herd, putting up several of my watches for sale. I decided to offer the Dubuis for sale on the second "culling." That could have been a very bad mistake. As it turned out, unbeknownst to me, my wife liked the watch. She was attracted by the unique style of the case. Fortunately, the watch did not sell. When I regained possession of the piece, I gave it to her, and she happily added it to her collection. A clear sign that her ambivalence toward watches had changed from when she sported a Victorinox watch.

Sympathie by Roger Dubuis

That watch is number 28 of a series of twenty-eight. Dubuis had a penchant for producing limited series of twenty-eight pieces. I was told there were several reasons, including the twenty-eight days in the lunar cycle and the number of days in a woman's menstrual cycle. The reason that seems most likely to me is that during his stint at Patek Philippe, Dubuis worked in the haute horology department and his bench number was twenty-eight, so his choice of that number honors that work bench.

On the Face of Things

The dial is the first part of the watch that the consumer typically looks at when shopping for a watch. It is the canvas upon which the designer is given the opportunity to demonstrate artistic prowess. The beauty of the dial is determined by the synergy of the design and decoration. The combination of base material, engraving, enameling, painting, or **guilloché** contribute to the gestalt of the dial. What features attract the eye of a particular collector are based on individual taste for sure. The more watches the collector is exposed to, the more likely the collector will be able to establish their own aesthetic That said, it is fun to try to have some variation, as variety is the spice of life, except (as I have assured my wife) when it comes to spouses.

The feature of a particular dial that affects me can vary. Sometimes it is the complexity of the workmanship. At other times, it is the simplicity of the dial that can make an oversized impression on me. Years ago, I saw and held an original Breguet pocket watch. I was at a get-together, and one of the attendees brought it for all to see. It was a time-only watch with an enamel dial, Breguet hands, and hand-painted numbers. Of course, the dial had the "hidden signature" (Breguet dials all have a second signature in very small font engraved somewhere on the dial). The dial was very simple, yet it was stunning. I have seen other, much more complicated original Breguet watches in museums, but the simplicity of this dial left an everlasting impression upon me. To me, that watch represented the ultimate example of Breguet.

I have been a bit conflicted about the modern-day Breguet brand. The current company produces watches that are attractive and well executed, yet I feel that connecting the marketing of the name Breguet and the modern-day brand to Abraham Breguet is somewhat of a stretch. A belief that I am sure my friends at Breguet will readily debate.

Some companies, such as Ulysse Nardin, have a traceable lineage to their initial founding. At the time of the purchase, Ulysse Nardin still employed several watchmakers working on marine **chronometers**. In my opinion, these companies are justified when they claim linkage between the present and the original founder and namesake. There are a number of brands, however, that try to connect their modern-day company to the namesake watchmaker from centuries ago when it is nothing more than an advertising contrivance—one that annoys me. There are companies that are purchased with the sole purpose of instant name recognition. The watches subsequently produced have no bearing on previous product lines under the previous ownership. I am more bothered by other companies created after acquiring the rights to a name and then, in their advertising campaign, insisting that they have a direct connection with the long-passed watchmaker, which is not remotely the case.

There are a few companies created and named for historically prominent watchmakers without creating fictional direct connections between past and present. They acknowledge that the newly formed company is using the name in order to honor the past and produce watches that memorialize the watchmaker's talents and historically notable creations.

Despite my conflicted opinions regarding the current-day brand, Breguet has a historical significance when referring to the watches produced by Abraham Breguet and his workshop. Virtually any museum that displays historically significant watches will include one or more two-hundred-year-old Breguets in their exhibition.

A friend owned a Breguet Classique, model 7147, with an enamel dial. It was reminiscent of the pocket watch I remembered, but the watch did not immediately attract me. His was in a white gold case. I much prefer red gold, and the Breguet pocket watch that was seared into my memory was in a yellow gold case. Maybe that lack of contrasting color influenced my opinion. There was another version of the same reference (watch model) that featured a silver **guilloché** dial. That did not attract me at all. Over time, the memory of my friend's watch weighed on me. I wondered if I should have gotten one, but by the time I decided to find one, it was no longer produced, and I did not want to enter the preowned marketplace.

A number of years later, Breguet introduced another version of the 7147. This model also had the enamel dial with the Breguet hands, hand-painted Arabic numbers, and the secret second signature. In this model, the secret signature was located at the three o'clock position rather than the twelve o'clock position on the dial of the pocket watch or my friend's version. When I saw this release, I had a couple of immediate reactions: I was glad that I did not get the prior version, and I wanted this watch.

Classique 7147 by Breguet

What drew me to this particular watch was the off-center seconds **sub-dial**. In the prior release, the seconds **sub-dial** was attached to the main dial, a standard approach when creating an enamel dial. There was clear separation of the enamel between the main dial and the **sub-dial**. In the new release, the enamel coating the main dial sloped into the seconds **sub-dial**. Visually, there was a beautiful and smooth continuity of the enamel between the dial and the **sub-dial**. The similarity to the old pocket watch and the sensuous curving enamel leading to the **sub-dial** made it a perfect piece for me. When the piece is right for me, I know, and there is no hesitation. The watch had to be mine.

Revisiting Seiko

My wife and I periodically drive to Los Angeles and visit the Jaeger-LeCoultre boutique on Rodeo Drive in Beverly Hills. We like to go there to visit friends and, at times, conduct business. On one occasion, after our visit was concluded, I suggested a stroll down the street to do the obvious, look at more watches. I was particularly interested in stopping at the Grand Seiko boutique. Several members of the Alphabet Soup Gang were fans of the Seiko brand and always brought some of theirs to our get-togethers. Typically, the Seikos were vintage, but occasionally a Grand Seiko would make an appearance. Reading about the Grand Seiko brand, I appreciated that they were producing interesting watches that were expertly constructed and nicely finished.

Whether it be art or watches, looking at pictures is not the way to fully appreciate an object. Stopping at the boutique would be a great way to expand my knowledge of the brand and give me firsthand experience with their product. We were warmly welcomed by the boutique manager, who stood by as we walked the store and inspected what was in the showcases. Nothing *spoke* to me. I guess the manager saw that I was not enthusiastic about any of the watches on display and offered to show me several "special" pieces that were in the safe. The first one he showed me was interesting but did not move me. He then brought out a watch that figuratively stopped me in my tracks.

The watch he handed me was from the Elegance collection, model SBGK004. It had a nicely finished manual wind movement housed in a rose gold case. What took my breath away was the dial. The dial was coated with a special lacquer obtained from a specific tree in Japan. The urushi lacquer has iron ore added to create a deep black color. The production and application of urushi is very labor intensive. A traditional, painstaking application process is used to apply the material to the dial. There is only one master at Seiko who has the proficiency to apply the lacquer with such perfection. Layer upon layer is carefully applied to build up the dial. When finished, the dial has an incredibly deep black coating.

Although black is the absence of all color, there can be different qualities and purity of black. The depth of the dial created by the absolute black drew me in, much as light is absorbed by a black hole. On the dial the GS and the numerals six and twelve were created with rose gold powder. The other hour indices were created with multiple applications of platinum dust. Both were applied using the classical maki-e technique, once again a process of slowly building up the numbers, letters, and indices with precious metal powder. Seiko has their own movements that are nicely finished, but with this watch, it was all about the dial that made it irresistible.

The edition was limited to one hundred fifty pieces. Grand Seiko had produced a second model with a red urushi dial, also limited to one hundred fifty pieces, but that edition was already sold out. The boutique manager told me there were very few black-dial versions still available in the market. To the best of his knowledge, the one in my hand was the last one available in the US, at least within the Grand Seiko boutique system. Forever the skeptic, I wondered if this was not-so-subtle sales hype.

I thanked the manager, and with his card in my hand, we left the boutique. I knew that I had found my next watch, and the hunt was on. Within a week, I was able to track one down at a better price than I was quoted at the boutique. The search for a watch consists of finding the right watch at the best price. That said, price should not be the sole determinant when purchasing a particular watch because availability and after-sales service are critical elements that need to be factored into the purchase. I have certainly bought watches at a discount, the more the better, but that doesn't mean I have always received the steepest discount, and certainly I might have been able to save some extra money had I kept hunting. But for the cost of a few extra dollars, I invested in the development of relationships with particular retailers with whom I continue to work. Those relationships have been invaluable over the course of time. That is one of the reasons that I have shied away from cruising the internet and searching for the perfect deal. I would rather spend the extra money and know that if I have a problem with a watch (not an uncommon scenario for me, it seems), I have access to get the problem handled without unnecessary hassles. It is very useful to have the retailer play intermediary when dealing with a brand. I am not sure this is the same experience when making a purchase from some anonymous business online. The development of such relationships has also led to access to some very special watches, something I have been quite grateful for.

Had my hunt for the urushi-dialed Grand Seiko been unsuccessful, I planned to return to the boutique and purchase the watch from them, so haunted was I by that dial. After the successful conclusion to my hunt for the black dial, I continue my search for the red urushi dial.

SBGK004, urushi dial by Grand Seiko

After bringing home the urushi-dial watch, I started to follow the Grand Seiko line with greater interest. I was impressed by their workmanship and the quality of their watches. Grand Seiko is said to be the finest collection within the Seiko constellation, except for the Credo models, which are only available in Japan.

The Credo line is Seiko's most exclusive and highest-quality line, especially when it comes to finishing and construction, but Grand Seiko is a close second. I was shown a Credo watch with an incredible blue enamel dial. The enamel fades toward the edges of the dial, revealing the white enamel underneath. An incredible effect and very tempting. My enthusiasm waned when I was told that the Credo line contains the Spring Drive movement. The Spring Drive movement is mechanical, including a **mainspring** for power storage, a gear train, and a **rotor** for winding. However, it uses an electric regulatory system that helps to control the **mainspring's** energy release and create a magnetic force used to regulate the glide of the hands of the watch. The result is a very accurate timepiece with a second hand that runs incredibly smoothly. That said, I am a purist and am willing to sacrifice some degree of accuracy for a completely mechanical movement.

As I followed the Seiko brand, I was overwhelmed by the number of new models released on a regular basis. When I was at the boutique, I told the manager how overwhelming the brand was to me. I asked him how to find the right watch. He recommended that I first decide on which movement I wanted and then what case design suited me and then look at dials. In that way I would be able to whittle down the number of choices. From that point on, the choice should be easier.

I knew that I wanted a model that contained their high-frequency movement. That movement vibrates at 36,000 vibrations per hour and is said to be more accurate than their standard purely mechanical movement. I found out that a friend purchased a specific Grand Seiko with a high-frequency movement, the SLGH013. We share similar taste, so I figured that would be a good starting place. When I read about the watch he acquired, I was pleasantly surprised. The watch came with a light-blue dial textured to represent snow. The case and bracelet were constructed from a special highly polished high-grade steel. Most impressive was the description of the movement and the upgrades made to it to improve performance and **power reserve**. I knew I found the watch that fit my search for a Hi-Beat model. It does not bother me that I have the same watch as my friend. This is not a limited edition but just a really nice watch with a great movement.

I know women do not want to go to an event and see someone in attendance wearing the same gown. This is not the case with watches. I am quite okay if someone else is wearing the same model watch as I am.

In fact, it could be an entrée to meeting a fellow collector and having an interesting conversation.

Hi-Beat SLGH013 by Grand Seiko

To the Moon and Back

There are many models of watches that display the moon phase. It can be argued that it is a useless **complication**. For sure there was a time in the history of humanity when knowing the phase of the moon carried a certain degree of significance. But now, not so much, except, perhaps, for astronomers. Despite the questionable utility, collectors continue to enjoy having the phase of the moon displayed on their timepieces.

I possess a number of moon phase watches even though I do not use the knowledge of the phase of the moon professionally or otherwise in my daily existence. The nature of the moon display varies among different models. There are differences in the image and detail of the moon surface. Some have drawings, while others have engravings, and still others are photographs of the moon surface. Some brands portray the moon in three dimensions, either with engraved images or globes. The background color of the sky or the use of jewels to portray the bright side of the moon can express the artistry of the brand.

Of course, there are differences in accuracy of the indication of the moon phase, ranging from one day's deviation within several years to one day in thousands of years (reportedly). Setting the moon phase correctly can be very challenging. Many watches are constructed such that the date and phase of the moon are integrated. Setting the moon phase when the date is also displayed is relatively straightforward with the help of a corrector, usually positioned on the side of the case, and a knowledge of the date of the last full or new moon. Set the date first, and then, with the use of a corrector, set the moon phase. A challenge arises if there is no date. Then the moon phase must be set according to best guess unless it is exactly a full or new moon. For a person with an obsessive need to have the displays on a watch dial be as accurate as possible, setting the moon phase correctly in that circumstance can be time consuming. It is not something done rapidly, and that can be an impediment when in a hurry to go to work.

Arnold & Son is a conundrum. The company bought its name in order to attain instant recognition. It has no relationship to its namesake, John Arnold, who was a very famous eighteenth-century British watchmaker. I first learned about the company Arnold & Son when it was part of the watch group the British Masters. Despite advertising that implied otherwise, the company had no ties to John Arnold or his descendants. Together the group represented, in my opinion, a contrived association of companies named after famous British watchmakers to present a suggestion of credibility and historical significance.

When the group disbanded, Arnold & Son ceased to produce watches. Subsequently, the rights to the name were purchased by the current company, under the Citizen Group umbrella. The new brand created a completely new line of watches that are distinctly different from those produced by the previous iteration of Arnold & Son. I highly doubt that the watches created by the brand have any relationship to those John Arnold conceived of centuries ago. Despite my disdain for that principle of marketing and "creative" advertising not borne out by historical facts, the current iteration of Arnold & Son makes some interesting watches. The fact is I found myself faced with principle versus passion when I began to learn about some of their products.

As common as moon phase watches are, it is uncommon for the moon to be represented in three dimensions. When I read about the Luna Magna, I was intrigued. Besides the fact that it was a limited edition of only twenty-eight pieces, the moon phase indicator fascinated me, as it reminded me off my youth. Growing up in Brooklyn in the '50s and '60s, my friends and I shot marbles. Marbles came in different varieties, mostly aggies and cat's eyes. The goal of the game was to shoot one's marble (with a shooter) and knock the opponents' marbles out of a circle drawn on the cement. The one with the last remaining marble in the circle was the winner.

Luna Magna by Arnold & Son

The size of the moon in the Luna Magna, as the name suggests, reminds me of the marbles from my yesteryear. It is not quite the size of my marbles, but it is significantly larger than any moon representation created to date for a watch. For this watch, setting the moon phase is uniquely easy, even though there is no date indicator. On the back of the watch is a dial that indicates the days of the lunar cycle. Using the dial, setting the watch to the correct phase of the moon is easy and stress free, something I completely appreciate. There are few designers that take into account the collectors who have an obsessive need for accuracy.

Swag

Many collectors enjoy receiving various brand-related paraphernalia, otherwise known as swag. Over the course of time, I have been offered my share of branded gifts such as hats, pens, key chains, paperweights, loupes, cups, and catalogues. Some I have kept, but most, over the course of time, I have passed on to others. Except for books. They continue to be useful reference material I refer to on occasion. Special gifts, such as the autographed article from TAG, I treasure as keepsakes. Then there is the gift from Parmigiani.

Chad informed me that Parmigiani was going to release a new model labeled the Tondagraph GT. The model combined a **chronograph** with an **annual calendar** function. It was to have a big date and an integrated bracelet. I was definitely interested when I saw pictures of the piece. Making it even more special, Parmigiani planned to produce a very limited run of forty pieces for the US market. These watches featured extra fine finishing of the movement and a special gift. Already a fan of Parmigiani, the "special deal" was too much for me to pass up. The limited series was gobbled up in a short time. When I received mine, it did indeed have very fine finishing, which was especially obvious when I compared it with a regular production piece. Engraved on the back **bezel** was "HF," which signifies hand finishing.

The special gift that Chad spoke of was a design sketch of the case with the **lugs** and detail features of the lettering with explanations (in French) hand drawn in pencil. It seemed to be taken from the actual design work done during the development of the watch. The drawing was personalized, inscribed with the case number of my watch and my name. Next to my name was Michel Parmigiani's signature. This is swag that is not the typical souvenir one expects to receive. As promised, it is special and a definite keepsake.

Tondagraph GT by Parmigiani

Chapter 8
Adventures with Independents

In the world of watches, there are a number of large conglomerates: Swatch, LVMH, and Richemont, to name a few. Each of these holding companies own a number of watch brands. Typically, these corporations have other luxury brands under their umbrella, and the watch department is but one component of a much larger operation. There are large single-brand companies that are owned and operated as solo entities, such as Patek Philippe, Audemars Piguet, Parmigiani, and Chopard. Then there are smaller brands that produce a modest number of watches per year, such as Armin Strom, Bovet, and Richard Mille. Typically, these companies are privately held, although there might be partial ownership by outside investors.

On the other end of the spectrum, are the independents. There is an ongoing debate as to what defines the independent watchmaker. My preference is someone who produces watches either on his or her own or with the assistance of very few employees and is unassociated with any larger entity. Typically, an independent's production numbers are very small. Unlike the big companies that can produce tens to hundreds of thousands of units per year, the independent watchmaker will produce several to several hundred watches per year.

When it comes to creativity and innovation, independent watchmakers tend to be the ones pushing the envelope both stylistically and mechanically. Some of the larger brands have been able to develop significant innovative changes as well, but they often evolve in a slow and deliberate fashion. By virtue of their size and flexibility, independent watchmakers are capable of developing innovative pieces in much shorter periods of time.

The principle of buying the seller, as recommended to me when dealing with the preowned marketplace, also applies to working with independent watchmakers, in my opinion. When buying the watchmaker, one is buying their creativity and ingenuity as well as supporting their livelihood, as they often operate on a shoestring budget. Also, because the collector deals directly with the person who is designing and constructing the watch, the collector has a greater opportunity for personalization, the chance to obtain a truly singular piece. Such an experience is much less likely to occur when purchasing a watch from a major brand, where there can be many layers in the corporate structure between the collector and the actual watchmaker. Trying to convince a major watch brand to create a unique watch can be a herculean task. Granted, recently, certain brands began affording selected collectors the opportunity to obtain one-of-a-kind pieces, but that is the exception and not the rule.

Some independents portray themselves as the sole creator; they let the world believe that they are actually at the bench, making the complete watch by themselves from start to finish, when that is not the case. Often, they use commercially available base movements, which they then modify to a varied degree. If a collector knows what to look for, it is not difficult to identify commonly utilized movements, such as the Unitas 6498, that have been decorated or finished to a watchmaker's specifications. Other independents market watches under their name that are completely designed or even built by outside entities.

That said, it is normal for independents to outsource at least some components for their watches. Their low production numbers make it economically unfeasible for them to produce every part, such as the **jewels, mainspring, hairsprings**, crystals, and, on occasion, cases. It is a practical consideration to purchase these components from experts in the field rather than trying to master a task for a very limited number of movements.

In fact, few watchmakers are capable of or willing to make a complete watch from start to finish. Those who do tend to produce in very low numbers, resulting in the creation of very expensive pieces due to the time requirement and overhead expenses involved. However, there is a growing cadre of watchmakers who are willing to take on the task of building a watch from the ground up. Establishing their workshops—at the minimum they need computer resources and a rudimentary CNC machine, but often they seek machines to manufacture the smallest parts of the watch movement, such as screws and pinions—requires a significant upfront investment. Additionally, frequently the machines are old and require some degree of rehabilitation to bring them to working order. While that may sound like a detriment, when speaking to some of these watchmakers, there is often a twinkle in their eyes as they describe the latest machine they purchased and what it took to rehabilitate it.

My entrée into the sub-world of independent watchmaker happened through Paul Gerber, from whom I received the Retro Twin Power Reserve. Making a direct connection to the actual watchmaker, rather than to a salesperson separated by many levels of an organizational chart from the person or persons who built the watch, created a completely new experience for me. Working with Paul, I obtained my first true limited edition: the **power reserve** added to the movement was only found in twenty watches. Once that series was done, no more were created with that **complication**. There would not be others with different dial or **bezel** colors or any minor alterations in the design of the watch. That, to me, is the definition of a real limited edition. And down a new corridor of the rabbit hole I went.

After Paul, Came Peter, and then Tim

By 2004, driving to Los Angeles to attend a watch event was a common practice for me. So when I learned a dinner there would be hosted by a watch retailer from the San Francisco Bay Area, it was an easy decision to attend. The featured young watchmaker was Peter Speake-Marin. Peter started his career as a watch restorer in London and then moved to

Switzerland, where he did a stint working at Renaud & Papi before starting his own brand.

His initial focus was geared toward developing a watch that would be very robust: by his own words, he highly modified a standard ETA movement and placed it in artfully appealing cases. Throughout the evening, I peppered him with questions, mostly involving the technical aspects of his watches. While he definitely intrigued me, I am told that I managed to make quite an impression with him. Ever since, whenever we meet, he invariably describes to others how I grilled him that evening. He continues to joke that he still gets a bit concerned about what I might ask whenever I raise my hand or open my mouth in his presence.

Even though the highlights of the evening were Peter and his watches, another significant consequence was that I met the host of the event, Tim. At that time, Tim owned a store near San Francisco, where he sold watches from several brands, but his true passion lay in the area of independent watchmaking. Subsequent to that first meeting, Tim became a dear friend as well as a guide in the world of the independents. With his assistance, I have had the good fortune to acquire some incredible watches and friends.

It has always been the independents that have stretched the borders of watchmaking, pushing the world of horology to new heights. They have played no small part in redefining the standards of quality now expected in the production and evaluation of all fine watches. Their influence upon collectors and the industry as a whole has led to a much greater emphasis on excellent finishing of all watch movement components. Thanks to the reach of the internet and the greater appreciation of fine watches by the general population, independent watchmakers are better able to gain prominence. In earlier days, however, it was Tim and other forward-thinking retailers and journalists who spread knowledge about the work and skill of these watchmakers.

At that dinner, Peter presented half a dozen of his newest creations. Internally, they all had his same movement. The dials, however, had different, beautiful presentations. There was a variety of **guilloché** patterns in gold and silver. Some watches had incredible engravings; one in particular that stood out was a three-dimensional dragon.

Once the event concluded, Tim, Peter, and several of us adjourned to a nearby bar to continue the evening's festivities. During the dinner, I had to share Peter's watches with the other attendees. At the bar, I was able to spend more time with them uninterrupted. While the others sipped their cocktails, I resumed my adoration, focusing particularly on one piece: a Piccadilly in a red gold case with a red gold dial and a wave **guilloché** pattern. The others continued talking to Peter—about what I have no idea. I wanted to be part of the conversation to be sociable, but I could not help focusing on the watch. That took precedence. However, the lighting where we were seated in the bar was too dark for me to fully appreciate the workmanship of the dial. With nowhere else to go, Tim and I adjourned to the men's room, which had better lighting. You could say I was completely smitten. So much so that it became the first time that I committed to a watch in such an odd place. (It would not be the last unusual place where I'd find myself buying a watch.)

Picadilly by Peter Speake-Marin

Besides the watches, that night had another lasting effect on me. When we all sat down in the bar, the server asked what I wanted to drink. I did not know what to order. I knew I did not want a beer, but what else does one order at a bar? The only thing that I could think of was an Irish coffee, which I ordered. I do not go to bars to hang out and had at best a rudimentary knowledge of the usual selections offered in such establishments. No one in the group seemed to take any notice of my discomfort; nonetheless, it was an uncomfortable sensation to be my age and not know what to order in a bar.

After that evening, I told my wife that it was time for me to learn to be an adult. In particular, I wanted to learn about whiskey. A couple of weeks later, we were relaxing at home one evening when I suggested that we go to a local restaurant for some dessert. When we got there, I decided that it was time to start my education about scotch and told the server something to that effect. The server sent the bartender to our table. She then brought a flight of scotches. As my wife ate dessert, I had my first exposure to different types of scotch from a very patient bartender.

The next day, we went to a nearby wine and liquor store, where Forrest, an employee, graciously spent forty-five minutes giving me my second in-depth lesson about scotch and whiskey. Since then, I have learned enough to be conversant about the various types of whiskey. One drink a week, if that, is average for me at home, but at least I can now go to a bar and order something comfortably, thanks to Peter, Tim, Forrest, and a certain watch.

Under the Influence of Tim

Over the next couple of years, Tim partnered with the Purists to present two other events that brought together independent watchmakers and collectors. Watchmakers in attendance included Peter, John and Stephen McGonigle, Vianney Halter, Marco Lang, Nicolas and Christophe Delaloye, and Maria and Richard Habring. The watchmakers brought several examples of their work to the events to illustrate how they were pushing the boundaries of creativity technologically and artistically. Being able to talk with the individuals responsible for these creations was a mind-expanding experience. Having the ability to see so many independently created watches in one place gave me a greater appreciation for the world they occupied, one different from that populated by the major brands. It was a world that, more and more, I knew I wanted to explore and support.

Enticed by discussions with Tim and the watchmakers he introduced me to, I started to read about the Académie Horlogère des Créateurs Indépendants (AHCI). Established in 1985 by watchmakers Svend Andersen and Vincent Calabrese, the AHCI is an organization that supports and promotes independent watchmakers and clockmakers. As I read about the organization and its members, I began to create a list of those I found interesting. For sure the AHCI does not encompass all independent watchmakers, but it was a starting point. As each of these independents produce small numbers of watches per year, securing a piece from them, I knew, would require persistence, luck, and possibly connections.

Where does one start but at the beginning? If I was going to use my AHCI checklist, why not start with one of the founders? I read more about Svend Andersen and discovered several of his watches that contained novel technology and were artfully constructed; he was known for watches that depicted erotic scenes on the underside. Those absolutely did not appeal to me; however, a different model did strike my fancy, the Orbita Lunae. It featured a moon phase indication and had a striking blue gold **guilloché** dial. The moon phase is displayed through an aperture that rotates around the dial as the days pass. In most watches, the moon phase dial rotates under the main dial to reveal the phase of the moon. In the Orbita Lunae, the reverse was true. At midnight or when the **crown** was pressed, the dial shifted to indicate the next date number, and the phase of the moon changed in the aperture.

The challenge presented to the owner was in adjusting the displays so that the correct date coincided with the correct moon phase. It was not always an easy task. Svend packages his watches not in presentation boxes but on winders for a very good reason. Keeping the watch running on a winder made setting it easier if the watch was not continuously worn. What bothered my sensibilities, given my obsessive tendencies, was when the month changed. Jumping the watch forward a day when the month was only thirty days long meant that the indicator was not precise. The discrepancy was more pronounced when the month changed from

February to March, whether or not it was a leap year. The disparity in the moon phase indication was bothersome. Eventually, although I continued to like the dial and the **guilloché**, I decided to sell the watch because of the challenges in setting the correct moon phase. It was a beautiful piece, and I may have been guilty of user error, but I succumbed to my peculiarities. Sometimes having compulsive tendencies can be a blessing, but other times it can be a curse.

Orbita Lunae by Svend Andersen

Continuing my research into Svend Andersen's offerings, I read about his Perpetuel Secular Calendar. I like **perpetual calendars**. They are watches that record, at a minimum, the month, day, and date and are able to account for the number of days in each month and correct for leap years. **Annual calendars**, on the other hand, account for the number of days of the months, thirty or thirty-one, but do not correct for February, forcing the owner to adjust the date displayed on the watch once a year. The problem with most **perpetual calendars** is that they do not know the one-hundred-year correction. The earth does not circle the sun in precisely 365 days. It actually takes 365 days, 5 hours, 59 minutes, and 16 seconds to complete an orbit around the sun. The leap year every four years corrects for the error; however, it overcorrects. This results in a further needed correction every hundredth year such that it is not a leap year. Once again, this overcorrects for the error, so every four hundredth year is a leap year. Svend Andersen's Secular Perpetuel Calendar claims that it is "programmed" to account for not only the leap year but also the hundredth-year and four hundredth-year adjustments. The corrections built into this watch fascinated me. Those corrections are not mysterious and are very well known. Computers can easily account for them, as can the atomic clock. To have those corrections programmed into a watch, however, is masterful, even though it is not very useful.

When I discussed a possible purchase with Svend, I mentioned one design concern. The case that the Secular Perpetuel Calendar came in was the same as the Orbita Lunae, which I still owned at the time, and I requested a different case design. Graciously, Svend put my Secular Perpetuel Calendar in a different case. Although the number on the dial says "No. 30," as it is the thirtieth Secular Perpetual Movement produced, on the back of the case is inscribed "Unique Piece" to indicate that the case is unique to my watch.

As is the case with the Ulysse Nardin Moonstruck, the Secular Perpetuel Calendar is a watch that requires my longevity, the necessity to stay alive for many centuries. Whoever purchases the Secular Perpetuel Calendar accepts the concept that the watch knows the four-hundred-year correction, but we are only taking Svend's word for it. How do we know if his claim is true? I feel it is my obligation to the world of horology to monitor the function of the watch through time to be sure that come the year 2400, it does what it is supposed to do. I need to prove that the watch correctly indicates that the years 2100, 2200, and 2300 are not leap years, while 2400 is. Unfortunately, I did not buy the watch until after 2000, so I missed seeing if the watch knew that 2000 was a leap year. Oh well. I will have to be patient and wait more than three hundred years due to that misfortune.

Secular Perpetuel Calendar by Svend Andersen

Getting Service

When working with independent watchmakers, it is, at times, challenging to get a watch serviced. The brands have boutiques or retail partners that ship a watch to a service center or back to the manufacture for necessary repairs or service. Many of them even have service centers in the US, which makes shipping to them relatively straightforward. Granted, that relative ease of sending in a watch does not always equate to rapid turnaround at the repair center. It can take many weeks or months, if not longer, to get a watch back.

When it comes to the independents, there is no such service infrastructure in place. Servicing requires direct contact between the collector and the watchmaker, which can take some time, and then there's the real and great concern over whether the watch will arrive safely at its destination. The same is true when the watch is ready to be returned to the collector. While there are ways for the collector to get some insurance for the watch, it is difficult to get adequate coverage. When faced with this predicament, I have, on occasion, asked one of the retailers I work with to ship the watch for me, as their insurance coverage is better than any I could obtain.

However, on one occasion, I needed to ship a watch of significant value to the watchmaker for adjustments. Thankfully, the watchmaker made the arrangements for the piece to be picked up and securely shipped back to him. The courier service he'd hired arrived at my house when my wife was home and I was not, as I was at work. I did not want the courier to come to my office, where I'd have to explain to the staff what was happening and why it was necessary.

The courier arrived on the appointed day. At the sight of him, my wife was taken aback, to put it mildly. "Are you packing?" she asked, momentarily shaken by the sight of the holstered gun on his hip.

"Yeah. These are valuable things," he responded, and off he went, leaving my wife a bit uneasy. The situation passed, but it led to a conversation between us about why these watches were in our house. Ultimately, it led to the renting of a safe deposit box for watch storage.

Another watch that needed servicing was the Andersen Secular Perpetuel Calendar; the date was not changing properly. When I contacted Svend, he initially suggested sending the watch to Roland Murphy of RGM watches in Pennsylvania. I was told that Svend had an arrangement with Murphy to service the Andersen watches in the US. As instructed, I sent the watch to RGM, which was relatively easy—I asked Chad to send it with the hope that the store's insurance would adequately cover the watch in transit. Unfortunately, once received, Roland Murphy called to tell me, in a quite abrupt fashion, that he would not service the watch, and he immediately shipped it back to me.

When it was back in my hands, I reached out to Svend again, who recommended I send it to him. Suddenly, I was challenged with the task of getting the watch to Switzerland safely and securely. Fortunately, Don Corson happened to be in the Los Angeles area to visit his son. After a three-way conversation with Don, Svend, and me, Don agreed to transport the watch to Switzerland and deliver it to Svend in Geneva. That certainly was fortuitous. What better way to transport a watch than in the hands of a watchmaker such as Don? The watch successfully made it to Geneva and was serviced to full working order.

As it turned out, when it was ready to be returned, my wife and I were traveling in Germany, with the intention of ending our travels in Munich for Oktoberfest. Svend had a good friend, Erwin Sattler, a clockmaker of repute, in Gräfelfing, an area in the district of Munich. He arranged to send the watch to Sattler's business address by French Chronopost. Happily, when we arrived at the Sattler showroom and workshop, we were able to tour their facility and meet some of the clockmakers. Once the short tour was completed, I received my Secular Perpetuel Calendar as good as new. The watch completed its world tour in my possession, safe and sound. But, again, this shows it's not always easy to get these pieces serviced!

Getting Personal

It is my preference, when considering an addition to my collection or purchasing anything of value, to see the object in person prior to making a commitment. There is a significant difference between seeing a piece of art or a watch in a photograph and seeing it live and in color. When it comes to deciding whether to purchase a watch, there is the added variable of its fit on the wrist. There is no way this can be done when looking at a picture or a drawing. If a collector hopes to make an emotional connection with an object as part of the purchasing process, it is usually only going to happen if the piece can be experienced—if the watch can be seen in the metal and put on the wrist. I firmly believe in this principle; however, there have been times when it has not been possible. I have had to take the word of others and commit to a piece sight unseen. Fortunately, to date, when I have been faced with such situations, it has worked out well for me, as happened one day when I received a call from Tim.

My wife and I were at a craft fair one day when Tim called. By then I was well acquainted with the McGonigle brothers. I had read about them and, of course, met them at the events organized by Tim. On the call, Tim informed me about an opportunity he thought might interest me: the McGonigles planned to produce their own watch called the Tuscar. Their goal was to build it from the ground up. They were looking for ten collectors to support their efforts by purchasing one. The design for the first ten would be unique, guaranteed to be different from the production model that would follow. In addition to a movement built from scratch, the finishing would be the best in the industry. As an added attraction, the movement was to be engraved with a typical Irish pattern by Stephen and John's sister, Frances.

Tim, aware of my aesthetics and what I was searching for in a watch, strongly recommended that I consider the piece. Yes, as I walked around a fair looking at different knickknacks, I held a discussion about horological art. Once again, an unusual location for such a conversation. While I believe it is best to take advantage of opportunities when they arise, this would truly be a decision made sight unseen. There were no computer images or even concept drawings to refer to that could help me understand what I was being offered. The idea of a uniquely designed, well-constructed watch by watchmakers I knew to be very well respected made the offer so much more enticing.

Besides the price, which was reasonable, the question of production time was also discussed. I was told that the watches would take about eight months, more or less, to produce, though there was a possibility that it could take longer. Amid faux leather belts, pottery of all sorts, wood boxes, utensils, and metal sculptures, I committed to the watch. This would not be the first time I relied solely on Tim's advice. To celebrate the decision, my wife and I purchased a funny-looking sculpture of a dog made from a propane can, which remains on display in a sitting area outside our living room.

The Tuscar is quite unique in construction and is beautifully finished, as promised. Different from other limited series, when the ten watches were produced, they were all numbered "one in ten." This avoided the inevitable debate about who should get what number. Of the ten collectors, everyone received number 1. My "one in ten" watch taught me patience.

Watches tell time. To get a fine watch takes time—exactly how long is affected by the vagaries of the industry and the watchmaker. The eight months turned into more than two years. Whenever I spoke to Tim, regardless of the subject, invariably, the anticipated date of delivery of the Tuscar was brought up. After an uncomfortable clearing of his throat, Tim would admit that he did not have a clue, share a laugh, and move on to other topics.

Asking about the timing of delivery became a sport I carried over to enjoy during other purchases. Some watchmakers, including major brands, seem to be able to complete and deliver a watch in the promised time frame, while others are not able to commit to a specific date. Not infrequently, a brand will announce a new model and collect orders but not deliver the first watch until a considerable period of time has passed, longer than promised when the order was taken.

One challenge for the independent watchmaker is their commitment to quality and attention to the smallest of details when creating a watch. Even more impactful and unpredictable is that they often need to source certain parts. Since they are dealing in small volumes, they are not the highest priority for their suppliers, which can result in unanticipated delays. For the McGonigles, the new movement, especially the unique bridge that held the escapement, presented construction challenges that led to prolongation of the production time. Also, as I grew to learn more about the McGonigles, I found they are obsessed with perfection and fine hand finishing, which was an additional factor. The bottom-line lesson I learned was that a watch will be delivered when it is completed to the watchmaker's satisfaction and no sooner.

Tuscar by McGonigle

It so happened that this watch was ready for delivery during the time when I was in Barcelona with my family to celebrate my wife's birthday. After some back-and-forth communication with Stephen and John, we agreed that another brother, Conor, would deliver the Tuscar to me while we were there. The fourth McGonigle met us for lunch near the harbor. We had a great meal of fideuà, and I received the beautiful timepiece. As I inspected the watch, I immediately understood why it had taken so long to create. The Tuscar is a true McGonigle family project. It was not a simple timepiece. It was, and is, a work of art.

Ireland

Several years later my wife expressed the desire to visit Ireland. Some of her family came to the US from Ireland, and she wanted to visit the old sod. I was dubious. I expected the food to be bland, and I had no burning desire to see the countryside, but we went nonetheless.

To say the least, the trip was fantastic. Ireland is beautiful and a joy to behold, even though it rains often. Actually, it only rains twice a week, once for three days and once for four. The people were very friendly, and surprisingly, the food was terrific. Driving around Ireland, however, was quite a challenge.

First of all, they drive on the wrong side of the road. Usually, when I rent a car, my American Express card or our personal car insurance will cover us for damage that may occur. Not in Ireland. Both expressly stated by that they provide no car rental coverage in Ireland. Consequently, the car rental was the most expensive I have ever paid for because I was required to accept all the coverage layered on by the rental company.

Second, the car came with a GPS program that was several years old, so the recently completed high-speed roads were not in the system. Driving around the country, we never turned on the radio; maneuvering from one destination to the next required all our attention, as we had to remember to stay on the correct side of the road and manage the roundabouts. Should a tour bus, and there were quite a few, or truck come toward us on the supposed two-lane roads, we were challenged to negotiate around the oncoming vehicle without landing in a ditch. There are no curbs, only shallow (usually) ditches to mark the edge of the road. My wife and I made the joy of driving there a two-person affair, taking turns at the wheel. We even had a competition to determine who drove into a ditch more often. My wife won, her three times to my two, but no car damage occurred. A true miracle.

In the center of Ireland is the town of Athlone. For watch collectors, Athlone is significant as it is the home of the McGonigle family. That's where John and Stephen grew up with their three siblings. Those two brothers moved to Switzerland to ply their trade. After a while, Stephen remained there, and John moved back with his family to Athlone. As part of our itinerary in Ireland, we arranged to visit with John and his family.

With a little help from the GPS, we found our way to John's house up a single-lane dirt road in the rural outskirts of the town. The house was guarded by a ferocious guard chicken who roamed the lot, protecting his charges.

John and Linda welcomed us into their home, where we had a nice chat before piling into John's car for a tour of Athlone. With wild abandon, John drove over the narrow single- and two-lane roads. After surviving the drive, we went for a pleasant walk to see some of the highlights of the town and then went along the banks of the Shannon River.

We stopped in Sean's Bar, said to be the oldest pub in Ireland, as registered by *Guinness World Records.* The pub was preparing for the annual Arthur's Day, the day designated to celebrate Arthur Guinness, the founder of the Guinness brewery. John and I talked about life in general and how to further popularize his brand. Perhaps I was a bit pretentious, but John was kind enough to at least humor me with his attention as I spouted off my opinions.

Back at their house, we went into his atelier, which, typical for independent watchmakers, was in his converted garage. The garage was bright, with natural light shining in through the installed windows, including a large one overlooking the backyard, where I could see the guard chicken on patrol. We met his assistant and discussed the work that he was engaged in at the time. On the bench was a Tuscar, one of the one in ten, in the process of being assembled. John went to the safe and brought out a presentation box with a beautiful watch. It was a **tourbillon** in a rose gold case with a dark gray dial, a color combination that I favor. He told me that it was one of only a few **tourbillons** they produced under the McGonigle brand, of which only two were in rose gold cases. Unlike the Tuscar, which came in a round case, the case for the **tourbillon** was oblong, wider than long by a difference of one millimeter. The shape of the case is very subtle—one only a keen eye might detect it—but it does demonstrate the minute details the brothers feel are so important for their watches.

The movement was based on a Christophe Claret **tourbillon** movement that the McGonigles modified. The watch was dated the year of its completion, 2006, which, John proudly informed me, was the year that the Ryder Cup was held in Ireland. Europe won that year (not a fan of golf, I could appreciate the significance of the victory but did not share the enthusiasm). In fact, the hotel that John arranged for us to stay in that evening had numerous pictures on the walls memorializing that Ryder Cup victory. Like the Tuscar, the underside of the movement plate of the **tourbillon** was engraved by their sister, Frances, with ancient Celtic patterns. Also, as with the Tuscar, the family name was etched into the **crown** in Ogham, the ancient Gaelic written language. I previously saw this watch when John and Stephen came to the presentation in Los Angeles years earlier. I was struck by the piece even then but was, at the time, in a different frame of mind with regards to finances and did not consider purchasing the watch. Seeing it once again and being more receptive to the price of the watch, the memory of the **tourbillon** weighed heavily on my mind throughout the rest of our time in Ireland.

After we arrived home, I gave in to temptation and let John know that I wanted the watch. He was very happy with my commitment but asked for my permission to postpone delivery. He wanted to take the watch on an upcoming visit to Asia to demonstrate the quality of the McGonigle work. He, as with most independents, did not have a stock of watches that he could put in a showcase for clients to see and buy. The independent's production is dictated by the orders they receive, and they sell virtually everything they produce as soon as it is completed.

After the trip to Asia, John insisted that he take the watch apart to fully service the movement and put it in top shape before delivering it to me. Of course, I agreed. The watch was delivered within several months. Notably, according to John, Stephen originally built the watch and John did the service, so I have the only McGonigle **tourbillon** watch worked on by both brothers.

Tourbillion by McGonigle

The Basel Watch Fair

Once a year, in the early spring, the Basel Watch Fair was the place to be for those interested in watches. The big brands constructed large exhibit structures. Some created buildings two stories high within the confines of the exhibition hall. As the popularity of independent watchmakers increased, they were provided space in an adjacent hall to present their newest creations. Unfortunately, I was not able to go to the Basel Fair for a variety of reasons. As much as I would have liked to have gone, the show was geared toward those involved with the industry: retailers, journalists, and, of course, VIPs. Attendees of the fair, in order to see the new products, had to schedule appointments with the individual brands. Those appointments were hard to come by as they were typically reserved for the target audience and high-valued clients. If the attendee did not have an appointment, he or she was left to stroll through the exhibit hall and see window displays of the brands' standard products but not the new releases. This would be no different than going to a retail outlet or a boutique anywhere on the planet. Of course, being at the fair did give the attendee some bragging rights, after paying a significant entrance fee and being able to afford the exorbitant prices for coffee and lunch or snacks. I am told that the prices for hotel rooms were also inflated sharply during the time of the fair. Once again, many visitors bolstered their egos by getting a reservation in "the right" hotels and spending a ridiculous amount of money for a room.

I knew that Tim attended the Basel Fair annually to visit several of the brands but, more importantly, to check in with the watchmakers that he represented and to search for new talent. Before he left for Basel, I typically asked him to keep a lookout for something special. I am positive that I was not the only one of his customers to make such a request, but once again, it could not hurt to ask. Besides, our relationship had matured to the point where he had a good sense of what I preferred and what might be a good addition to my growing collection.

One year, shortly after the Basel Fair opened, I was sitting in my backyard when I received a text from Tim saying he'd found a watch for me. It was a piece by Peter Speake-Marin, a one-of-a-kind prototype **jump hour** called the Marin 3. It was unlike anything Tim had previously seen. He sent me pictures, and we agreed that he would call me later that day. When we spoke, Tim told me that I had until the next day, Geneva time, to decide whether I wanted the piece. If I refused or delayed my decision, the watch was going to be sent to Vietnam for sale.

I do not respond well to pressure sales, but this was a different situation. Once again, I was being asked to decide on a watch without seeing it in the metal. Tim described the watch, saying it had the same dimensions as one that I already possessed, so I knew how the watch would feel on my wrist. Having met Peter on several occasions, I was also comfortable with the quality of his work. The **jump hour** module was unique. It was totally exposed, sitting on top of the main plate that covered a standard Speake-Marin movement. The sweep second and minute hands were mounted on the central post, and the **jump hour** display was at the twelve o'clock position. As the minute hand circled the dial, the gearing could be seen preparing for the jump of the hour hand. Unique to this watch, the hour hand could safely "jump" forward or backward. This feature is very rare in **jump hour** watches. In most **jump hour** watches, the owner is specifically instructed to only advance the time forward and not go backward. Such a mistake could damage the movement and force its return to its birthplace. With this watch, the wearer could move the minute hand forward or backward without concern for the integrity of the movement.

From the pictures I could tell that the finishing on the movement was finely done. The movement was Peter's, but the unique **jump hour** module was designed, built, and finished by an Irish watchmaker, Stephen McDonnell. With less than twenty-four hours to decide, and with no further information available, I put my faith in Tim's opinion and committed to the watch.

When I finally received the watch, there was no doubt in my mind that I had made the correct decision. It is truly a unique piece, one that has garnered many comments from fellow collectors and watchmakers alike. Besides the one-of-a-kind movement, its finishing was expertly crafted. On the back of the watch, the case is engraved to indicate that it is a prototype for the Marin 3. As part of the **jump hour** module, there is an interesting feature that I did not appreciate in the pictures. At the three o'clock position on the **jump hour** module, there is a small aperture. When the minute hand moves around the dial and approaches the twelve o'clock position, a red dot appears in the window. Once the hour jumps forward, the red dot instantaneously disappears. Clearly the dot had something to do with the **jump hour**, but exactly what message it was delivering was not apparent to me or to Tim.

It was only several years later, when I met Stephen McDonnell, that I found out the true reason for the red dot. When the minute hand is pointing toward the twelve, there is a brief period of time when the wearer might not know whether the time is just before or just after the hour. Stephen's concept to resolve that problem was to have the red dot indicate that the time is before the hour. If the red dot is visible, the hour is the old one and about to change. If the red dot is not visible, the wearer will know that it is the new hour. There is no other watch that I know of that has such attention to detail. That is the brilliance of Stephen McDonnell. Another small mystery regarding the red dot was the nature of its composition. Tim and I were not sure whether Stephen used a special type of paint or other compound that would hold its brilliance and not deteriorate over time. When I asked Stephen, he shrugged and said that it was a dab of his wife's nail polish.

As it turns out, the Speake-Marin Marin 3 prototype is the only one of its kind. Peter decided not to market the watch due to financial considerations. He told me it would cost too much to put into production, and he did not think that he could sell the watch at a price that would make it worthwhile to produce.

Jump Hour Prototype by Speake-Marin

The Watch That Wasn't

After one of the Purists tours, several of the attendees and I took a side trip to Twann, a small town in the Canton of Bern, on the banks of the Bielersee in Switzerland. We went to visit Thomas Prescher, another independent watchmaker. Thomas is the creator of a number of innovative watches but is best known for the production of a set of three watches, each with a unique **tourbillon**. One has a single-axis **tourbillon**, while the second has a double-axis **tourbillon**, and the last contains a remarkable triple-axis **tourbillon**. He is credited for having produced the very first triple-axis **tourbillon** within a wristwatch.

I was unaware of Thomas's body of work until we visited, when I quickly discovered his watches to be mechanically extraordinary. What initially attracted me was his proposal to build a QP (Quantième Perpétuel), a perpetual calendar, where the five hands for time, day of the week, and date come off the central post, something not previously attempted. There were to be no **sub-dials**. The challenge to design and build this watch was obvious even to me. I was captivated.

Thomas gave us a comprehensive tour of his workshop with a detailed explanation about each piece of machinery. We were shown some of his completed watches and the dials for others. After the tour we were invited to lunch. We were offered the choice of an Italian restaurant or a restaurant that served local fare. Collectively we chose the latter.

Over lunch, Thomas explained that the region that we were in, historically, had been a lower-socioeconomic area of Switzerland. As a result, the inhabitants traditionally ate horse meat, as it is a cheaper source of protein than beef. The restaurant he chose was known as the best place to get this local delicacy. When we sat down for lunch, we were not asked what we wanted to eat but rather how many grams we wanted: 250, 350, or 450. So we all ate horse and chips, washed down with local beer.

The restaurant was actually a tavern. We sat outside around a wood table on a cement pad under a wooden trellis. Separating the cement pad from the wall of the adjacent building was a ten-foot-wide strip of grass.

As we worked our way through our horse steaks, two cows walked by on the grass path. Bells clanging, they sauntered past, seemingly on their own accord. Chewing on a piece of horse, I looked over at the first cow; I believe she winked at me.

During and after lunch, Thomas and I discussed his plans for the QP 1 **perpetual calendar**. In detail, he explained his challenges with the movement, using very technical terms. Not being an engineer and still only having a rudimentary understanding of watch movements, I struggled nobly to follow. Despite his concerns and uncertainty about when the watch could be finished, I only grew more intrigued. By then I had several **perpetual calendar** watches but nothing as innovative as what Thomas proposed. Once again, the collector in me saw an opportunity to acquire the number 1 or maybe even the prototype. I was hooked.

When I returned home, I contacted Tim. Tim knew Thomas well and represented him. He knew about the perpetual and thought that it was a good find. After several discussions and some back-and-forth emails with Thomas, the three of us agreed I would receive the first Perpetual QP 1 built. With all parties in agreement, the one factor left open was the time frame for production; the determining variable was when Thomas could solve the issues with the movement. Regardless, once again, I jumped into the independent world. Agreements were made; the order was placed, and I waited.

By this time, I knew that patience was the operant word. I was ordering a watch that was conceived of and partially built but had features not previously created. I understood that Thomas was going to need time to perfect the movement.

Apparently, more than time was required for this watch. For reasons not fully explained, Thomas could not overcome some of the technical challenges to get the watch to function as desired. (Had he tried to explain the problems to me, I doubt that I would have fully understood them.) I learned about the situation when he came to the States to visit Tim and break the news that the QP 1 was not going to happen. When I met Thomas in Tim's store, I could tell he felt bad that he was not able to complete what he promised me. In exchange, he offered me a single-axis **tourbillon** he had with him, as he'd brought several of his other watches. I was disappointed and asked Tim if we could take a walk. We left the store, leaving Thomas and my wife to talk about non-horological topics.

Tim and I discussed my options: cancel the order and be refunded the deposit, or accept the offer of the **tourbillon** at a very reasonable price. On inspection of the **tourbillon**, it, too, was something that I had never seen before. Subsequently, friends labeled it the "**tourbillon** on a stick," as it was in a large see-through aperture balanced only on a single post. As Thomas later explained, the post was composed of a tube within a tube. The power for the **escapement** went up the post, and the time impulse generated by the **escapement** went down the post by way of the second tube. The total diameter of the tubular structure that held the **tourbillon** in space was less than two millimeters.

The watch had other attractive features. It was the first ever created with a **constant force** mechanism in the **tourbillon** carriage. The underside had a unique pattern of decoration not seen in any other watch, a hand-engraved solid-gold plate composed of multiple pyramids. Initially saddened by the reality that the dream of the QP 1 was gone, I grew to understand that I still had the opportunity to obtain something distinctive and rare. Oh, and by the way, it was number 1.

Single-Axis Tourbillon by Thomas Prescher

Later, I learned from my wife that Thomas was very nervous when Tim and I left the shop. He was much relieved when we returned, and I told him that I very happily accepted his offer.

It is a large watch. The case is 43 mm square and wears big, but it is truly a unique piece of horological technology and art.

Gearing Up a Level

Vianney Halter was also at that first meeting Tim hosted, and he brought several of his avant-garde watches, including the Antiqua, the Trio, and the Classic Janvier. As is true with many of the independent watchmakers I have met, Vianney is very interesting. The son of a trainman, Vianney has a fascination with engines and gauges, which perhaps explains his passion for steampunk. That style is reflected in the design of some of his watches, where different "gauges" are used to display different indications, and industrial-looking cases are held together with rivets instead of screws.

At the time of the event, I was not as adventurous as I am now. I tried on the Trio, but it did not sit well on my wrist. The rectangular case, built to represent an ingot of gold, was not comfortable. It felt as if I'd strapped a brick on my wrist. The Antiqua was unlike anything I had seen, and although it did wear comfortably, at that time I could not see myself wearing it because of its avant-garde design, even if I could afford it. What caught my eye was the Classic Janvier. It was in a round case, beautifully executed with interesting astronomical **complications**. Besides time and an **annual calendar**, it shows the **equation of time**, the moon phase, and a lunar calendar. Interested as I was, the price put it out of range for me, yet I kept going back to look at it.

There are multiple considerations that go into selecting the "right" watch, whether it be the first one or an addition to a growing collection. One factor, clearly, is finances. It is important to understand one's own comfort level regarding price and be aware of how easy it can be to get swept up with desire for a particular watch, only to have reality strike when struggling to come up with the funds to pay for the indulgence. For that is what it is: an indulgence. There are attractive watches in all price ranges. The amount of pleasure engendered by the purchase of a watch should never be determined by the price paid for it but rather the joy that it brings. When someone shows me a watch they recently acquired, they will, at times, downplay it with the excuse that they are sure it is not something that interests me or something I would want to own. That may be true, but it is their watch, and it is what they like and can comfortably afford. I always assure them that their happiness with the watch is all that matters, not what I might think. If they're happy, then I am as well and support their choice.

Some collectors start out acquiring entry-level pieces and gradually increase the price range that they will consider as time passes and they refine their taste. Others start with entry-level watches and choose to stay at that level and price point because of financial considerations or because they prefer to obtain a greater variety rather than fewer, more exclusive and expensive ones. Still others jump into the deep end at the outset, choosing to go for an upper-end watch as their first purchase. Clearly the choice is the individual's. There is no right or wrong decision.

When I started collecting, I had a comfort zone that was very conservative. As time passed, I gradually expanded that zone. There are always limits to what I am willing to spend on a watch, but as time progressed, I expanded my comfort zone. Once I cross to the next, albeit arbitrary, price range, I tend to favor watches in that general level. Of course, I am always willing to consider a new piece in a less expensive price range if it interests me.

My tolerance and willingness to consider a more expensive watch and further expand my comfort zone usually comes about when I am presented with a special watch that entices me for whatever reason. Of course, the increased price requires a fair amount of consideration and often rationalization, as I must justify it to myself and to my wife. Regardless of my decision on the purchase of an expensive watch, I know that there are even more expensive watches that are incredible. There is a broad range in haute horology, and I know that I will never be able to attain the highest heights, and I am okay with that realization. I can still appreciate those watches for the marvels that they are—from a distance.

I know that the same can be said by virtually anyone; it is just a matter of where one draws the line for what is and is not comfortably affordable.

At the time of my first exposure to Vianney Halter's watches, I was not in a position to consider purchasing any of them. In fact, the McGonigle **tourbillon** that I eventually purchased was at that same event, yet I wasn't able to wrap my head around the concept of spending the money on it until I saw it again in Ireland years later. Even if I'd had the capacity to pay the price at the time for a Vianney Halter watch, I am not sure that I would have bought one, with the possible exception of the Janvier, given their design and fit on the wrist.

Robert from the Watch Connection offered me a preowned Antiqua at a reasonable price. I thanked him for the opportunity but did not pursue it, as I, again, was not sure that I would wear it because of its design. Times change and tastes change. If the same offer came my way now, I might strongly consider the purchase. I have become somewhat more adventurous with regards to what I am willing to wear, but even now there are limits.

A number of years after I first met Vianney, Tim called to offer me the opportunity to obtain a Classic. First presented by Vianney in the early 2000s, it is a simple time-only watch in a case reminiscent of the Janvier without the complex astronomical features. It has a modified movement that is highly finished and features his "mystery mass" **rotor**, a weighted ring that seems unconnected to the central pinion but is still able to wind the **mainspring**. Tim had two available that represented some of the last to be produced in the series. Of the two, one was in a yellow gold case and the other a rose gold case. The yellow gold watch was the last of thirty-four pieces Vianney made in that metal case. As a nice complement, the hands were blued. The rose gold option was one of a 140-piece series. Tim told me that he wanted one for himself, but I could have the pick of the two. I jumped at the opportunity to see and potentially get one of the watches. We agreed to meet for breakfast, and once again, the purchase of a watch occurred in an odd locale. At least this time it was not in a bathroom but rather in an outdoor restaurant on a pleasant Sunday morning.

I do like to be social and enjoy conversations that have to do with things other than watches, but when I am considering the purchase of a watch, I tend to be hyper-focused on the new temptation. Once we were seated at the table and gave the server our order, I moved aside the silverware, and Tim laid out the two watches. Much to Tim's dismay, within several heartbeats, I grabbed the yellow gold Classic and claimed it as mine. Tim was left with a great second choice, the rose gold, though he had hoped I would take that one. He saw the yellow gold model as more exclusive and, we both agreed, more alluring. That said, I do believe that he is still happy with his red gold watch.

Classic by Vianney Halter

In the Company of Dogs

As you may have noted, opportunities to find a watch can occur in strange locations: bathrooms, restaurants, and craft fairs are not the typical venues for deciding to commit to an expensive purchase. That said, one must seize the opportunity when it presents itself and not wait for a better or optimal setting.

Case in point, one day when my wife and I were enjoying an afternoon at a playground with our grandson, I received a text from someone I'd recently met: Aren Bazerkanian. We'd met at the F.P. Journe boutique in Hollywood, where he was a sales associate. Since our meeting, he'd decided to leave the boutique and was in the process of fulfilling his goal of starting his own watch brand, Havid Nagan. He designed his first watch and was working with suppliers in Switzerland to start production. The purpose of the text was to inform me of his new venture and ask for my opinion of the design. Of course, he also wanted to know if I was interested in purchasing one.

We had a nice conversation, initially via text, and he sent me several pictures of his watches, which were hard to fully appreciate because of the bright sun and glare in the park. Based on his description, the project sounded interesting. Once I got home and was better able to appreciate the pictures he had sent, I was intrigued. The case shape was interestingly curved, with dial options of blue, plum, and green with a very attractive **guilloché** pattern. The movement, I was told, was from Schwarz-Etienne, a much more substantial movement than what is typically found in a watch in the price range he quoted.

We had several more conversations over the next couple of days. I found his passion for his nascent brand, not to mention watches in general, to be infectious, and I thought I might want to support his efforts. I said that I was interested but I told him I would not commit to a watch purchase without first seeing one in the metal. I wanted to be sure that the design of the case was to my liking and that it wore well. He understood my point. He lives in Southern California, as do I, and was familiar with where I lived; he and his wife took their dog to a dog park not far from my house, even though it was quite a distance for them to drive. His wife's friends lived near that park, so going there was more about his wife socializing with her friends than the dog's preference. However, as it turned out, we frequented the same park with our dog. Aren's dog would go to the small dog section while ours to the big dog enclosure. We agreed to meet there on the following Sunday.

While our wives watched the dogs, Aren ventured to the big dog area and showed me the Havid Nagan HN00. Of the three dial colors, he was wearing the plum one. I immediately saw that the pictures of the watches he sent did not do the dial justice. The dial glowed. Although the **guilloché** was stamped rather than hand done, it had great three-dimensionality. Aren told me that he considered having the **guilloché** done by hand, but that would have increased the cost of the watch to a point that did not fit his desired price point. I had not thought to bring a loupe, as it is not standard equipment when taking our dog to the park. A ball is essential for a golden retriever to chase but not necessarily to retrieve. For sure she had no interest in watches, so a loupe was unnecessary.

The movement, with a micro-**rotor**, seemed to be nicely finished, according to Aren, to his specifications. The unique arc of the cushion-shaped case fit nicely on my wrist. Without much of a sales pitch, I agreed to commit to the purchase, in the dog park on a fine Sunday afternoon.

HN00 by Havid Nagan

The Right Watch at the Right Time

Our younger son attended the University of California, Berkeley. From Southern California, we drove to Berkeley on a regular basis, especially after, upon my wife's insistence, we bought season tickets to the California

Bears football games. She decided we should be season ticket holders when Aaron Rodgers was the quarterback for Cal. Thanks to Aaron Rodgers and Cal Bears football, my wife became and remains a rabid football enthusiast. Subsequently, after Rodgers became the starting quarterback for the Green Bay Packers, she transformed into a diehard Packer fan. So dedicated was she to the Packers that the boys and I bought her a share in the Green Bay Packers team. She is, as she proudly tells anyone who might care, an owner.

During several of our visits to Berkeley, since we were nearby, I took the opportunity to visit Tim in his Bay Area store. On display he had watches from the brands he represented and from some independents. On every visit he had several pieces made by Richard Habring (the company is Habring[2], so named to represent Richard and his wife, Maria), and often I would try them on.

I had long admired their work. In fact, well before any visit to Tim, I had met Richard and Maria when they came to California from their home in Austria to join one of the early presentations of the independents. Before starting his own company, Richard helped create the **tourbillon** for Lange & Söhne, and, when at IWC, he developed their Doppelchronograph.

Over time, Tim showed me different offerings built by the Habrings. I admired Richard's technological prowess and wanted to support them but could not pull the trigger. At one point, I gave serious consideration to purchasing their **tourbillon**. It was similar in layout, I thought, to the Lange & Söhne **tourbillon**, but at a much more attractive price. In the end I decided against it. Richard's ability as a watchmaker is unquestionably top notch. He is able to produce watches with a variety of interesting **complications** and offer them at very affordable prices. However, even with all the available color and layout variations, I was not attracted to the watches. The dials were machine pressed, and the finishing of both the dials and the movement were not what I preferred. The finishing of a watch dial and movement has become very important for me when selecting a watch. Of course, the degree of finishing affects the price of the piece, but it is a cost that I am willing to absorb.

To celebrate the anniversary of the release of his split-second **chronograph**, Richard produced a limited series of watches with that very special **complication**. I wanted to support and honor Richard's creativity with the purchase of one. Also, I saw it as a good opportunity to obtain a **rattrapante**, a **complication** I did not have in my collection. Unfortunately, once again, I could not bring myself to acquire the Habring². The aesthetic of the watch did not suit my taste. At the same time, IWC released the Ingenieur Doppelchronograph. It contained the same movement that was in the Habring² anniversary piece; after all, it was the one that Richard had developed for them. Mainly because of aesthetics, I chose the IWC model. I realize that by picking the IWC, Richard achieved no benefit.

The IWC Ingenieur was more of a sport watch, and its dial design attracted me. The blue highlights on the **bezel** and second hand against the black background caught my eye at first glance and continue to give me joy. They are a small feature of the watch but seem to have an oversized effect on me. Also, the fit was very comfortable, especially since it is built for a more casual or sporty look. It came on a rubber strap with a titanium case, making it form-fitting and very light to wear. In addition to the split **chronograph**, the Ingenieur displayed the day of the week as well as the date, a feature that the Habring² model did not have.

Because it shows the day, the IWC has become one of my preferred travel companions, even though it is not a **GMT watch**. When I travel, knowing what day it is tends to be more important than knowing the specific date. On one vacation, my family and I arrived at a hotel on the wrong day simply because I lost track of the day of the week. This watch helps to eliminate that confusion. As an unintended consequence of that mistake, however, I learned an invaluable lesson. When we arrived at the hotel a day early, after initial confusion, the hotel manager uttered what for me are famous words, "No problem," and arranged for our accommodations. I subsequently realized that when someone says, "No problem," there is not a problem, and any issue is resolved. If, on the other hand, someone says, "Well, let me see what I can do," or something similar, then there very well might be a problem. That theory has been proven on quite a number of occasions. Now if someone says to me, "No problem," I breathe a sigh of relief because I know that the issue at hand will be resolved to everyone's satisfaction.

Ingenieur Doppelchronograph by IWC

Eventually, I had the opportunity to speak with Richard about the finishing of his watches. He was very open and honest in his response, admitting that he considered the finishing of his watches to be about 80 percent done, and he was fine with that. His rationale was that in order to create a greater degree of finishing, the time required would force him to raise the prices of his product. He thought that the price point of his watches was in a place where, given the nature of his products, he did not have competition. He did not want to change a business model that was working well for him and Maria. It was refreshing to get such a transparent response, one that demanded ultimate respect. Interestingly, this is the same rationale Aren gave me later when he and I spoke about the **guilloché** on the dials of his watches.

It was at an event that Tim hosted for Richard and Maria when I had that frank conversation with him. For the occasion, they brought a broad sample of their current inventory. One of the watches caught my eye, the COS ZM Pilot. On the surface, the watch was a typical pilot's watch: black dial with white numerals, indices, and hands. I was told that it was a **chronograph**, but it had no **pushers** or **sub-dials**. Instead, turning the

197

crown counterclockwise activated the **chronograph**, and the second hand started counting the seconds. Another hand that was hidden under the second hand counted the elapsed minutes on the dial, and the dial served as the minute counter. When the **crown** was turned in a clockwise manner to the neutral position, the **chronograph** would stop. Another counterclockwise turn would set it moving again, or a further clockwise turn would reset the **chronograph**. To wind and set the time of the watch, the **crown** had to be pulled into the second and third positions, respectively.

The COS in the name stands for Crown Operating System, a Richard Habring innovation. Brilliant. With most **monopusher chronographs**, the system has only start, stop, and reset functions. This COS, which could be considered a **monopusher** since there was only one **crown** that controlled the **chronograph**, had the addition of a restart function. The dial was simple in design but technologically complicated. For the first time, a Habring² watch unequivocally attracted me. Even better, the back of the watch was closed, so the quality of finishing of the movement was not an issue. Perfect. I'd finally found my Habring² watch. I committed to it immediately. To make matters even more interesting, it was the prototype. Between the **lugs** at six o'clock, the case was engraved "piece unique." What more could I want? Within minutes of seeing and learning about the watch, I gave Tim my credit card. I went home very happy after spending a lovely evening with friends, the Habrings, and a new watch.

Typically, I do not wear the same watch two days in a row. For that reason, I am not very concerned about the accuracy of timekeeping over the course of days, to a reasonable degree. That said, I set the watch to the correct second in the morning and check it at the end of the day. A few seconds' variation is acceptable, but I admit to getting a thrill when, in the evening, the time on my watch matches, to the second, that on the clock I used to set it hours earlier. I set the watch precisely to assess the health of the watch. If a watch is losing or gaining too much time, especially if it is a recent change in accuracy, it may be an indication that servicing is required.

An exception to my typical watch-wearing pattern is when I bring a new watch home, I tend to wear it for a few days in succession to enjoy and celebrate its arrival. When I brought my Habring home, that is exactly what I did. Of course, I played with the **chronograph** repeatedly since that was the novelty of the watch. Shortly, I discovered that the hands of the **chronograph** did not reset properly when the **crown** was turned. Once again, the risk attendant to acquiring a first of its kind became apparent. After confirming that the **chronograph** did have a problem, I notified Tim, who in turn notified Richard.

Chronograph COS ZM Pilot by Habring[2]

The watch was returned to Richard who sheepishly admitted that before coming to the States for the event, he hurriedly assembled the movement with parts available to him on his bench. I suspect that he did not plan for this particular watch to be sold. Unlike many other situations I have experienced where a watch is gone for months for repair, adjustment, or servicing, this watch was returned to me in a matter of several weeks, working perfectly, and it has since that time. This is one of the benefits of working with an independent who is the designer, builder, and service center all in one. Communication is easier, and resolution of a problem is usually much faster.

Marco Goes Solo

The first time that I met Marco Lang was many years ago in Los Angeles. Marco was the Lang in the company Lang & Heyne until he left the company. Subsequently, I've been fortunate to meet him several times when he traveled to the US.

Earlier, I mentioned that my wife and I took a trip to Germany. We started in Berlin and took a meandering course through the country in our typical fashion; we followed no preconceived plan or route. We wanted to visit certain places but the exact timing for these stopovers were left to the spirit of the moment. On the Autobahn, driving toward Dresden, we passed signs for Glashütte, the town famous for German watchmaking. As we were not on a trip geared toward watches and watchmaking, I did not think it would be fair to my wife to divert us toward that destination. Definite husband points were gained from that decision. Besides, if I'd wanted a tour of a manufacture, planning in advance and booking one prior to arrival is always the best strategy. Alas, advanced planning is not always my strong suit when it comes to vacations. What had previously happened in Switzerland, when we'd knocked on Audemars Piguet's door and received a tour of the facility, was the exception and certainly not the rule when dealing with watch manufactures.

We had a pleasant visit in Dresden, where we came upon a watch store that was established by Marco Lang. At the time, it was one of a very few retail establishments in the world that exhibited the work of independent watchmakers. It was a pleasant, though brief, stopover in the store because before arriving in Germany, I actually did a little pre-planning and made arrangements to visit Marco in his atelier. *That* was where I wanted to spend the time allotted for a watch experience.

Marco's atelier was located in his house and this time not in the garage. On a residential street across the River Elbe from the Dresden city center, a small brass plate on a fence announced the presence of Marco's atelier. Shortly after we rang the doorbell, Marco came to the door and welcomed us. He introduced us to his wife and then began our tour of the part of the house that served as his workplace.

Marco is a fifth-generation watchmaker. In the reception area of the workshop, there were framed mementos of the generations of watchmakers in the family, including, interestingly, his grandmother, who was a master watchmaker. A woman in such a position was not common in those days. There was also a beautiful clock that was part of the Lang family heritage.

The atelier was composed of several floors where watchmakers were busy at work. Of course, there were the obligatory computers and a CNC machine, but much of the work and finishing was being done by hand. He took us through the construction process of his watches, along the way introducing us to the team members responsible for the various stages of creation. The result of their combined efforts was beautiful watches that I'd admired since first laying eyes on them during Marco's visits to the US.

It was a wonderful visit with Marco, and my desire to bring home a watch created by him and his team was affirmed. But which one?

For quite some time I was attracted to a model called the Albert. It is a **monopusher chronograph** that is elegant in all respects. Interestingly, the **chronograph** utilizes the main dial to count the seconds and minutes of elapsed time for the **chronograph**, while the hour and minute hand continue to show the time of day. A very clever execution, one that predated the Habring[2] COS ZM pilot **chronograph** by a number of years. Everything about the watch checked all the boxes for me: the white enamel dial's classic design with Roman numerals perfectly proportioned to the dial is magnificent; the platinum case work is beautiful; and the **chronograph** movement unique and exquisitely finished. The **pusher** that controls the **chronograph** in the Albert is incorporated within the **crown** to start, stop, and reset the **chronograph**, but unlike with the Habring[2] **chronograph**s, there is no option to resume function.

Function aside, from the first time I saw the Albert, I gave it serious consideration. The issue that prevented me from committing to the watch was the fit on my wrist. At 44 mm, the watch felt big when I strapped it on. When considering the purchase of any watch, the diameter of the case is an important variable to take into account. However, the number alone does not always dictate the fit of the watch; the design of the **lugs** is key to how the watch sits on any wrist, large or small. I have a couple of watches with 46 mm cases that fit well because the **lugs** curve down in such a fashion that the straps wrap comfortably around my wrist. I will not, on the other hand, wear some watches that have a smaller diameter case because the **lugs** lay straight, which, in turn, sends the bracelet away from the case horizontally. In those circumstances, the watch feels as though it is protruding beyond my wrist and wears bigger than its measurement, and it is uncomfortable.

I was given the opportunity to wear the Albert in a platinum case for a day to see how it felt on my wrist. Throughout the day I kept admiring it. It is absolutely stunning. Pure elegance. As a fun coincidence, the Albert I was lent was number 23, a favored number as it is my birth date. Beautiful though it was, I could not commit to the purchase even with the special number. The experience was an interesting lesson for me. A watch is made to be worn. A watch may be beautiful and the subject of daydreams, but if it does not feel right on the wrist, then it is not the right choice. Trusting one's instincts is critical when deciding whether to buy something. Regardless of my ability to put into words why I am interested in or hesitant about a potential purchase, having faith in my sixth sense has not led me astray.

Despite my experience with the Albert, I knew I wanted something representative of Marco's skill and art. When he launched his first rectangular-cased watch, the Georg, I thought I found the one for me. The dimensions of the watch, 40 x 32 mm, would certainly fit better on my wrist. The reverse side had a uniquely designed movement whose finishing was outstanding. When I tried on an example, it fit perfectly. It was a winner.

I spoke to Tim about the watch, and he agreed that it was beautiful, and, in fact, he eventually got one for himself. However, after considerable discussion, he advised me to wait and not get the Georg. He said that while the Georg was great, Marco was going to release his first **tourbillon** in the same-sized case, and that was the watch I should strongly consider. With that information and the agreement to keep it secret, I waited. It turned out that I waited a year before Marco was ready to announce the new watch that he called the Anton.

By the time the Anton was publicly announced, I had an agreement with Marco that I would receive number 1, a great honor. Often companies will number the cases of different metals separately. There can be several number 1s based on the metal of the case or the color of the dial or some such variation in the model. Not so with Lang & Heyne. Marco numbered the movement so there would only be one number 1. Once the number was agreed upon, I needed to choose the of metal for the case of my Anton. After consulting with Tim, who had seen the different combinations of metal cases and colored hands that were available, albeit in the context of the Georg, I chose rose gold and blue hands. That done, I requested that Marco do something extra special for my watch. I wanted something to set the watch apart from others besides the number 1 since I had been waiting patiently for so long. Generously, Marco agreed. It was his intent to include a small diamond chip in each of the top corners of the underside of the base plate in every Anton. For me, he offered to replace the diamonds with blue sapphires, and of course I accepted. In addition, he blued the hairspring to match the blue of the hands and the sapphires.

To say the least, I was and remain entranced by the beauty of the Anton, front and back. The piece has all the features that I require in a finely made watch: excellent technology, in-house movement development, an enamel dial, and a movement that was expertly hand-finished.

As I awaited completion of my Anton, I did not know that there was a major change in Lang & Heyne coming. Very shortly after I accepted delivery of my watch, Marco announced that he was leaving his eponymous company. Lang & Heyne was to continue as a brand but without Marco's association. It was a major shock to me personally.

As it turns out, my Anton may be the only or at most one of two Antons ever touched by the master himself. The company continues, and Marco went on to establish his own brand, Marco Lang Watches, with a single employee, Marco Lang.

Anton Tourbillon by Lang & Heyne

Marco may have been done with Lang & Heyne, but certainly he was not done with his creativity as a watchmaker. Two years after the separation from the company that bore his name, I learned from Tim that Marco was ready to announce the first model to be produced by his new company. It was called the Zweigesicht-1 and was to be uniquely designed. The watch displayed the time on both sides, one with a solid dial and the other **skeletonized**. It could be worn with either face exposed by way of manipulating the **lugs** and straps.

Ever inventive, Marco designed a novel four-way shock indication system. This system provided information regarding any shocks the watch might sustain that could affect timekeeping. It gave the watchmaker the ability to adjust the movement appropriately should a shock occur. Even more impressive, the information regarding this system was open sourced so that any watchmaker could have access to it.

The series consisted of eighteen watches, and Tim gave me the opportunity to grab one. Once again, I had to make my decision by studying pictures since there was no prototype to see. This time I had an advantage. I knew of Marco's skill and his attention to detail and design. I realized that this was a unique project that I wanted to join. I was not concerned about fit, as the case was 40 mm, which is a very wearable size for me. It is fortunate that I made the decision to proceed, as the series sold out rapidly. This time I was an early bird that got the worm.

Zweigesicht-1 face and reverse by Marco Lang

Chapter 9
The Visit

Several years after my introduction to the independent watchmaking world, I took a bold step. One New Year's Day, I was not working and had little to do. The football game on television did not interest me, and as is frequently the case when my.thoughts are not otherwise engaged, my mind drifted to watches. At the time, I had been reading *Masters of Contemporary Watchmaking* by Michael Clerizo, which profiles some of the most prominent watchmakers of our time. The work by some of these watchmakers interested me. I decided to email several whose work intrigued me, expressing interest in their work. While I was at it, I also sent emails to a few not mentioned in the book but whose work I admired.

To my surprise, several days later, I received responses from Roger Smith and Kari Voutilainen. With nothing to lose and only friendships to gain, I started communicating with both. Separate from Clerizo's book, I was familiar with Kari's work, having met him on several occasions, but I knew very little about Roger, except what I had read. Roger was the only apprentice employed by George Daniels. I had learned from several people knowledgeable about such matters that George Daniels is considered by many to be the Abraham-Louis Breguet of modern times. He is credited with the creation of the first new watch movement in over two hundred years, the co-axial **escapement**. First developed in the 1970s, George eventually sold the movement to Omega, which uses it in most of their watches produced today.

Because George lived on the Isle of Man, Roger was compelled to move there so that he could work with George, who taught him how to build a complete watch from start to finish. It was George's belief that all of the parts must be made and assembled in-house, from cases to the tiniest of components, that all parts were finely hand-finished, and that the dials were to decorated with **guilloché** using the rose engine.

On Befriending Roger

In 1999, George and Roger built a watch called the Millennium Watch, which contained a modified Omega co-axial movement. A series of fifty watches were constructed. After completing his apprenticeship with George, Roger remained on the Isle of Man, where he started his own brand in 2001.

When I began communicating with Roger, he had just launched his second model, the Series 2. All I knew about his watches was that they were built to the strict standards of George Daniels, and, based on the few pictures I saw of the Series 1 and Series 2, they were stunning. Again, with only my inner voice advising me, I decided that of the two models, the Series 2 was the one I favored.

Initially, our discussion was only by email, but in short order, Roger suggested that he call me. Of course, I immediately agreed, and we set up a time for the following Saturday. At the appointed hour, Roger called, and we had a very pleasant conversation; I walked around our local farmers market while he was eight time zones away. During the conversation, I innocently, though foolishly, inquired if there happened to be something of George's, like a watch, lying around that might be available. Roger was gracious and diplomatic; he completely ignored the question. Once again, one never knows what may result from an innocent question, so why not ask? I am sure I was not the first person to ask such a ludicrous question. I believe that there are no dumb questions, but there are absolutely silly ones.

By the end of our forty-five-minute phone call, I was pretty much convinced about the Series 2. Nonetheless, we had several more conversations before I finalized the decision to proceed with the purchase. Before I did, I asked Roger about the possibility of having him build a

perpetual calendar as an alternative to a Series 2. I was particularly interested in **perpetual calendars** and owned several at that time, so I thought it worth investigating. He promised to get back to me about it.

Our next call occurred while my wife and I were about to enter a motel, on our way to visit our son in Berkley. Roger said he would be willing to make the **perpetual calendar** for me. Great news. To do that, he would have to build one from the ground up, starting with the creation of hand-drawn renderings for each component of the movement. Great. To construct the watch, he would need to build a completely new movement, and that would require retooling some of his equipment. Uh-oh. He did not consider it feasible to use one of his "standard" movements and add a **perpetual calendar** module. As I entered the lobby of the motel, he told me the approximate price. I immediately turned around and went outside to finish the conversation. It was not good news. I still had a child in college and a wife who was, at best, skeptical about my hobby. Sadly, it was not going to happen.

Once the **perpetual calendar** idea was put to rest, we struck a deal for the Series 2. I was committed; the case would be made of rose gold; the dial and **sub-dials** would be decorated with the standard (if you can call it that) engine-turned **guilloché**; and he agreed to add engraving to the **barrel bridge** and balance cock. A deposit was requested and sent. There was no defined delivery date, but I was assured that the watch would go into production within several months and would take six months to complete.

Once again, I committed to a watch I had not seen in the metal, but here, at least, I did have pictures that helped with my decision. It was Roger himself who ultimately sold me the piece. It is not that he is a salesman; Roger did not convince me to buy anything. Rather, it was because of the type of person he is. In his softspoken manner, he explained his dedication to the principles Daniels preached. He was patient with me when I peppered him with questions. Without hesitation, he gave me details of the movement, particularly the adjustments to the original co-axial movement he was considering, with George's approval, of course. Little did I know how wonderful the watch would ultimately be. That inner voice of mine, once again, did not lead me astray.

A short time after I wired my deposit for the Series 2, Roger announced to the world that he and George had designed a watch to celebrate the thirty-fifth anniversary of the creation of the co-axial movement. The announcement took the watch world by storm. Roger was going to produce, under George's watchful eye, a series of thirty-five numbered pieces. Per George's preference, and to honor the pieces he had built, the cases for the series would be made from yellow gold. In addition to thirty-five yellow gold watches, the plan was also to produce up to four sets of four watches each with the movement cased in a different precious metal: white gold, yellow gold, rose gold, and platinum.

After reading the announcement, I had a few restless nights of sleep. Ultimately, throwing caution to the wind, I gave in to temptation and contacted Roger. We had another telephone call, this time to discuss the Daniels Anniversary watch. Pacing in my backyard, I listened to Roger describe the watch. He said that, unlike the Millennium project, this watch was going to be original from the ground up. It would not contain an off-the-shelf movement, but rather Roger, with George's absolute approval, had designed an original movement to include changes to the co-axial that would never again be used in any other watch. He described the changes to me, but I must admit it was beyond my level of understanding.

I swallowed the bait and asked about the availability of an allocation. It is said that one should never think they are going to only look at puppies. Invariably, when one does so, a puppy comes home. It is the same thing for me with watches. When I ask about availability, I may think that I am asking for curiosity's sake, but in truth I am asking if I will need to plan to make room for it when it comes home, eventually. Yes, there was availability, as I had called early enough. Number 1 was taken, as were other preferred numbers, but number 35 was still available. I asked if the deposit I sent for the Series 2 could be transferred to the Daniels. Roger said yes without hesitation. I asked for a couple of days to consider the opportunity, and he agreed, saying he would reserve the number 35, pending my decision.

The cost differential between the two pieces was substantial and gave me more than a moment of pause. Up until then, I had never spent anywhere close to the amount of money being asked for a Daniels on a single watch. It was crossing a boundary I thought impassable. It defied logic. It was also the first time I thought about a watch with regards to its historical significance. I never purchase a watch with any thought of financial gain. However, given the reality of the numbers being discussed, I felt I needed to at least take financial factors into consideration. I contacted several people whose opinions I trust; something that I had not done previously. It was during those discussions I was told Daniels was the modern-day Breguet.

Taking more than a few deep breaths, I committed to the watch, although I did make one request of Roger. The thirty-five Daniels Anniversary watches were going to be numbered with the inscriptions "No. 1," "No. 2," etc. George was in his early eighties, and I figured this would most likely be his last project. With that in mind, I asked if my watch, as it would be the last of the series, could be engraved "35/35" instead of "No. 35." In my mind, it would represent the last of the last, the last watch of the last series. Roger agreed. I had no idea how prescient that request would turn out to be.

The number of the watch in a series does not relate to the order of production. Watch companies tend to produce watches in the sequence that orders are received and not by the engraved case number, even in a limited series. Although collectors make a big deal about the case or movement numbers, there is no real significance to them. The numbering becomes more significant after the watches have been produced. It is more a case of bragging rights than anything else. My watch was not the first one produced, as there had been orders placed before mine, yet it was one of the earliest ones completed.

When I placed my order, it was not far from my sixtieth birthday. My dream for that significant birthday was to arrange a trip to the Isle of Man and have George hand me my watch. That would be a fantastic birthday present, albeit from myself. The only one I told of that wish was my wife, as I thought that it was not wise to place any expectation upon Roger—not that it would have made a difference. There is no way to rush excellence.

As time passed, I communicated with Roger and his wife, Caroline, a number of times for updates on how the project was progressing. As they were working on the first watches ordered, it became apparent my dream was not going to come to fruition. I also periodically asked about George's well-being. Roger would respond that George had good and not-so-good days. He would not provide more details, and I, of course, would not ask for them.

Meanwhile, my wife and I decided to take a trip to England. The trip was unrelated to anything to do with watches, if that is ever possible. While planning our trip, my wife suggested we include a visit to the Isle of Man. We had already met Roger and Caroline, but my wife thought it would be a good idea to see them again, and I could take the opportunity to meet George Daniels. I am not the kind of person who seeks out celebrities to have my picture taken with them or ask for an autograph. Besides, why would George want to meet me, and what would I talk to him about? I resisted, but my wife insisted. She repeatedly reminded me about the varying state of George's well-being. She argued that if something was to happen to him and we did not take advantage of the opportunity to meet him, I would be forever disappointed. I finally relented and emailed Roger to ask if it was a possibility. In short order, Roger replied that we absolutely should come for a visit, so plans were made.

After arriving in England, we spent a few days in London, which included a stop at the British Museum. One of the top museums in the world, it contains an overwhelmingly vast collection. During our wanderings we came upon rooms thirty-eight and thirty-nine, exhibits dedicated to English watchmaking. In one display case were pocket watches constructed by the most famous watchmakers in British, if not world history, such as John Arnold, Thomas Mudge and George Graham. International historical figures were represented as well, including Abraham-Louis Breguet. There, among the elite, hung a watch built by George Daniels.

On Meeting George

The Isle of Man lies in the Irish Sea midway between England and Ireland. There are two ways to get there, by ferry or air. Fortunately, we decided to fly. Had we ignored my wife's propensity for seasickness and taken the ferry, we would have been stranded on the island. There was such significant wind when we were scheduled to return to England that the ferry was canceled for the day.

When we landed at the Douglas airport, Caroline met us and took us on a driving tour of the island. We went through remote parts with idyllic scenery of windswept fields ending at cliffs overlooking the Irish Sea. After stopping for tea, we headed to their house, located in a remote area at the intersection of two roads, neither traversed by many vehicles. Roger was there to welcome us. Once again, the workshop was in a converted garage divided into several rooms. The largest contained a large table that served as a communal bench, where two watchmakers sat working, with space for two more, one of which being Roger. In a separate room was Roger's technician, who was responsible for operating the CNC machine that produced the needed components for the watches.

After pleasantries were exchanged, the technician pulled out a sheet of metal and, speaking directly to my wife, told her how creating a watch started with a sheet of metal. For the next forty-five minutes, he patiently and expertly took my wife through the process of making a watch from start to finish. For me, that was the most valuable forty-five minutes ever spent in a manufacture or atelier because when he finished, my wife looked at me and said words I have cherished ever since: "Now I understand why watches cost so much." I cannot count the number of times I had to talk my wife off a ledge when she found out what I was paying for a watch. That moment of clarity has markedly lessened the frequency of these discussions, though they still do occur at times.

While my wife received her tutorial, Roger and I discussed more pedestrian subjects: watches and watch movements. On the bench lay two Daniels Anniversary watches ticking away. Neither was mine, but there they were in the metal, and, of importance, they had been carefully inspected and approved by George Daniels.

After the visit to the atelier, the four of us went into the town of Douglas. Caroline and my wife chatted as Roger and I walked ahead, continuing our conversation. Accompanying us was Mac, Roger's terrier, otherwise referred to as "the terrorist." Roger related, with Caroline's concurrence, the story of Mac's conniving ways that earned him his moniker. It was an unforgettable moment: me walking with Roger Smith, one of the most well-respected watchmakers on the planet, having an in-depth conversation interrupted by him needing to scoop up his dog's waste. I doubt there are any journalists, watch collectors, or enthusiasts who have had a similar experience.

After dinner we retired to the bed-and-breakfast Caroline had arranged for us, and the following morning, Roger picked us up and drove us to George's house. George lived in a Georgian mansion with several outbuildings on four acres of land. Our first stop was the garage that had been converted into George's workshop. In the anteroom, Roger showed us some technical drawings for a watch movement—done by hand by George. He never used a computer to design his movements or do the necessary calculations. All plans were conceived and worked out by pencil and paper.

We next went into the workshop itself. In so doing, it was as if we'd entered a time portal to when George had just walked out of the workshop after a long day at the bench. There, amid various tools of the trade, were his glasses with attached loupes. A wine glass, minus its stem, covered a partially deconstructed pocket watch, with various parts strewn about on the bench. I am sure that in the chaos was organization known only to the watchmaker. There were two partially completed silver dials and a case back for a pocket watch. Sitting on a block of wood was a co-axial **escapement** that apparently was destined to be included in the disassembled pocket watch. It would have been romantic to think that it was one of the first co-axial **escapements** made, but no claim of that possibility was offered. In subsequent conversations with Roger, I could not resist the impulse to ask if there was a possibility of acquiring half-finished dials. Once again, Roger was incredibly gracious in the way he said no.

Around this large room, there were various pieces of watchmaking equipment. Among the machinery large and small, there was a notable absence of a computer. There was no CNC machine and no CAD drawings. On one side of the room sat a rose engine used to apply the **guilloché** to the dials. Roger showed us step by step how to operate the cams of the rose engine and how to create the complex patterns for the dials. Extreme concentration, Roger told us, was required to produce a flawless dial. He would spend hours deep into the night working on a single dial. If his attention was distracted, he risked making a mistake that would result in the dial having to be discarded and the process restarted. Once the explanation was done, Roger gave my wife a turn at the rose engine machine to give her a sense of its operation. It was a memorable moment as she operated the machine George used to decorate the dials of his historic watches and Roger would use to create the one for my watch.

When we finished our exploration of the workshop, we headed toward the side entrance to the main house. As we entered, my wife asked me what I was going to talk to George about. Under my breath, I responded that I had no idea. I handed her my camera for safe-keeping and continued carrying my copy of *Watchmaking* written by George. The book is considered the bible of watchmaking. It seems to be de rigueur for watchmakers to have a copy of *Watchmaking* in their workshop, readily at hand for reference. (It also seems to be customary for watchmakers to have an Atmos Clock by Jaeger-LeCoultre, whether or not it is in working condition, on a shelf somewhere in their shop.)

Except for the ticking of a grandfather clock, the house was quiet as we walked down the carpeted first-floor hallway toward the sitting room where George was waiting. As we approached, we could hear soft voices emanating from a television. Roger had previously explained to us that George was having issues with significant pain and was scheduled for surgery the following week. We entered the sitting room and found George in a wheelchair, opposite a hospital bed.

The decor was decades old, but the room was neatly kept. Several pictures of George in various settings were hanging on the wall. In one corner, a television was on, the volume of the broadcast turned down. A bedside hospital table stood next to him with a plate of petit fours left untouched, along with a cup of tea.

Introductions were made, and Roger asked George how he was doing. George responded that he was bored. I sat down on the bed opposite George and inquired about his general state of health and his upcoming surgery. I asked if he was nervous about the surgery, to which he replied, with an acerbic wit, he was not, but his surgeon should be. In fact, he was looking forward to it because the pain was an incredible distraction from his work. He added that if anything bad should happen, he would not care because he would be dead; rather, the surgeon would have to deal with the aftereffects. Definitely dark humor and a very British perspective.

Changing subjects, I asked what he thought about when he went to sleep at night. He replied he thought about cars and watches. As far as he was concerned, cars were done (this was before the advent of electric cars), but watches were not; there was more to do. Roger mentioned there was a vintage Bentley parked outside the bed-and-breakfast where we had spent the night. Being such an expert about the brand, without hesitation, George knew the model and all the particulars about that car.

As we continued talking, sometimes George would drift off for a moment, but otherwise he was sharp and very detailed in his answers during our forty-five-minute visit. Of course we spoke about his co-axial movement. He proudly and emphatically stated that the accuracy of his movement was better than anything else in the market, reminding us his movement had an error rate of about one second a month and had a service interval that was much longer than what is recommended for other movements. I have several Omega watches with the co-axial movement in addition to the Daniels, so I can testify to the truth of George's claim. They are very accurate timekeepers.

When Roger and I had spoken about the Anniversary watch, he told me that the **power reserve** was limited to about thirty-six hours. Most modern watches have **power reserves** that last at least forty-five hours, if not more. Some watches have **power reserves** that have been extended to seven to ten days. In fact, A. Lange & Söhne produced a watch with a thirty-day **power reserve** and required a crank to wind the **mainspring**. I asked George why the **power reserve** for his watch was relatively low. He gave two reasons. The first was that the limited **power reserve** was to guarantee accuracy of timekeeping. As the **mainspring** unwinds, there can be a point where there is deterioration of power transmission and a decline in the **amplitude** of the **escape wheel**, thus affecting the accuracy of timekeeping. The other reason was George believed that when someone bought one of his watches, the owner was expected to wind the watch daily. That was George's concept of the responsibility of the watch owner. In fact, one of the enjoyments of handling a mechanical watch is the tactile pleasure of winding the **crown**. Whenever I look at a watch, I invariably wind the **crown**, of course with the permission of the owner and being careful not to overwind it, in order to feel the winding mechanism. So I agree with George: winding a watch is an expectation, pleasure, and responsibility of the owner.

I asked George what, in his opinion, would comprise an optimal watch collection. With a twinkle in his eye, George responded, "Two Daniels and a pocket watch." I immediately looked at my wife to make sure she'd heard his response. Without missing a beat, he offered to give me the name of someone to see on Bond Street who would find me the right pocket watch. I did not take him up on his offer, as we didn't have plans to return to London after our visit to the Isle of Man. We had already been to Bond Street and the watch stores that were there. In retrospect, not getting the contact information from George was truly a wrong decision.

We could see that George was tiring, so we made our farewells but before we left, I asked him to autograph my copy of *Watchmaking.* Graciously, he complied. On the title page, he inscribed, "George Daniels 6th October 211." Yes, he left out the 0.

As we headed to the car, I commented to my wife that she had not taken any pictures during our visit. Her response was she did not think it was appropriate. I absolutely agreed with her. There are plenty of pictures of George Daniels. There is no need for a picture of me with my arm around his shoulders. Even had Roger been included in the picture, it was not important to me. I have the memory of those forty-five minutes and will always treasure it. That was our history and all I needed.

Our flight from Douglas back to Luton was later in the afternoon, so we had enough time to have a nice lunch. As we ate, I remained in a state of euphoria from all that had transpired over the previous twenty-four hours. I knew I had made the correct decision to get the Daniels watch. I knew I would not be able to get a second. I knew that my wife appreciated what we had just experienced. Also, I knew that the Daniels Anniversary watch purchase was rational, a once-in-a-lifetime opportunity.

Over lunch, I told Roger I still wanted one of his watches. He asked me what I was thinking about. I wanted the Series 2. The next question was what size, a 38 mm case or 40 mm case, and what metal. The metal was easy. The Daniels was in a yellow gold case, so I immediately chose rose gold. As far as size, I did not know. Roger chose the 40 mm case. Then, after thinking for a few moments, Roger stated that he had an idea. He had been thinking about working with a fellow in England who engraved shotguns and wanted to make a watch with a dial engraved by him. I did not have any idea what he was talking about, but he said he would look into it and let me know. I figured that meant I would be part of the design project and have some input if I wanted it or not.

We returned to England and continued our trip. Out of concern, we called Caroline several times over the course of our travels to inquire after George's well-being. The surgery was successful, we were informed, and he was recovering well.

We flew home on October 21, with the first leg of our return flying from London to New Jersey. While heading to Passport Control, I received a text message from a friend informing me that George had died. Saddened, it occurred to us that we may have been one of the last, if not the last, people who were not friends, family, or care providers to see and speak with George. The significance of that realization was not lost on us. My choice of number and the 35/35 became more significant to me. The last of the last. In a number of ways, so very true. Thank you, Roger.

I continued to communicate with Roger and Caroline during the production of my Daniels Anniversary piece. When I was notified of the expected date of completion, I booked passage to England with plans to meet Roger at a place of his choosing for him to deliver the watch to me. The flight to London seemed to pass in a flash. Roger and I met the following day for lunch at a restaurant in the Mayfair section of London. After ordering food, Roger presented the Daniels to me. It was magnificent. I could not have been happier, but I was faced with a dilemma. The watch was wrapped in a protective covering and secured in its presentation box. I just stared at it. I knew I was looking at a historically significant piece. Number 35 of 35. Daniels on the dial, no other writing. Simple and to the point. The question was what to do next? If I unwrapped the watch and put it on, the watch would no longer be in mint condition. How would that affect its value? Putting on the watch, there was the risk of scratching the case or otherwise damaging the watch. What's more, I would be creasing the strap.

But why was the watch created? It was built to be worn. It was made to serve a purpose: to tell time. This watch cost as much as a high-performance car. That car, for most of its existence, would not be put to the use for which it was designed and built. Not so a watch. I do not believe in *safe queens*, watches bought but never unwrapped or worn. They are kept in a safe as investment commodities as you would a stock certificate. I did not tell Roger any of my internal deliberation. The whole debate took a matter of seconds. I unwrapped the watch and put it on. Roger had made the strap to my specifications. It fit perfectly.

A couple of years after George died, an auction was held to sell George's personal watches. It was impressive how scratched the cases were and how used the watches appeared. Clearly George believed in wearing all his watches, even the prototypes and other historically significant pieces. Those watches confirmed my bias about wearing watches and not "saving them."

During our lunch, we revisited the discussions we had started when we were on our walk with Mac on the Isle of Man. We discussed Roger's business model. I was fascinated when he said his goal was to produce approximately fifteen watches per year and no more. He wanted to follow the Daniels business model, producing a very limited number of pieces, assured that his watches would be the finest in quality. He could not conceive of producing more. Once again, he was following in the footsteps of his mentor. George Daniels only built approximately thirty-seven watches in total over the course of his career. Each of them was built with the notion of making changes and advancing horological knowledge and experience. Yes, he did supervise and approve of the Millennium series and the Anniversary watch projects, but those were built in Roger's shop.

I did the math, not hard to do. If Roger was to produce watches for forty years, then he would only be producing about six hundred in his career. When I mentioned my calculations, he said he would be totally fine with such a limited production. Roger's goal was to produce watches that would stand the test of time.

We discussed the expanding use of silicium components in watches. He did not use them, nor was he in favor of doing so because his concept was that a watchmaker in the future should be able to service the watch. He believed that the availability of silicium components in the future might be problematic, as may be true for whatever other materials might be developed over time. Brass and steel will always be present, along with technical knowledge and tools to make any replacement parts.

As lunch progressed, Roger gave me a preview of his plans for the next model he would release. He told me that he was planning to develop a new model, the Series 4. The new model was to include a novel way to display the date. He did not go into any specific details, keeping the discussion in broad generalities; nonetheless, he asked for total secrecy, which, of course, I promised. It was not the first time, nor would it be the last, I was told something watch-related in confidence and told that the information was not for public consumption. I will admit to being compulsive about keeping the promise of confidentiality when requested.

Anniversary Watch by George Daniels

The Dial

After lunch, Roger suggested we stroll around Mayfair. He needed to run an errand before flying back to the Isle of Man; a pair of shoes required servicing. He explained he only wore handmade shoes from Church's. They come at a considerable price, but they are built to last and can be reconditioned, for a "nominal" fee, when needed. This was my second of two lessons I have received about the finer points of high-end shoes, both from important people in the watch community. Might there be a connection between watches and high-end shoes? I am not sure.

Now that the Daniels was in my possession, my attention turned to the matter of the Series 2. Roger said he would honor our previous contract. He would build the watch for me to the specifications and price we agreed upon prior to changing the order to the Daniels. I remembered he was thinking of a special dial for my watch, but we did not discuss it at the time. I figured when he was ready, Roger would show me what he had in mind.

Months later I received an email from Roger with an attached of picture labeled "your dial." Without my knowledge, and I am not complaining at all, Roger took it upon himself to send a blank German silver dial to the shotgun engraver. I can only assume they discussed Roger's ideas, and here was the result. The dial was rough and dirty, but the engraving could be seen and, per Roger, needed a fair amount of finish work.

There are times when it is better to have faith in the artist than step in and give input. I acknowledged receipt of the pictures with appropriate affirmations. Little did I know what was coming my way. I had a similar situation when the landscaping was being done for our house. We discussed building a pond with a waterfall in our courtyard. Apparently, while my wife and I were at work, there was a meeting of the landscape architect, gardener, pool contractor, and sub-contractor who constructed rocks. They came up with a plan and set about their work. When we got home that evening, there was a big hole in our courtyard. The pond and the waterfall they constructed continues to give joy so many years later. I am very happy I did not try to interfere with their creativity.

Approximately a year and a half after the lunch on the Isle of Man with Roger and Caroline, I was presented with my Series 2, Shotgun edition. There were no words to describe my reaction when I saw the watch and put it on my wrist. It literally took my breath away. I later learned that Roger produced five such watches with the engraved dial by the same shotgun engraver. Mine was clearly the first. Including the Daniels and the Series 2, if Roger makes only fifteen watches per year, there is a possibility that I accounted for thirteen percent of Roger's output for one year. I cannot imagine having such a percentage of output from any other brand.

Years after our visit to the Isle of Man, I was invited to appear on several podcasts. Around the same time, a couple of articles were published about me, but in the written work, I was identified by a pseudonym. During the interviews and in talking with friends, I took pleasure in relating the tale of our visit with Roger Smith and George Daniels. I was always sure to give my wife the credit she deserves for being the inciting force behind the visit.

Series 2 by Roger Smith

A few years later, after a get-together of the Alphabet Soup Gang, we decided to visit a nearby Omega boutique several of the group frequented. Those of us not known to the Omega staff introduced ourselves and went about looking at the wares. When there was a break in activity, one of the boutique staff members approached me and asked if I was the person on the podcast who talked about meeting George. I guess the story of our visit to the Isle of Man had a lasting impression on others, not just me.

Chapter 10
Boutiques

As mentioned, and perhaps made obvious by my stories here, the experience of buying a watch from an independent watchmaker is quite different than purchasing from any other source. An important difference is independents or micro-brands allow for more flexibility when it comes to change in design features than possible from a bigger brand, whether you're purchasing the watch from an authorized retailer, a gray-market dealer, a private source, or a boutique. There are times, however, when the collector might develop close enough ties with a brand representative who, in turn, has sufficient connections within the leadership structure of that brand so he or she can try to accommodate the wishes of a collector. Certainly, Ahmad is such a person, but the nature of his relationship to the leadership of Ulysse Nardin was an exception and not the rule in most other brands. Complicating matters is the fact that the watch industry, in general, seems to have a relatively rapid turnover of sales and administrative staff, making it difficult to develop long-lasting relationships.

Over time, a number of the major brands have made the decision to move away from working with independent retailers and authorized dealers in favor of opening their own single-brand boutiques. Despite that, there remains a hybrid model for most brands, so some retailers can also carry the brands' products, particularly in regions where brand boutiques are not available.

When working with a boutique, the customer needs to accept certain realities, including the difficulty of finding the right watch at the right price. It is important to realize that when buying a watch from a brand, whether from a boutique or from an authorized dealer, the price of the watch includes the cost created by the layering of staff positions within the corporate structure, such as administrative staff that handles sales, marketing, and accounting. Also contributing to the cost of each watch is the advertising budget. The fascination that many brands have with celebrity endorsements and sponsorships of festivals, sporting events, and teams does not come cheap. I do not care what a particular celebrity is wearing or what they have to say about a particular watch; I probably know more about the brand or the watch than they do anyway. But that's me. I understand that marketing any luxury product involves selling an image that frequently includes an endorsement by celebrities. That is a scene I just do not care about, and I wish I could separate out the percentage of the cost of an "ambassador" or spokesperson from the cost of a watch.

Depending on the watch and the particular dealer, discounts may be available to a varying degree, but due to the economics of the watch industry, the margins that authorized dealers have to work with are growing narrower, so the discounts offered have become much smaller. The boutiques have minimized or completely abolished any price discounts. The advantage of shopping with them is they can provide access to special or "boutique" editions, limited editions and limited production pieces, as well as those in high demand and not readily available in the general marketplace. What distinguishes boutique editions from regular production pieces may only be the color of the dial or other decorative features, but by controlling the release of those editions, boutiques create increased demand that helps to fuel their market.

Boutiques also have access to watches that are unique and truly special. Typically, these are not available to even their best retail partners. The other advantage to working with the boutiques, at least according to the brands, is the difference in the buying experience. They may offer other benefits to select clients in place of price discounts.

226

Coffee and Chocolate

When I worked at the Watch Connection, I frequently noticed that when a customer was considering a purchase of a watch, beads of sweat would form on their upper lip, or their hands would shake. This response occurred regardless of the price of the piece. In fact, the actual price was irrelevant; it was an expensive purchase for that particular customer and, for some, a nerve-racking experience. I know from experience.

Soon after it opened in a shopping center not far from where I live, I wandered into the Jaeger-LeCoultre boutique and met the staff, including one of the managers, Stephanie. At our first meeting, Stephanie politely ushered me to the desk in the main area of the boutique and offered me something to drink. I accepted her offer and asked for an espresso. Before Stephanie went to get the espresso, she presented to me the Extreme Lab 2. The one she showed me was, according to her (here we go again), one of the last available in the company. I liked the watch and gave serious consideration to purchasing it.

When Stephanie reappeared with the espresso, I spilled some onto the newly installed carpet. Faced with the possibility of making a purchase, especially since it would have been spur of the moment, I admit that I was a bit nervous, and my hands were shaking, which resulted in the spill. She was very understanding as I tried to clean up the coffee from the brand-new carpet, and she assured me the cleaning crew would take care of it, and I was not to worry.

The next time I visited the boutique, there was no sign of a coffee stain from my attempt to christen the new carpeting, and, by the way, the watch had been sold. Forgiving as she was, the spill of the coffee continues to be an ongoing joke between me and the staff of the boutique. Even with my storied past, they still offer me a coffee when I visit, and I have successfully avoided a repeat performance.

Despite the awkward start, we did have a nice discussion about watches, and I discovered her knowledge and appreciation of watches extended well beyond the Jaeger-LeCoultre brand. During my visits, she presented other watches for my consideration, but nothing seemed to stick. She knew I already owned a couple of Duomètres. Previously, I owned a Reverso Grande GMT but sold it in favor of another watch. At the time I found the Reverso GMT uncomfortable to wear because of its large case. When I wanted the second time zone on the **verso** side while traveling, the **crown** on the left side of the watch bothered me. Interestingly, I once wore it to a dinner attended by then-CEO of Jaeger-LeCoultre Jérôme Lambert. He told me that, at that time, the Reverso Grande GMT was the most complicated watch that the manufacture produced. This was before the Duomètre line or other haute horology models were developed. Despite his comments, the discomfort wearing the watch overcame the technological advances that the watch represented.

As stated previously, in modern day watches, I consider the single-axis **tourbillon** to be "eye candy" or a conference watch (a watch to serve as a diversion and to be enjoyed during a particularly boring meeting). A more practical application of the concept of a **tourbillon** in a wristwatch movement is when the **tourbillon** functions is multiple axes, like the Sphérotourbillon by Jaeger-LeCoultre.

Since I first laid eyes on it, I have found the Sphérotourbillon to be as beautiful as it is functional. The **tourbillon** rotates on two axes, making it more appropriate for the purpose for which it was designed. It displays two time zones, local and home time, thus it could function as a travel watch, if one is comfortable wearing such a valuable piece when traveling. It also fit my obsessive tendencies, as it has a **pusher** that automatically resets the second hand to zero, making the setting of time more precise. Part of the Duomètre line, the movement has the practicality of two separate power sources for the different functions of the watch, ensuring better timekeeping. The finishing is best in class, as is true with all the models in the line.

It is not uncommon for me to become obsessed with a particular watch. Day or night, when my thoughts are not otherwise engaged, my mind drifts to the particular watch of the moment. George Daniels told me that he thought about watches when he lay down at night. I, too, think about watches when I close my eyes at night. Such was the case with the Sphérotourbillon. It is incredibly elegant and mesmerizing. Such a marvelous piece was not cheap. I started to rationalize that with the purchase of the Daniels, I had crossed a psychological price barrier. I was able to make the finances work that time. Therefore, I should be able to do it again, right?

As an added incentive, I was told that since the Sphérotourbillon is within the Hybris Mechanica line, the brand's most complicated and highly prized watches, if I purchased it, I would be one step closer to qualifying to be eligible to order a Grande Sonnerie. The Grande Sonnerie is the most complicated Duometre. It takes more than a year to build and retails for seven figures. I only had to purchase two more watches from the Hybris Mechanica line, and I could apply for an allocation. Needless to say, the preposterous suggestion that I come up with the funds to buy not just the Sphérotourbillon but two more very expensive watches, no matter how complicated and desirous, in order to be able to spend a crazy amount of money for the Grande Sonnerie, no matter how fantastic a watch it might be, was not a selling point—at least for my wife. This time, there was no disagreement between the two of us, only shared laughter at the nonsensical hypothetical question. After much to and fro, I ultimately committed to the Sphérotourbillon watch with the understanding that it was not going to be my first step toward ordering the Grande Sonnerie.

Sphérotourbillon by Jaeger-LeCoultre

Since bringing the Sphero home, I have given a few talks about watches and have said, as I truly believe, that the Sphérotourbillon is one of the most complete watches I have and, dare I say it, one of my favorites. That question, "Which is your favorite?" frequently comes up, and my typical response is, "Which of my children is my favorite?" I acquire a watch because of a connection that I made with it, whatever that might be. The watches I possess are with me because that connection remains strong. Each watch has meaning, and designating a favorite is difficult at best. The saving grace is that watches do not have opinions or feelings, so if I was to designate one as a favorite, then no egos would be hurt. All this said, the Sphero remains one of my most favorite watches, art and function beautifully mixed together.

As a side note, the other answer I give when asked to pick my favorite is the answer given by many collectors: "Either the last one I got or the next one I will get." Yes, collectors can be a fly-by-night group of people with ever-altering allegiances.

When I met Stephanie, I did not own a Reverso, but my wife did. My Reverso GMT was long gone, and I had not yet gotten the Reverso 101. At that time the two Duometres were the only ones I owned by Jaeger-LeCoultre. I also had an Atmos clock, but that would be very difficult to wear on my wrist.

There are iconic watches that might be considered essential elements of any watch collection; one is a Reverso. I decided that I wanted to replace my Reverso GMT. What caught my eye was the Grande Reverso Ultra Thin 1931, commonly referred to as the Chocolate Reverso because of its brown dial. The combination of the brown dial and the rose gold case, markers, and hands on a brown leather strap was beautiful. A classic combination and presentation.

At the same time, Stephanie showed me a Grande Reverso Lady Ultra Thin Duetto Duo for my wife. Both watches were very appealing, and I thought it would be a nice pairing for my wife and me. Surprisingly, she did not need much convincing this time. I made the sale, not Stephanie.

When I ordered my Reverso, I was enticed by the blank case on the **verso** side. The Reverso was originally designed to protect the watch while playing polo. Prior to the creation of the Duoface Reverso, the **verso** of the case was typically blank. It can also serve as a canvas for the owner to personalize the watch. There are many options available, and Jaeger-LeCoultre promises they can accommodate a client by engraving or painting whatever the client requests on the back of the Reverso, something I'd born witness to when my wife and I toured the Jaeger-LeCoultre Manufacture. The first time I was there, the art department responsible for all the painting, enameling, and engraving, whether it be on the dial or the **verso** of the Reverso case, was in a separate building some distance from the main factory. At some point, the department was relocated to the main building, where it overlooks a set of train tracks. Not the location one would think of as optimal given the delicate nature of the work the artists are required to perform. How they dealt with the rumble of a passing train beneath the window I do not know; I just know they do.

There are several stations in the department for the different artisans. One young woman, probably a junior member of the staff, had her work set out in her workspace. In front of her was a photograph of a Pomeranian in a Santa Claus outfit she was tasked to copy in enamel onto the back side of a Reverso case. She did not speak English, and we do not speak French, but the communication between us was very clear. Her plea for pity was obvious. We had a good laugh then and still do now when we remember the preposterous image and imagine it adorning a watch.

I knew I did not want my initials or anything very personal engraved on my watch. Early in my journey, I purchased an IWC Mark XV pilot's watch. Simple, clean, and very legible, it is a nice counterpoint to more complex watches I found myself attracted to.

When I decided to purchase the watch, the retailer offered to engrave my initials on the back of the watch. I accepted the offer, and off I went happily. A number of years later, I decided that I wanted to part with the watch and tried to sell it. The endeavor was not successful; there are not very many people collecting watches with my initials. Eventually, I gave it to my younger son to wear. He and I do not share initials, but he enjoys wearing the watch and does so every day. It does give me joy to see him providing the watch with a purposeful existence.

Mark XV by IWC

When I ordered my Chocolate Reverso, Stephanie and I discussed the option of having it engraved. She told me I had some time before I needed to decide if and what I wanted for an engraving. After some consideration, I decided I indeed wanted to proceed with an engraving to make it a unique piece. Specifically, I wanted it to complement the dial on the Smith Series 2 I was yet to receive. It had been a while since Roger sent me pictures of the dial, and I did not have a clear recollection of the design. To get close to what I remembered, I decided that a fleur-de-lis pattern would be nice.

Soon thereafter, I attended a lecture that was not engaging; frankly, I was bored. Left to my own devices, my mind started to wander. With the assistance of Google, I searched for an image of a fleur-de-lis pattern. I came upon one I particularly liked; however, it was in a circular format. I thought the composition would be challenging given the fact that the Reverso case is rectangular. I showed the image to Stephanie, and she suggested we send it to Switzerland and see what the engravers thought. We received no word from them, but when the watch arrived, the **verso** side was beautifully engraved with a rectangular interpretation of the circular picture. I was delighted.

A month later, I showed my Chocolate Reverso to a friend. After extolling its beauty and appreciating the workmanship of the engraver, he pointed out that a segment of the design was incomplete. Some of the stippling seen in the other segments of the pattern was missing. Sadly, the watch had to be sent back to Switzerland. Fortunately, the turnaround time was short, and the watch was returned with the engraving satisfactorily completed.

Chocolate Reverso by Jaeger-LeCoultre

Although my interest in other Reverso models grew, I continued to be enamored by the Duomètre line. The next Duomètre model released was the Unique Travel Time, or UTT, with the first model being a limited edition of one hundred pieces. It came with an enamel dial and was to be released only through the Paris boutique located in the Place Vendôme. The seven and nine of the second time zone are highlighted in red while the other numbers are in black, as a nod to the address of the boutique. Many GMT or world time watches indicate a second time zone solely by adjusting the hour indicator, and indeed the UTT had that same function by way of **pushers** on the side of the case. However, the UTT also allowed the second time zone to be adjusted to the minute by moving its minute hand by way of the **crown**. There are several places in the world where the time zone is different by thirty minutes, so this enabled the world traveler to be prepared for all contingencies.

Yet another new feature for this Duomètre was incorporated, no doubt with me in mind. When setting the time, pulling on the **crown** zeros the second hand so that the watch can be set to the correct second. Thanks to the design of the dual-wing movement, I am able to know the precise time to the second throughout the day, as the watch functions within a second deviation over the course of the day.

There were several challenges for me, and hence Stephanie, when I asked for this watch. The first was whether I could get one without having to travel to Paris and, and another was whether I could I get number 94. As it turned out, not only was I able to get the watch from the local boutique and not have to travel six thousand miles, but I was allocated number 94 as well. Fortunately, 94 is not a popular number. Why would it be?

Unique Travel Time by Jaeger-LeCoultre

More than One

Some collectors like to have different versions of the same watch. The varieties could be in case composition, dial color, or design. There is nothing wrong with that approach, but I prefer to have distinctly different watches. There are so many choices and only a finite amount of funds, so I favor variety. A watch is the combination of design, function, and movement. Many watches from different brands have the same identical movement or one that has been modified to a degree, while the dial configuration or case design is the difference. My preference is to look for watches that are distinct from ones I already possess. That said, Jaeger-LeCoultre released another version of the Duomètre Quantieme Lunaire that caught my attention.

The new version, like the UTT, came with a **grand feu** enamel dial. Although the basic features of the new edition were the same as the original Quantieme Lunaire I already owned, the case was smaller. The original was 42 mm in diameter while the new version was 40.5 mm. Due to the smaller case, the design of the moon phase **sub-dial** had to be changed. Both had the **foudroyante** counting sixths of a second. The new version had one difference with regards to the movement: like the UTT, it could be set to the second with a pull of the **crown**. This model was released as a limited edition of two hundred.

Because of the smaller case size, it fit my wrist differently, and there was enough of a difference in appearance that I decided to ask for number 94. Once again, good fortune was mine, and home it came. I now am the proud owner of five Duomètres. I am told I may be the only or, at most, one of only several people in the world to own five Duomètres. The number I own is not important to me; rather, it is the nature of the line that makes me hope for more in the future. At one point, I was told the manufacture had on the drawing board another model for the Duomètre line that incorporated a **perpetual calendar** as the second function. I wait and hope.

I have had the pleasure of attending a number of events and dinners with the leadership of Jaeger-LeCoultre. At every opportunity I make a plea that they produce another Duomètre. I usually receive a noncommittal response that one is coming but no date is provided, but hope does remain eternal.

Duomètre Quantieme Enamel Lunaire by Jaeger-LeCoultre

Special Events with Jaeger-LeCoultre

I was invited by the then-US brand president for Jaeger-LeCoultre to be interviewed at a meeting for the staff of all of the boutiques that reported to him. Representatives were there from South America, Mexico, and across the United States. His purpose was to interview me so that his team could hear the voice of a consumer. It was a fun half-hour conversation. During the course of the interview, I was asked to name three of my favorite watches in my collection. Of course, I was sure to list the Sphérotourbillon as a perfect watch, both in form and function. I was also asked by one of the group if I wanted to design my own watch. I thought about the question for a moment and said that I did not think so. I can appreciate art, and certainly I know what appeals to me, but I do not think I can create art, and the same goes for watches. I may have been wrong, at least when it comes to watches.

Not long after that interview, my wife and I attended another watch function. We were invited by Jaeger-LeCoultre to attend the Shanghai film festival, which they were sponsoring. At one point we took a break from the event and wandered off to get lunch. We found a pleasant restaurant in a garden setting, and as we waited for our food to be served, not quite sure what we had ordered, I sketched an idea for a watch on a napkin.

The Duomètre was still very much on my mind, so you could assume I was under an influence. I drew the dial layout for a new Duomètre model, one I named Duomètre Alarme du Jour. The dial layout was typical of the line with the time on the right side of the dial and the settings for an alarm on the left. My idea was that the alarm could be set to ring at a specified time within the twenty-four hours of a day. As an added feature, the alarm could be set to ring on a specific day of the week or every day. That evening at the gala hosted by Jaeger-LeCoultre, I excitedly pitched my idea and showed my drawing to several senior members of the company including the CEO. They appeared interested, but I suspect they were only being polite.

After I got home, I eventually gave the drawing to the US brand president after, once again, pitching my concept to him. Later he told me he kept my drawing in his desk and was waiting for an opportune time to introduce it to the higher-ups. When he left the company, I was told he passed my drawing to a senior-level person in the US office. Unfortunately, I have no idea what became of it after that. When I introduced the idea, and still to this day, all I wanted was the ability to spend a couple of hours with a designer and perhaps an engineer to see if my design could work. Once again, I can only wish.

While that Duomètre dream faded, a special Reverso materialized for me. I was asked to be a guest on a podcast to discuss my experiences collecting watches. Before heading to the interview, with some time to spare, I stopped at the Jaeger-LeCoultre boutique to say hello to Stephanie. She showed me an interesting Reverso she had just received, the Grande Reverso 1931 Seconde Centrale, built, as the name suggests, as a reproduction of a model released in the 1930s. Unique compared to any other Reverso model at the time, it featured a multilayered dial construction and had a central second hand rather than the more typical seconds **sub-dial** at the six o'clock position. Most notably, it was powered by an automatic movement, something unique in the Reverso line.

It was released in a limited fashion to mixed reviews. Some collectors did not like the fact that it had an automatic movement, insisting that

Reversos should be true to their history and only be made with a manual wind movement. Also, because of the automatic movement, the watch was thicker than usual. I, on the other hand, found the model intriguing. I guess Stephanie figured that during the interview I might be asked to talk about what I was wearing, and she offered to lend me the watch for the evening. I can well imagine lending a watch was a rarity for any boutique. Gratefully, I accepted the offer and wore it for the interview. Indeed, I was asked about the particular piece and discussed it during the podcast.

Reverso 1931 Seconde Centrale by Jaeger-LeCoultre

Over the course of the evening, I became more enamored with the watch. As a special edition available only through the boutique, I knew the number produced was limited. Subsequently, I have never been able to find out the exact number produced; watch companies are frequently reticent to disclose such information. Why? I do not know. Meanwhile, to make the acquisition even more tempting, the company offered to adorn this watch with the same engraving that was on my Chocolate Reverso. I was informed that the particular engraving was exclusively mine and would not be applied to anyone else's Reverso cases. Once again, by participating in an attempt to sell a watch, I wound up buying the piece. I really am a great salesman...to myself.

###

Another event my wife and I were invited to attend was the opening of the Jaeger-LeCoultre boutique in New York City. It was a great chance to visit the city, so we jumped at the opportunity. The event took place toward the end of what had been a long winter for New Yorkers, one with back-to-back snowstorms that made life challenging. We, on the other hand, were excited to have the opportunity to see the city in the snow. In fact, when we went to the Guggenheim Museum and it started to snow, it seemed we were the only ones in the museum, if not the whole city, who were excited by it. Once we were finished at the museum, we walked down Fifth Avenue playing in the snow like children.

At the opening, many of the Jaeger-LeCoultre corporate staff were in attendance. By that time, my wife and I had become friends with most of them, and it was great to reunite. For the opening, the brand brought in a number of special watches to fill the display cases, and several celebrities, said to be "friends of the brand," were in attendance, including Clive Owen. He did not seem to be interested in meeting me, which was fine because I was more interested in the watches anyway. We were ships that passed in the night. I believe that there were several other celebrities there, but I did not recognize them, and they did not acknowledge me.

Cruising around the cases, I spied a Grande Reverso Ultra Thin SQ (Squelette). Stephanie accompanied us to the opening, and when I pointed out the watch, she told me she had showed it to me previously. Apparently, I did not show interest in it at the time. Sometimes I have to see something several times before it strikes the right chord, or maybe I was just, for whatever reason, more receptive that evening than before. She took it out of the case so I could get a better look. It was beautifully **skeletonized**, with hand-engraved decorations on the front and back of the movement, framed by an attractive blue enamel **bezel**. It was produced as a limited edition of fifty pieces, and this was number 1.

Once again, boxes were checked. I expressed serious interest in the piece and continued to carefully inspect it as people pressed into the space and the festivities began. Despite the noise and energy around me, I was so focused on the watch that on the front of it, something caught my eye between the markers at six and seven o'clock. I requested a loupe and to take a closer look. Sure enough, there it was, a small piece of white material under the sapphire crystal. As best as I could tell, it looked like a piece of lint.

A wayward piece of lint, no matter how small, could be the death knell for a movement. One of the features of the newly opened boutique was that they had a watchmaker on site, Natalie. Stephanie called her over, and she confirmed the presence of the piece of lint. Without skipping a beat, she looked up and said that the watch needed to go back to Switzerland. Clearly, the watch could not be sold as is. Amid the ongoing festivities, several of the administrative staff involved themselves in the discussion about the watch and the foreign body. Obligatory apologies were made. They fell over themselves promising to get the problem rectified and assured me of a quick turnaround. We agreed I would be in line to purchase the watch pending the outcome in Switzerland.

Several months later, Stephanie contacted me to let me know that the SQ was back from the manufacture. It was shipped not to the New York boutique but to the one closest to me, where Stephanie was. In short order, I made my way over. Based on prior experiences, I examined the watch with a loupe and was relieved to see that the piece of lint was gone. However, on further inspection, I found scratches on the eleven and twelve index markers. It seemed that someone, in the process of servicing the watch, had not been careful with a tool. Once again, the watch was not in the condition to be sold, so back to Switzerland it went. The third time hopefully would be a charm. When it came back to the boutique, I was finally, with a small celebration, satisfied with its condition to bring the watch home.

My wife continues to insist that I should get a job in quality control for a watch company. I am not sure why I tend to find problems with watches. Is it bad luck, or am I more careful than most when inspecting a watch? I do not have a clue, but it does seem that I have a knack for discovering quality issues with a number of watches across different brands. It might be fun to do quality assurance, as long as someone else fixes the problem. I can find the problem, but I know I do not have the talent, hands, or eyes to work as a watchmaker. I have learned from my experiences that before laying down a credit card, it is best to carefully examine the watch and not be embarrassed to ask for a loupe. Even a novice can find defects in a watch that should be repaired prior to completing the sale.

Reverso SQ by Jaeger-LeCoultre

Goodbye Wave

In 2018 Jaeger-LeCoultre unveiled a trio of watches called the Reverso Tribute Enamel. The set of watches featured different paintings on their **verso** sides. One had a reproduction of the *Great Wave off Kanagawa* by Hokusai. The second had a painting of horses inspired by Xu Beihong, and the last had a reproduction of George Seurat's *A Sunday Afternoon on the Island of La Grande Latte.* Eight of each model was to be produced.

When the trio was presented to me, I immediately agreed that the paintings were exquisitely executed. But what captured my attention was not the paintings but rather the dials. Each of the three models had a specific dial in blue, green, or white, and they were stunning. The blue and green dials had a **guilloché** lozenge pattern with a translucent **grand feu** enamel coat that had never-seen-before depth.

I immediately decided I wanted a watch with the blue dial. However, none of the paintings had meaning to me. I had no connection with the horses that were on the case of the white dial version. The Seurat reproduction, on the **verso** side of the green dial, missed the point of the painting. I have seen the masterpiece in the Art Institute of Chicago. It is a large painting done in pointillism. Reducing the painting to the size of a Reverso case, though very well done, lost a lot in translation. The painting on the back of the watch with the blue dial I lusted after was the Hokusai *Wave*. In my opinion, the *Wave* is an extremely overcommercialized image. It is reproduced by other artists, and many luxury brands feature it on various baubles. Commercialized imitations of all sorts can be found all over the world on every surface and souvenir imaginable: mugs, posters, t-shirts, playing cards, and the like. I like ukiyo-e and even own several original prints by a different artist, Hiroshige, but the overuse of this picture has ruined its artistic appeal for me. As much as I wanted the blue dial, I did not want the *Wave*. It did not make sense to me to pay for something that I did not connect with, yet the dial haunted me.

I sweetly asked if it was possible to get a Reverso with the blue dial without the *Wave*. With little hope for success, I waited for a response. After a couple of weeks, to my great surprise, I was told that the company was willing to take one of the blue pieces out of production and sell me the watch without the painting. Everything about the watch would be exactly the same, and instead, they would put my engraving on the back. Score. I asked if they would engrave the watch with "piece unique," as that was what it was. They refused. It was against company policy to label any of their watches as "piece unique." A fair compromise.

Of all of my watches past and present, this one cannot be photographed in such a fashion to give a true picture of its depth and beauty.

Unique blue Enamel Reverso by Jaeger-LeCoultre

Another Reverso

The Reverso Tribute Small Seconds has been produced with different-colored dials. By the time of its release, I had acquired a number of Reversos, but when I saw the burgundy-dial rendition with the complementary burgundy-colored leather strap, I got that feeling again. In no time I decided I wanted the watch.

Previously and since there have been several Reversos released with a red dial, but the fire-engine red did not attract me, even though I have always wanted to be a firefighter. However, there was something about the burgundy coloring that immediately drew me to it. Something else: the case is stainless steel; I did not have a Reverso in a stainless steel case. The company ultimately released a burgundy-dialed Tribute Reverso in a red gold case, which is stunning, but I am happy with the steel case. There was no question about its fit on my wrist, as the chocolate Tribute Reverso had the same dimensions.

Of course, I wanted my engraving on the case back. All was good, except, I was told, the manufacture initially refused to do the engraving. It is company policy to guarantee that a design would belong to an

243

individual client and not be repeated on anyone else's watch. The requested engraving was only for one Jaeger-LeCoultre client. Stephanie reassured the engraving department that I was that client. Only after they were fully convinced of my identity did they proceed to do the engraving. Although the design of my engraving, and indeed it is mine, is the same on all four watches, each is slightly different. That is probably due to a combination of different metals that had to be worked and the interpretation by different engravers. That in itself makes it more fun to appreciate.

Reverso Burgundy Tribute Small Second by Jaeger-LeCoultre

Accidents Happen 1

In the shopping mall not far from my house, there has been an ever-expanding number of single-brand boutiques. Tourbillon, a Swatch Group multibrand store, used to be there, and I stopped by multiple times but never made a purchase. I did get to know some of the staff at the store, including Brad and Slah. After Tourbillon closed, both moved to the new Vacheron Constantin boutique.

In the past, Slah had tried to interest me with several watches, but I never was tempted enough to bite the bullet. After some time elapsed, along with a number of conversations, he got an understanding about what type of watch interested me, so when he started working at Vacheron, I decided to give him a challenge. I had read an article about a model called the Sputnik, a watch celebrating the fiftieth anniversary of the first Sputnik launch. I do not have any interest in the Soviet space program but found the watch attractive, and it contained a movement that interested me. It was designed by the Métiers d'Art department and was produced in a limited quantity of ten pieces. To make the challenge even more difficult, it was distributed by the Moscow boutique only. It was a perfect example of a watch that whets the appetite of a collector: rare and unavailable. What does the collector pine for? That which he or she cannot get.

Slah took on the challenge and went on the hunt. I figured he would not be successful. Only ten pieces made and released a number of years earlier. What were the chances of finding one? You never know.

As predicted, he was unsuccessful. We settled by agreeing that eventually I would like to get a watch with that movement. Subsequently I tried a couple of times to secure different models with the movement, but it is included only in rare watches of very limited production and at a significant price point. However, one day Slah called me to tell me that he had found a watch that might interest me. Indeed, he did find a very interesting watch, the Copernicus.

Also produced by Vacheron's Métiers d'Art department, the Copernicus had a novel **complication**. The earth rotated around its axis over a twenty-four-hour period, which served as a day/night indicator. Simultaneously, the earth traveled around the sun over the course of the year. In its travels, the earth traversed the various astrological signs, as engraved into the **bezel**. Three versions of the same theme were created. One had a dial with an astronomical map created in Grande Feu enameling. The second had hand-engraved astrological signs on a white gold dial. The third version had laser etching of the astrological signs on the back of the sapphire crystal, while the earth had highly detailed hand engraving on a hand-painted blue dial. I was told that twenty total samples were produced. I am not sure how many of each model were created to add up to a total of twenty. The movement had the Geneva Seal and Vacheron claims that the rotation of the earth is so accurate it will require a correction of a single day after eight thousand years have passed (an incredible feat assuming the watch never stops working, ever.). Without a second thought, I knew I wanted the third version. A definite find by Slah.

The Copernicus, like most watches, is a piece of machinery that has a built-in shock absorption system. The most delicate component in the movement is the balance staff, which supports the **escapement**. With a significant shock, the balance staff can be dislodged, which, in turn, causes the **escapement** to stop. Each end of the balance staff rests on a ruby whose function is to eliminate friction. One of those rubies is incorporated into a shock absorption system.

To set the Copernicus, first I adjust the hands to the correct time, and then I ensure that the Earth is in the correct orientation to the sun for the day/night indication, something easily accomplished by looking out the window. Once the time indication is correct, I need to be sure that the earth is in the proper orbital position around the sun by aligning it within the section for the current astrological sign. I do not know the order of astrological signs, so I need to refer to a calendar for the current sign. I usually search for the calendar on my wife's computer, which can be found in our bedroom. Sometimes, however, I use my mobile phone that is charging in the kitchen instead, especially if I am in a hurry to get out of the house.

One morning, several months after bringing home the Copernicus, I set the time and then went to the kitchen to set the position of the earth in the proper astrological house. With the watch in hand, I reached for my phone but lost control and juggled the phone and the watch. I caught the phone, but sadly, the watch hit the ceramic tile floor face down. If there is one thing to be sure, watches do not like to hit hard surfaces from any height. When I picked up the watch, it was at a dead stop. The expletive-laden explosion I elicited did not change the situation. I had a sick feeling in the pit of my stomach that accompanied the sight of my damaged watch. It is a feeling that occurs regardless of the value, rarity, or significance of a precious object. Denial, shaking it, exhorting a higher spirit—nothing made the second hand move.

On several tours of manufactures I saw how brands test their watches for shock resistance. I have seen various drop tests and impact tests, which was impressive, but nothing mimicked the fall from a height, dial down, onto a hard surface.

When I visited the Chopard Manufacture, the group that I was with visited the Fondation Qualité Fleurier (FQF). It was established as a joint venture by Chopard, Parmigiani Fleurier, and Bovet to serve as a certification organization. The mission of the Fondation is to test specific watches with regards to quality of production, finishing, and performance within fixed and rigid guidelines. More common is the COSC (Contrôle Officiel Suisse des Chronomètres) certificate that many watch companies strive to obtain and advertise when they receive it. That certification tests only samples from a production series—uncased movements to assess whether they perform within established guidelines and meet certain specifications. If the movements are certified, the movements are then encased, and the certification is applied to all watches in that series, whether or not they have individually been tested.

Of course, the process of encasing the movements, even the ones tested, risks an adverse event that can affect the function of the movement. On the other hand, the FQF certifies only the individual watch it tests. When put through testing, the watch is already encased and ready for final sale. They require that all components be 100% Swiss made, and there is also a finishing requirement to the certification. It was interesting to see how the FQF tested the chronometry of the watch. As part of the process the watch was secured to a mechanical "arm," which then went through twenty-four hours of robotic simulation of arm movements to assess stability and accuracy of timekeeping. At the conclusion of their process, the Fondation documents the test results of the individual watch and stores the results in ledgers that they keep in their facility.

There is also the Geneva Seal certification, or Poinçon de Genève, which includes twelve criteria a watch must meet in order to be granted the seal. It requires that the watch movement be assembled within the Canton of Geneva, and the watch must meet established criteria set regarding technical and finishing aspects. The certification is not geared to performance, as with the FQF certification or even the COSC certification.

Sadly, none of these certifications, or others that are available, evaluate watches for their ability to withstand the shock of a watch falling five feet, dial down, onto a hard floor. There have been watch companies that have advertised the durability of their products, such as the early Timex commercials, "Takes a licking but keeps on ticking." And Richard Mille has athletes wear their watches during athletic competitions. But there is no formal quantification of the degree of shock resistance. Maybe there should be?

I try to be very careful with my watches. I try to be situationally aware in order to minimize the risk of damaging my watch. However, I have experienced that gut-wrenching feeling one other time. I was at work wearing my Corson Dresdener when I entered an area that required me to take off my watch. Dutifully, I followed regulations and had the watch in my hand. Before I could slip the watch into my pocket for safekeeping, I lost control of my phone (sound familiar?) and, when I went to grab for it, lost control of my watch. It hit the ground, a linoleum-tiled floor this time, face down. Instantly, the watch froze. It had to be returned to Don for repair. Even though Don was very understanding, I was very embarrassed. Don confirmed that the shock of the fall dislodged the balance staff. The repair was relatively simple, and to my relief, no other damage occurred.

I was mortified at the concept of what I did to my Copernicus. Such carelessness. I was so sickened and embarrassed that I asked my wife to take the watch to the boutique, fully expecting that it would have to be sent to Switzerland for repair. I could not bear the thought of suffering the slings and arrows from my friends in the boutique, even though I knew it would be in good humor. They would be much nicer to my wife.

The next time I visited the boutique, the staff was very kind to not give me a hard time. In fact, they were quite sympathetic. Once repaired and returned to me, lesson learned. I now set any watch over carpet, using the nearby computer for any information that is needed such as the moon phase or astrological sign. I still use the window to check whether it is day or night.

Copernicus by Vacheron Constantin

Accidents Happen 2

Despite best intentions, wearing a watch is always associated with the possibility of scratching or damaging the case, bracelet, or buckle. It is virtually unavoidable. But using some care lessens the chance of incurring significant damage. Fine scratches on the case or buckle is a sure sign that the watch has been worn. That is not a problem because that is why the watch was built in the first place. Fine scratches can usually be buffed out if desired anyway. When I worked at the Watch Connection, I saw several watches that were brought in for repair with deep gashes or dents in the case. Sometimes the customers complained that the watch was not working properly and requested that the service be covered by the warranty. They had to be told that clearly the watch had been damaged from misuse, which, in turn, was the cause of the dysfunction. No, the warranty would not cover the repair. It was not an easy conversation to have when the customer feigned ignorance. Fortunately, I did not have to have such a discussion with a customer. I am not sure I would have been very tactful.

I admit to the fact that even though I know tiny scratches are inevitable, it does bother me to see them on the case of one of my watches. This is especially true if the scratch is more than a simple hairline. I am particularly bothered when I see a scratch on a watch I recently, acquired and more so if it is something that resulted because of carelessness.

I was fortunate to obtain a Jaeger-LeCoultre Reverso Tribute Nonantième, a limited edition produced to celebrate the ninetieth anniversary of the creation of the Reverso. It is a very attractive watch with a novel display on the **verso** side. Unlike other Reverso models that have dual time, the front has a classical display of time, but the **verso** shows time in a digital format for the **jump hour** and an analog minute display along with a day/night display positioned between the two.

Several weeks after bringing it home, I decided to wear the watch to work. When I pulled into the garage, I dropped a pen, which rolled under the driver's seat. Without thinking, I reached under the seat with my left hand to retrieve it and felt the watch scrape against the undercarriage. When I withdrew my hand, I saw a gash in the watch case across one of the linear grids at the lower aspect of the front and felt that all-too-familiar sinking feeling (one only has to have that sensation once to have become familiar). I flipped the watch over to the other side so that I did not have to look at the scratch. Every so often, over the course of the day, I would peek at the scratch—maybe it was not really there—but it was. Despite my efforts, it did not rub off. I felt embarrassed and dreaded taking it to the boutique for it to get repaired.

That evening, I put the watch in its storage place and tried not to think about the damage I had caused. Several times I had some very choice words for myself. After a couple of weeks, my desire to wear the Nonantième overcame the embarrassment caused by the sight of the scratch, which was still there. The scratch was not as large as I remembered, but it was still very noticeable.

Driving home from work that evening, while stuck in traffic, I started picking at the front of the watch case. To my surprise, I peeled off a piece of plastic I had neglected to remove from the original protective packaging. It was a small piece that was on the lower portion of the case. When I got home, I looked at my watch. Miraculously, the deep scratch that so troubled me was gone! The scratch was in the protective plastic and not on the case. Relief flooded over me. Even weeks later I periodically looked at the watch for reassurance that there was no scratch. It was truly gone. That is called dodging a bullet.

Lesson learned. Don't reach into tight spaces when wearing a watch. Either take it off or use the other hand. The question remains: when receiving a new watch, is it a good idea to take off all the plastic protective covering or leave it on for such a situation?

Reverso Tribute Nonantième by Jaeger-LeCoultre

Hallmarks

During one of my visits with the staff at the Vacheron boutique, I asked Slah and Brad what they considered to be the iconic model of the brand. Most, if not all, brands have different model lines, but there is often one model that is the hallmark. Jaeger-LeCoultre has the Reverso, Audemars Piguet the Royal Oak, Girard Perregaux the Triple Bridge **tourbillon**, A Lange & Söhne the Lange 1, and so on. After some thought and consideration, they decided that it was the Historiques American 1921.

Designed in 1921 as a driving watch, the dial is rotated forty-five degrees clockwise so that when a driver has his or her hands on the wheel in the proper ten and two positions, he or she can read the watch in proper orientation. There are a number of brands that make watches built with driving in mind, but few, such as one from Longines, make a watch with a similar orientation as the 1921. Despite that, Brad and Slah felt that the model was a hallmark piece by Vacheron Constantin. After I gave their recommendation some thought, I embarked on a discussion with them about what version would be best to get. There were several versions to consider. One of the staff had a sporty 1921 variety where the Arabic numbers were filled with luminescence. Released in a yellow gold case, it was a close replica of the original model, but it was produced as a limited edition that was long sold out. As the discussion continued, conspiratorially, it was suggested I wait a year to purchase a 1921. To celebrate the hundredth anniversary of its creation, a limited edition was scheduled to be released, this time in a platinum case.

Patience paid off. The platinum 1921 edition was limited to only one hundred pieces, and Brad told me that the boutique was allocated only four. When he told me what numbers were available, he apologized that the case numbers were all high and listed them off. One of the numbers they were allocated was number 94. It had to be destiny. I committed to number 94. I was able to carry the Jaeger-LeCoultre number forward for the sake of personal fun. Vacheron and JLC are subsidiaries of Richemont, so maybe it was destiny that brought me the 94.

When wearing a driving watch, the owner is faced with a challenge— when not driving, reading the time requires a bit of reorientation to read the dial. Certainly, when wearing the 1921, I have to adjust my brain so I can tell the correct time when my hands are not at the preferred ten and two position on a steering wheel. That would be true for any driving watch and the 1921 is not my only one. My younger son texted me one day and told me he was reading about an interesting watch, the Amida Digitrend. Produced in the 1970s, it was a mechanical watch that had a horizontally oriented movement with two digital dials to display the time, one for the hours and the other for the minutes. So that the driver could read the time with hands properly placed on a steering wheel, mirrors were used to project the time so that it was displayed in a vertical plane. It was a fascinating concept, and I had not seen anything like it. The movement itself was nothing special, but the construction and execution were interesting.

1921 Platine by Vacheron Constantin

I researched the watch and discovered that it was quite affordable; however, I could not find one available in any retail outlet I knew. To obtain one, I figured I would have to dip my toes into the preowned and vintage marketplace. My son sent me a link to an eBay auction for one. Previously, I had never bought anything off eBay and was skeptical, particularly because at the time there were no guarantees provided with the purchase.

Not really knowing what I was doing, I submitted a bid and then watched the auction. I was at work when the auction was ending and found it a challenge to surreptitiously make another bid. I lost it in the last seconds of the auction. When another Digitrend appeared on eBay, I was a more determined bidder and succeeded in making the winning bid. It was sent to me from Germany and worked for a week before it ground to a stop. I was able to get the watch serviced without a problem, since the movement was not complicated, and they replaced the **crown**. After that small investment, more in time than money, the watch worked. Its accuracy is not the best, but it is fun.

I wore it on occasion until several years later when my son, forgetting he was the one who pointed out that watch to me previously, texted me saying he was interested in a watch. Always excited when someone in my family expresses an interest in a watch, I anxiously called him. He was consistent; he told me that he was interested in a watch called the Amida Digitrend. What was I to do? I gave it to him.

Digitrend by Amida

What's Old Is New Again

More than four decades after the release of the Amida Digitrend, MB&F produced the Horological Machine No. 5. It is a driving watch, and fascinatingly, it is structurally similar to the Digitrend with the same concept to display the time: mirrors are used to reflect a horizontal time display to a vertical position. It serves to demonstrate the point that in the world of watches, there is very little that has not been done before. Case in point: on a trip to Geneva, I had time to tour the Patek Philippe Museum and spent a fascinating three hours going from one display case to the next. For anyone even remotely interested in watches, a trip to Geneva is incomplete without a visit to the Patek Philippe Museum, so amazing is the collection. I noted that many of the **complications** touted today by watchmakers as being unique were in evidence in watches built more than a century earlier. They were done in pocket watches, of course, so the tolerances were somewhat more forgiving as compared to those found in wristwatches. Nonetheless, the concepts were the same. Of course, to do the same **complication** in a smaller space, as in a wristwatch, certainly is a feat to admire. Rare is a novel **complication**.

I have had the pleasure of meeting Max Büsser, the MB of MB&F, on several occasions. I hope to have another opportunity so I can borrow the Amida Digitrend from my son and wear it to the meeting. Then I want to compare it with Max's Horological Machine. Why is one watch valued at eighty to one hundred times the other? An interesting and fun question to ask Max.

In a similar vein, Girard-Perregaux released the Casquette model, which is a modern-day version of a watch they released in the 1970s. Shaped similar to the Digitrend, it, too, is a driving watch with a vertical readout. This time, however, the watch has a quartz movement with an LED readout, so the mechanics are different than the mechanical Digitrend and the Horological Machine No. 5, but the design is the same, with a significant price differential.

Then there's Michel Parmigiani. Michel started his career as a watchmaker doing restoration of antique, high-value watches. When he started his own brand, the designs of many of his watches were based on watches he had restored. The quality of his work, especially the finishing of his movements, is excellent. Any watchmaker I have spoken to about Parmigiani is very complimentary about their products and particularly about the finishing of their movements.

Parmigiani produced a series of watches I admired for a few years, the Bugatti Type 370. As the name suggests, it is a watch created in partnership with the car company Bugatti. It has a unique construction, even for a driving watch. Once again, the movement is built in a horizontal orientation. Its ten-day **power reserve** is indicated by the **sub-dial** positioned on top of the movement. However, the time display is oriented on a vertical axis. There are no mirrors; the display is analog, meaning that there needs to be the equivalent of a universal joint to transmit the power from the horizontal "engine" to the vertical display. The movement is something special to behold and is visible at all angles by virtue of multiple windows set in the unusual but beautifully constructed case.

Ever since the model line was released, I have been a fan. It has a distinct design with a height of 18 mm, which is quite tall for a watch. It certainly is a statement watch and would not be worn comfortably under the sleeve of a sports jacket or any more formal attire. If seen, it will certainly attract attention, something that is not my desire. Yet the engineering skill required to build this watch fascinates me. In time, I have become more adventurous regarding the design of a watch that I might consider wearing. So I was not put off by the bold statement that the watch made. Unfortunately, the retail price for the Bugatti was not in my comfort zone, so I relegated myself to the role of admirer from afar.

Parmigiani had a ten-year association with Bugatti. When that association ended, Bugatti moved to a different brand, and Parmigiani had to stop selling Bugatti-branded watches by a specific date. Whatever watches were not sold by that day, would be sent to the crusher. As it turned out, there were still several Bugatti 370 watches available when that announcement was made. Chad had two in the display case, and one was exactly what I lusted after.

We embarked on a three-way negotiation: me, Chad, and the Parmigiani team. My argument was simple; they had a very limited time to sell the watch before it had to be destroyed, and I was offering something, which was better than nothing. After some give and take, we settled on a fair price.

Sometimes it is good to get the first of a new model when the brand is testing the marketplace. The price for the initial run might not reflect the true production cost, and they might not realize the demand for the for the particular model, both of which could result in a price adjustment. Other times it helps to be at the end of the run, when a brand is looking to recoup anything possible from the remaining pieces. Still at other times, a brand wants to maintain a certain value of a watch and will not agree to discounts even at the very end of the run. I can only assume that, in this situation anyway, Parmigiani was willing to work with me to cover some of their production cost rather than destroy the watch. Upon inspection of the watch, we all agreed that it was shopworn and needed servicing and reconditioning. I made a deposit, and off the watch went to Switzerland. I am told that Michel Parmigiani himself worked on this watch. Not bad, if true.

The Bugatti is a bulky and heavy watch. It is not a watch to be worn on a daily basis but when I do wear it, it is an enjoyable experience. It is a remarkable piece, beautiful in design and fascinating in construction. It is unlike anything else I own. Though not my objective, it does raise eyebrows when people see it. As with other driving watches, I have to remember to turn my wrist when I want to read the time as I do not spend the day with my hands in the ten and two position.

Bugatti by Parmigiani

The Psychology of Hype

There have always been brands that garner special attention from the public and media. Within those brands, specific models have been the subject of considerable hype, which results in a surge in demand. The hype has been further exacerbated by the brands themselves, who limit availability of the specific models either artificially or out of necessity due to production constraints. Again, what is it that a collector wants most of all? That which is not available. Fanning the flames of hype and desire is the ego boost that can occur when one is able to secure something rare, in great demand, and lusted after by others.

The secondary market is well aware of the fever pitch that can consume the marketplace for select pieces, such as steel-cased sport watches with integrated bracelets from the likes of Rolex, Patek Philippe, and Audemars Piguet. Those able to purchase such a watch know that they can then turn around and flip it for a substantial financial gain. The end result is inflated prices out of proportion to the watches' inherent value and to watches of similar construction and **complication**. This results in the influx of speculators only interested in profits and not in the art and beauty of the watches they have turned into a commodity. The introduction of cryptocurrency has also pushed up the prices for certain watches as those with electronic currency look to convert their investments into more liquid entities.

It is difficult to insulate oneself from this explosion of prices and the potential for quick financial gain. As I have said, I do not collect watches with the goal of financial remuneration; however, I will admit to being affected by the rush to riches.

For a period of time, the Watch Connection was an authorized dealer for Audemars Piguet. At that time I was interested in a new movement they had developed, the 3120, and considered purchasing a round-cased Jules Audemars model with it inside. A friend, knowledgeable about such things, recommended I wait for the Caliber 3120 to be released in the Royal Oak line. I waited and ultimately brought home the Royal Oak model 15300 with a black dial and the desired movement.

The Royal Oak line is the iconic model for Audemars Piguet. In recent times, these models have become highly sought after, and their value has escalated significantly. I have owned mine for more than ten years and used it as a work watch, a "beater," using the vernacular. As a result, the case and bracelet were scuffed and scratched. When I realized that the secondary market price for the watch had shot up, I decided it was prudent to send the watch to Audemars for servicing to include rehabilitation of the case and bracelet. It was returned to me in prime condition with all of its protective wrapping in place. I dutifully put it in the safe deposit box in the bank, where it has remained untouched and unworn. Was this the right thing to do? I have no plans to sell the watch, and, frankly, I have watches that are more valuable. So why am I not wearing the watch? Hype.

Royal Oak 15300 by Audemars Piguet

An Anti-Flip

As the availability of sport watches from Audemars Piguet, Patek Philippe, and Rolex has been so limited and relatively expensive, popular attention has turned to other brands' sport watches, with a concomitant increase in demand for those models. Vacheron Constantin has one such product line, the Overseas, especially the boutique edition with a blue dial. During a visit to the boutique, I was told by the staff that I could get the model that was in such demand if I so wished. It occurred to me that if I got one, even without a price discount, I could turn around and sell it for a nice profit. Surrendering to a weak moment, I said yes. I had not seen the watch in the metal but decided that this time, I would consider being a flipper and make some money that would, in turn, pay for another watch. As I waited for the arrival of my Overseas, I continued to have mixed feelings about my decision. Was I being honest to my principles of watch collecting?

Within several weeks, I received the call that the Overseas had arrived at the boutique, and I could pick it up at my leisure. As I headed over, my plan remained in place: flip it with the anticipation of a nice profit. However, when Brad handed me the watch, I changed my plans immediately. The dial was a deep shade of blue, and, as had happened with the Grand Seiko urushi dial, I lost myself in the depths of the dial. I have other blue-dialed watches but this was incredibly deep and alluring.

I had the steel bracelet properly sized because there was no doubt this was my watch; no flipper would I be. I then had the staff put on the rubber strap, and the watch fit my wrist like a glove. If watches could talk, this one spoke to me, insisting I take it home and wear it with the joy I felt. I did and I do.

Overseas by Vacheron Constantin

I absolutely enjoy the watch, but of equal, if not greater, significance was the lesson I learned. Although the hype brought me to the watch, I need to stay true to the principles that have guided me all these years and have brought me such joy. Avoid the hype. Let others get caught up in it and think they will make their fortune by flipping. Speculating on a watch is not for me.

Perks of Collecting

Of course, being aware of the hype is a necessary evil, as is paying attention to the results of auctions. The auction houses themselves help to contribute to the hype and drive the speculative market. It is a fiscal responsibility to my family that I am aware of the approximate value of my collection, as I am forced to acknowledge that there is an investment component to owning these watches given their inherent worth.

Certain brands have a corporate policy that requires a customer to "qualify" for the right and privilege to acquire particular watches that are in high demand, limited in production, or highly valued. The client first must purchase other, less desirable pieces from the brand. The rationale expressed to me by a boutique manager is that "to get married one first has to date several times." To a certain extent I can understand that rationale: when it comes allocating a specific watch that is in great demand, the brand does need to develop some criteria. That said, I still see this "dating" concept as a marketing ploy to move less desirable products. I do not subscribe to that sales approach. If I cannot get a watch because I have not made the proper foundational purchases and have not worked on my "résumé," so be it. To quote my dad, "There are many fish in the sea."

That said, I have established a purchase history with several brands and have built my résumé to the degree that I seem to have access to special pieces and other considerations. Even with that acknowledgment, the purchases that contributed to my résumé were made out of desire for the particular watch and not because of any ulterior motive (not as a résumé builder).

I have been subjected to this sales tactic since I started collecting watches, but it has become more prevalent recently and is used by a larger number of brands. Early in my journey, I was offered a special watch made by Patek Philippe. The retailer I used to frequent said I could have the much-in-demand piece if I purchased one or two other watches from the same brand first. Money is not endless, and I did not take the bait. I believe the watch in question was indeed a special piece, which, I am sure, is much more valuable today and would be a nice addition to any collection. At the time, I do not know if the mandate was emanating from the brand or, more likely, if it was store policy. Either way, I do not play that game. The interaction left a bad taste in my mouth that remains today and negatively affects my interest in the brand. It is one reason for the absence of watches from that brand in my collection. It is also why I never purchased a watch from that store.

Collectors are always looking for the right watch at the right price, whether new or preowned. Many collectors enjoy the hunt as much as they do the watch itself. There are those who take pleasure in showing off their latest acquisition and relating their story of the great deal they negotiated. I am not that kind of collector, though over time, I have purchased some watches at very favorable prices for a variety of reasons. At times the accommodations included me agreeing not to disclose the price I paid. If the seller ever wished to make similar accommodations for other potential clients, it is up to them, not me, and I do not breech confidences. I do not get any joy in flaunting my "connections." I would rather just share the joy of collecting and the pieces that come my way.

Conversely, I have been told that in certain circles, not mine, there is a reverse mindset such that collectors broadcast the fact that they paid more for a particular model than others did. This perverse logic is geared toward the ego boost of being able to say that they, the buyer, are more important and wealthier than others to the extent that they are able to afford a more expensive version of the same watch. No worries there for me. Within the groups of collectors I associate with, the topic of money rarely is discussed. When I am asked what I paid for a particular watch, I will usually deflect the question or, if necessary, say that I am not comfortable answering or just wordlessly stare at the questioner until they get the message. Regardless of the watch or the cost, it is no one's business. I do not show people my bank statement either.

Working with several boutiques, I have developed relationships that resulted in my wife and me being the fortunate recipients of a number of invitations to participate in special experiences at the generosity of the brands. We are often surprised and always grateful when these opportunities are presented to us, and to this day, we still marvel at the largesse of the brands. Obviously, we are included in the experiences not just because we may be nice people but rather because of the quantity of business we have done with the brands over time and the hope that more will occur in the future. We are not fools; such is the nature of the economics of the luxury marketplace. That said, there are many others who spend a lot more than we do. Maybe we are the comic relief.

The opportunity to attend dinners sponsored by different brands is not just an opportunity to have good food. For sure, the dinners we have gone to do not consist of banquet rubber chicken but rather excellent meals at notable restaurants. There, we have had the chance to meet like-minded collectors and have developed nice friendships with several of them. When attending these dinners, we have also met some people, at times quite young, who seem to have the attitude that luxury goods are a right and not a privilege. And we have met people who take joy in exhibiting their very expensive watches but clearly do not understand the functions of the watch. There is nothing that will disturb a watch purist more than to see a watch not properly set, such as a beautiful **perpetual calendar** with all the **sub-dials** indicating random days, date, and month or a watch with a home time that is set wrong.

Relatedly, once when I stopped by the Jaeger-LeCoultre boutique just to say hello, the staff was working with a client who was in the process of purchasing a lovely **tourbillon** with a second time zone at the twelve o'clock position. They were busy handling the transaction, with credit cards and cash on the desk, so they asked me to set the watch for the client. I properly set the home time to where the client was from on the main dial and the local time on the dial at twelve o'clock. I set the watch to the second. It was perfect, if I say so myself. Wordlessly, I handed the watch back to the staff, who presented the watch to the purchaser. She took one look at it and pushed it back into the hands of the staff member demanding that the time **indicators** be reversed They, in turn, gave it back to me to make the "correction." The boutique manager could see my agitation and simply murmured calming words to me as I made the requested changes. My wife, who observed this, could do nothing but laugh at me.

Our brand-sponsored experiences have extended beyond dinners to include incredible adventures thanks to a number of companies. We've have had tours of a number of manufactures in Switzerland and have been taken to film festivals in Los Angeles, New York, Venice, Shanghai, and Cannes. I have seen the US Open finals, and we went to watch the America's Cup. Attending a Rolling Stones concert, possibly one of the best concerts we have ever seen, was an incredible opportunity. We would never have imagined doing any of these had it not been for the generosity of different brands.

Of course, these opportunities do not come every day or easily. We are fun to be around, that is true. We have established a reputation after singing "Bohemian Rhapsody" on limousine rides, dancing in a Ferris wheel in Las Vegas, playing pétanque in Cannes, jet skiing in Bermuda, creating perfume in Provence and seeing newborn pandas in Chengdu, but I know that there are other reasons that we were invited to these events. One of those reasons was not for us to have the opportunity to try hot pot in Chengdu, the capital of the Sichuan province in China, one of the most painfully spicy eating experiences we have ever had, despite asking in several different ways for "little spice."

There is a component of quid pro quo that comes with these invitations. At the various events, we attend the required "commercial session," where new products are presented for consideration. I equate those sessions to the obligatory sales presentations geared to the purchase of a timeshare when one accepts a free weekend at a hotel or resort from a hotel group. Unlike the timeshare presentations, these commercial sessions come with a lot less pressure and are, of course, much more fun and interesting. We have never been sucked into a timeshare, but the same cannot be said for the commercial meetings. It has been at those sessions when I have been able to see watches I would not otherwise have seen in the metal due to rarity or exclusivity. It was on such an occasion I first saw the Reverso Tribute Enamel. There have been others.

On one occasion, we were invited to the opening of the Jaeger-LeCoultre exhibit "Sound Maker" in New York City, which celebrated the brand's watches that make sound: **minute repeaters** and the Memovox product line. We enjoyed a wonderful three days with the staff and like-minded collectors, some of whom have become lasting friends. During our "commercial meeting," I was presented with several new releases. One was the Reverso Tribute Minute Repeater. It was stunningly constructed. **Skeletonized** with excellent finishing, it displayed the time on both sides. The repeater chimes were clear and sonorous. What was particularly novel and fascinating was that the gongs had to be laid out in a rectangular fashion to fit the case. Quite unusual. I was told there were only going to be ten pieces made and most of them were already sold. When I asked about what serial numbers were available, I was told 1 and 10 were, of course, taken, but number 8 was still available. That was surprising because the number eight is very important in certain parts of Asia. In Chinese, the word for eight sounds similar to the word meaning "becoming rich in a short time." It is associated with wealth and status.

Fortunately, my wife was sitting right there and heard the conversation, the number still available, and, most importantly, the price. She looked at me and, stunningly, said I had to get the watch. I was dumbfounded to hear those words emanate from her mouth. She said that with all the watches I possessed, it was wrong that I should not have a repeater in my collection. It was my turn to have to be talked off the ledge. She has come such a long way. I asked for the night to sleep on it. They agreed and set a meeting for the following morning. At the appointed time the following morning, I met with the Jaeger-LeCoultre team and was told that they needed a decision because if I did not take the watch, it was going to be allocated to Singapore. The opinion of those present was that I would be foolish not to get the watch, and the availability of number 8 made it a no-brainer. I asked when the watch would be completed, and from behind me, the person in charge of national sales, someone I knew well, immediately said 2024. That was several years off and would give me plenty of time to arrange the funds. Looking into my wife's eyes, I agreed to commit, and off we went on the next watch project.

I have committed to a number of watches when they are released and then waited a significant amount of time after the promised delivery date to finally receive them. I figured that the 2024 date was probably optimistic. This time, the case was just the opposite. About six months after committing to the watch, I received a call informing me that my watch was about to be shipped. Sometimes I have been able to put off delivery of a watch for a period of time to organize finances, but Jaeger-LeCoultre was not going to hold off for a year and a half. I was able to make the finances work, but the downside effect was I had to cancel several other watch orders, which, I am sure, did not please other salespeople. Although stressful at the time, I have a watch that brings joy every time I engage the slide and listen to the chime of the repeater.

I am now prepared for the next blackout. I will always be able to know the exact time even when there is no light thanks to the beautiful chiming of the hours, quarter hours, and minutes.

Reverso Tribute Minute Repeater by Jaeger-LeCoultre

Chapter 11
Ribs and Kumquats

Traveling to the factories and attending brand-sponsored events and dinners has been fun and certainly educational. During those opportunities, I have had the pleasure of meeting CEOs, corporate executives, watchmakers, and sales staff. Despite all my interactions with the brands, I have not met a watchmaker from a major brand who actually built a watch that I own. The closest was when I visited Ulysse Nardin and discussed the issues involving my Stranger with the watchmakers in the haute horology department. Even then I did not meet the specific watchmaker responsible for my particular watch.

When working with independent watchmakers, as I've previously described, that is not the case. Rather, when I speak to the independent watchmaker, I am usually speaking to the person specifically responsible for the construction of my watch. Getting to know these creators adds an extra layer of significance to the watch I acquire and contributes its particular story. When admiring a painting by an old master, studying the brush strokes is fascinating. The brush strokes are a direct connection between the artist and the observer, though they may be separated by centuries. Much the same can be said about the watches from the hands of the independent watchmakers. These watchmakers imbue their own personalities, philosophies, and artistry into the watches that they create. This all becomes more apparent when given the opportunity to sit and talk with them.

House Guests

We have had the pleasure of hosting a number of watchmakers in our home. Several even brought their families to afford them the opportunity to enjoy touring the region. Others have come for a day or an evening to visit with us or to be the guest of honor among a gathering of collectors.

A lasting friendship is definitely more likely to develop in a relaxed atmosphere such as our family room or over the dinner table enjoying a meal prepared by my wife. Times like those are when conversations are free and easy and extend way beyond the world of watches, if that is at all possible. Of course, there will be the inevitable discussion about the technical and artistic aspects of the watchmaker's watches and probing to try to ascertain future plans—with, naturally, the pledge of confidentiality. Even with sincere promises made, the likelihood of prying new information is slim. Regardless, these moments in time, sitting on the family room couch or in our backyard, create relationships and indelible memories that years later are warmly recalled when I strap on the watchmaker's product.

Roger Smith and his wife, Caroline, stayed at our house before our trip to the Isle of Man. That was when we solidified our friendship and when I first laid eyes on an open dial Series 2 and a "standard" Series 2. With Roger's permission, I hosted a small gathering of friends and fellow collectors to meet him and see the watches. Roger was just starting to make a name for himself. At that time a mere mortal such as myself could still order a watch from him. Due to his low production numbers, his watches were rarely seen in the public domain, which made being able to see the two pieces a delight and special opportunity. In the end, it also helped to solidify my desire to eventually purchase one of his watches, much less two.

My wife and I also had the pleasure of hosting Serge Michel and Claude Greisler, CEO and head watchmaker, respectively, for Armin Strom. We'd already met at a reception in Beverly Hills. However, at such receptions, it is hard to get to know the featured guests. There are too many unavoidable distractions from other attendees to permit meaningful conversation. Also, the guests of honor are there primarily to schmooze all the attendees, not a selected few, to familiarize all those present with their brand. Equally, it is hard to fully appreciate special watches at such receptions, as it is necessary to share the "stars" of the show with others in attendance. My wife and I have similar experiences at art galleries. Gallery show openings are not times to appreciate the art. There are typically too many people around, too many getting in the way of experiencing the displayed works. We might go to an opening for social reasons and return at another time to fully experience the exhibit.

When Serge and Claude stayed at our house, we had a wonderful visit, and I was able to fully explore their brand, a completely different experience than when we met at the retailer. It is so much easier to learn about a brand, especially a new one, from the mouths of the company founders. They shared stories about their relationship to the man, Armin Strom, someone they knew for years, and how their philosophy for the future intersected with the concepts that began with Armin Strom. I was able to examine their watches while guided by the head watchmaker. It was definitely a unique experience and gave me a greater appreciation for the brand. Usually visits such as these do not translate into an immediate purchase. Rather, the education achieved—and, more importantly, the relationships established—set the stage for the possibility of a purchase sometime in the future.

It has never been my intent to use the visits for the sole purpose of achieving access. The main reason to spend time with these people is to develop friendships and to expand my knowledge regarding horology. There is the general perception of a watchmaker as someone huddled over a bench, loupe in place, tools in hand, working in a world the size of a postcard. Although that may be a true picture some of the time, watchmakers do get away from the bench and some can be true characters, as we discovered with Stephen McGonigle.

He and his partner, Cathriona, came for a stay during a trip around California. It was fun to watch the Super Bowl with an Irishman who had no idea what was happening. I learned later that Stephen is very passionate about sports, just not American football. He is passionate about rugby and Irish hurling (picture a mix of baseball, lacrosse, hockey, and

Gaelic). Beer and snacks made the afternoon more relatable for Stephen, while Cathriona and my wife chatted in another room, oblivious to the goings-on during the game. Watch talk would happen at other times. This was an exclusively social visit, as they were on their California adventure.

When watchmakers come to California, a majority of them make a trip to the desert. Originally, it was a mystery to me as to why. My answer came with the realization that Switzerland, with its beautiful topography of lakes, green fields, and snow-covered mountains, does not have a desert within its borders or in neighboring countries. Many of the watchmakers also enjoy hiking in the forests, hills, and valleys of their beautiful countryside, so when they come to California, they look forward to experiencing a different natural environment, as seen in the desert. Then again, the chance to see ghost towns and the Wild West depicted in movies might also be part of the draw.

Thomas Prescher; his wife, Heike; and their two sons also came and used our house to organize their visit throughout Southern California. During their time with us Thomas and I had several in-depth horological discussions that were rather intense. Sometimes, I have to work very hard to follow a watchmaker's train of thought. They start with a basis of understanding that I am only still trying to learn. One of my sons is an engineer and might stand a better chance than I do of following the detailed explanations of power transmission, minimization of friction, and other fine points of watchmaking. It is almost comical to me how they attempt to educate me on principles of engineering and physics. Thomas patiently put pencil to paper and drew a detailed diagram to explain how his **tourbillon** functioned, as it seemed to sit out there in the middle of space on a single post. I still have that drawing and refer to it periodically when I need a refresher or when I try to explain the magic of Thomas's **tourbillon** to a friend.

To a one, the watchmakers who stayed with us or paid us a visit have been so very grateful. A thanks is all that we require, but Thomas and his family took the thank you to a different level. My wife and I were at work when the Prescher family left our house after a several-day stay. When we got home that afternoon, we found the cabinets in our kitchen papered with the words "thank you" and a lovely arrangement of flowers on the table. It was a beautiful sentiment that we still warmly remember.

In our back yard we have two very large and proliferative kumquat trees. A kumquat is a small citrus fruit. Biting into one first gives a shock of sour juice that is then quickly followed by the sweetness of the rind. It is an acquired taste to eat a kumquat straight off the tree to be sure. My wife takes the bountiful harvest and makes kumquat marmalade in sufficient quantity such that visitors to our house are often sent off with a jar of marmalade and perhaps a bag full of the fruit. The watchmaking community has received their fair share. We have not gotten to the point of barter where we trade the kumquats and the marmalade for a watch. We did, however, trade marmalade for Prescher honey.

My wife loves to cook and enjoys feeding our guests. She is creative and willing to try different cuisines. On one occasion, while we were speaking with Tim Jackson, he was bragging about the barbecue ribs he makes. Rushing to my wife's defense, I claimed that hers were the most tender and flavorful ever. The gauntlet was thrown, and we agreed to a cook-off. Challenge accepted, the chosen time for the cook-off happened to coincide with a different visit by Thomas, the one when I agreed to acquire the Single Axis Tourbillon.

The parties agreed, much to Thomas's dismay, that he would be the judge. We convened the competition at our house, and both chefs did their very best. They produced a lunch that was filled with amazing barbecued ribs and all the fixings. Thomas did his political best and judged that it was a tie. To say the least, before making his judgment, Thomas was between a chill and a sweat. It was all for fun, though, and we all enjoyed the feast. There were truly no losers, only winners.

The joy of collecting is amplified by sharing a mutual passion with other like-minded people. Hosting watchmakers at our house has always been fun, and the ability to have friends join the festivities makes it even better. On one of his visits to California, Marco Lang came to my house for a get-together. By that time, I had already ordered the Lang & Heyne Anton. For that visit, Marco brought several watches for others to see. For me, the most important watch laid out on the coffee table was the number 1 Anton, my watch. It was great, but at the time I was asked to keep to myself the fact the Anton on display was to be mine. For fun, he had put it on a red strap, which made it look very casual. It is his creation; he is well within his rights to put whatever "shoes" he wants on his baby. Putting on different straps can change the aesthetic of a watch, and that can be an easy way to have different experiences with it. He was not ready to give me the watch, however. He needed to make some other commercial stops and needed it for marketing purposes. That said, throughout his stay at my house, I was barely separated from what was to be my watch. He promised, of course, that once he completed his marketing trip, he would service and recondition it to his high standards before handing it over. When it was delivered to me, it was not on the red strap. It was in perfect condition and has been an absolute joy to behold.

A Logical Decision

I first met Romain Gauthier when Tim hosted a dinner event in Santa Monica. It was also my first opportunity to see Romain's initial releases, the HM and the HMS. Romain is not a watchmaker; rather, he is an engineer with a business degree. He owns a company that produces specialized movement components for a number of watchmakers. In typical Swiss fashion, he refuses to reveal which companies he supplies. A secret is a secret.

When he shared the origin story of his company, we discovered that his path to forming his company was different from other nascent watch companies. Although not a watchmaker, growing up in the Vallée de Joux, he easily fell under the spell of that creative trade. First, he developed his parts company as a means to financially support his ultimate desire to create his own brand. His goal was to design watches that were unique, technically innovative, and finely finished. He did not have the skill to build the watch, but his talent to design very special pieces certainly was and is in evidence. He credited his passion for fine finishing to the influence of a neighbor and mentor in the Vallée de Joux, Philippe Dufour. Under Phillipe's tutelage, at least in part, Romain has received high praise for the quality of his product. Many collectors now consider Romain to have one of the finest finished watches in the market.

In addition to his finishing, he has designed features into his watches that are very unique. Not having the classical training of a watchmaker and being, instead, an engineer, he has not been bound by the conventions of traditional watchmaking. As was the case with Marco when we first met, I realized that someday I would have one of his watches, but it had to be the right one.

Subsequent to that first dinner event, I have met Romain on a number of other occasions and continued to admire his watches. Tim and I talked about Romain, and he knew that I was looking for the "right" Gauthier watch. In time, Tim let me know about a forthcoming model called the Logical One. The plan was for the first series, consisting of only twenty pieces, to be released in a platinum case. Tim strongly recommended that I consider the watch. He had never led me wrong, but I knew almost nothing about the watch, and Tim knew not much more.

Soon thereafter, Romain paid a visit to Tim's store in the San Diego region. Of course, I drove over to participate in the evening event Tim held. It was a very pleasant evening, but not much was revealed about the Logical One. The next day Romain planned to drive to Los Angeles, so I took the initiative and invited him to stop at my house for some one-on-one time. Our house is on the way to Los Angeles, and I offered him the opportunity to stay with us. He demurred because he already had plans; however, he agreed to stop by for a visit. This time I did not organize a get-together, but rather it was just him and me.

We spent several hours discussing a host of issues, including the proposed Logical One. Of course there was engineer-speak, but this time I seemed to have a better understanding about what he explained to me. I did not have to pedal quite as fast to keep up with him. Maybe his command of English was better than other watchmakers, or perhaps I was benefiting from a larger base of understanding I'd developed by that time. He gave me a detailed description of his concept for a chain to be used as part of the movement. It would function similar to a chain **fusée** except there would be a difference: the plan was for the chain to connect the **barrel** where power was stored to a snail cam that would transmit power to drive the **escapement**. There would not be the classical cone on which the chain was wound. Rather, it would wind around the **barrel**. He claimed that he'd perfected the design of the chain.

His testing confirmed a **constant force** that assured consistent power supply to the **escapement** via the chain whether the **mainspring** was full wound or nearly completely unwound at the end of the **power reserve**. He showed me graphs that demonstrated a consistent **amplitude** of the **escape wheel** and thus accurate timekeeping. With most mechanical watches with a standard movement and **mainspring**, there is variability in the power transmission to the **escapement** based on the tension in the **mainspring**. As it unwinds, the transmitted power from the **mainspring** can vary, thus affecting the **amplitude** and the timekeeping accuracy of the movement. There can be significant difference between a fully wound **mainspring** and one almost totally unwound. A **constant force** mechanism such as the chain he designed, however, avoids this problem; the power transmission is the same from beginning to end.

Also, what set the Logical One apart was his plan for a uniquely designed chain. All **fusée** chains are made from brass and steel and look like bicycle chains. This has been a consistent approach for centuries. Romain proposed making his chain with linked rubies, something never done before, as far as I know. As an added unique feature, sprouted from his creative engineering mind, he developed a revolutionary winding system that used a **pusher** instead of a **crown**. Only the time would be set by way of a **crown**. If I had a doubt, those few hours we spent together on the couch in our family room sold me on the watch. The only decision left was the dial. I had a choice of a white enamel one or a black **guilloché** dial. I chose the enamel dial. Subsequently Romain offered to change the dial to any other color I might like, but I chose to remain with the purity of the white enamel.

When I finally received my watch, there was no doubt that the Logical One was something extraordinary. As mine was one of the first Logical Ones produced, I did not have the opportunity to see one in the metal before mine was delivered. I immediately noticed that the chain was not as Romain described to me. Linking the rubies into a chain, as it turned out, was not possible, according to Romain. It was necessary to bracket each ruby with metal links that then formed the chain to ensure its stability. The change made absolutely no difference to me. When I pushed the winding **pusher** once, the **escapement** immediately jumped into action. Winding most watches takes at least several turns of the **crown** to start the **escapement** moving. Some require a bit of a shake, called the "watchmaker's shake," to start up the **escapement**. When I inspected the finishing, every part was beautifully hand beveled. When judging the finishing and **anglage**, the way to best appreciate the craftsmanship and skill is by examining the internal angles of the **bridges** and plates. Those are the hardest areas to do high-quality finishing. On close inspection of the Logical One, those areas were no less than perfect. That said, my favorite place to look at is the sharp angle of the **bridge** holding the **escapement** at the three o'clock position. Sharp to a point, with perfect **anglage** on both aspects of the **bridge**, it brings joy to my eyes. Even the screws are unique. Romain specially made the screws such that the slots were in an S-curve. His rationale for using such an unusual screw design was that a special screwdriver would be required to manipulate them. This served, I am told, to prevent an untrained watchmaker from working on the movement, which could have tragic ramifications.

Logical One by Romain Gauthier

The Americans

In the nineteenth and early twentieth centuries, American watchmaking was a vigorous industry. Much of that capacity was lost by the mid-1900s, as the watch industry developed in Europe and Asia. Currently there remain several American-based watch companies. Most design only the dial or even the case but the rest of the manufacturing occurs in other countries. For the most part, the movements are likewise imported.

Independent watchmaking in America is also quite limited, but there is a burgeoning community as a growing crop of watchmakers are making their own components and building their own watches. One such person is Keaton Myrick.

Keaton studied in the Rolex training program, and after working in the Rolex repair department for a period of time, he decided to form his own brand and moved to Oregon. Once again, Tim's store provided the site of our introduction. I initially met Keaton there, and subsequently have met him several other times when he visited the region. He, too, spent time with my wife and me in our home.

Later, on a trip to Oregon, my wife and I arranged a visit to his workshop in Sisters, which is in a remote part of that state. Watchmakers seem to be attracted to pastoral environments, and certainly Sisters is one. The area is dominated by mountains, called the Three Sisters, along with forests, rivers, and hiking trails to be explored.

While picturesque, the locale comes with a bit of a hardship. I've talked to Keaton, as well as several other US-based watchmakers, regarding the dearth of independent watchmakers on this side of the Atlantic and Pacific. They say the problem is getting parts from manufactures in Switzerland. Their orders are always small in quantity, which makes them a low priority, and because of distances, there is difficulty developing relationships with manufactures. Keaton made another interesting point: the distance between Oregon and Switzerland makes it hard for him to get desired assistance from respected watchmakers when faced with a challenge regarding a design element or mechanical question. Although they may be competitors in a sense, independent watchmaking is filled with camaraderie and support between fellow artisans. Master watchmakers, as far as I know, are always willing to give others the benefit of their knowledge and experience when asked. Keaton spoke of going to the Basel Fair with his watch in hand to show to others. He used the opportunity to get valuable input to improve his watch. It was very helpful for him, but unfortunately for Keaton and his American colleagues, now that the show is defunct, the opportunity to be in a concentrated gathering of colleagues with any degree of regularity is much less likely.

Keaton designed his own movement and is now capable of making most of the components, even cases, pinions, and screws. When talking with him, I enjoyed the excitement he manifested when he spoke about getting a new-to-him piece of equipment designed to make one component for his movement—those machines might be eighty years old when they come on the market. It was up to him to service the machine and get it into working order. The joy in doing so is only surpassed when he uses it for its intended purpose and successfully produces a screw, a plate, or a pinion. It always amazes me that relatively big and complicated pieces of machinery are needed to construct the tiniest part of a watch.

As yet I have not committed to a watch made by Keaton. As he produces more watches, his skill, design, and finish work will improve significantly. We have discussed the possibility of a watch for me, but we both agreed to wait until he has designed the right piece. I am sure that it will happen. I want to support homegrown, American watchmakers and see a resurgence of watchmaking in the New World.

Along a similar vein, more recently I learned about a dial maker based in Los Angeles, Joshua Shapiro. When I first found out about Josh, his day job was as a principal at a private school. With an interest in mechanical design since childhood, he taught himself how to use a rose engine and developed a proficiency in creating **guilloché** dials. In time he developed his own **guilloché** pattern designated the Infinity Weave.

After reading George Daniels's *Watchmaking*, Josh decided to set out to create his own watch company in Los Angeles. Over time, he has gained recognition for the art of his dials and has collaborated on several projects with other watchmakers. As he expanded his operation, he started to produce watches under his own name.

The article that introduced me to Josh's work referred to a watch he was going to produce with a special dial made from meteorite, engraved with his Infinity Weave. I contacted him on a whim (is there such a thing when it comes to watch collecting?). He responded quite promptly and wrote that the watch was a special subscription project he was doing in conjunction with a particular collector's group. He put me in contact with one of the group leaders, and left it to us to discuss whether there was an opportunity for me to get a watch with a meteorite dial.

I had several nice conversations with the leader, my goal was for him to learn that I am not a fly-by-night collector, that I am serious and have some special pieces. Of the limited series, there was one allocation left, and I was told that for me to be part of the group, I would need to buy this watch. Interested in the watch, I spoke to Josh, and we agreed that he would bring the watch to my house so that I could make a decision.

I was fortunate to see a couple of Josh's watches when he visited, including the one with the meteorite dial. I was impressed with his workmanship as a dial maker. Having had discussions with Roger Smith and Kari Voutilainen about the complexities of the rose engine machine and what it took to make a high-quality dial, I had respect for what Josh achieved.

Josh is transparent. He openly admits that his expertise is in dial work. At the time, his watches had movements supplied by Uhren-Werke-Dresden, a component company owned by Lang and Heyne. After some discussion, I decided that I did not want to proceed with the meteorite dial watch for a couple of reasons. First, the meteorite material did not lend itself to a good demonstration of Josh's skill with the rose engine—the weave of the **guilloché** was not very obvious on the dial. It was somewhat erratic, with gaps readily apparent, because of the nature of the meteorite. Another determining factor was the idea of buying a watch as an entrance requirement to join a club. I am very interested in being part of a watch collectors group. Over time I have joined several others, as I enjoy being part of a community and learning from like-minded crazies. However, there was no way I was going to buy a "club watch" so that I could be a member of this or any group. I already have enough reasons to buy a watch and enough sources of temptation.

As Josh and I talked, he showed me a completed watch in a rose gold case, part of his "Infinity" series. That dial was beautifully done to be sure and demonstrated his skill with the rose engine machine. I could see why Josh was getting noticed by the watch world. I did like the piece, but Josh suggested I wait. He told me, in confidence, he was in the process of designing his own movement and intended to use "the Daniels method." His intention was to produce all the components of the watch (except for springs and **jewels**) in his shop and build the movement from the ground up. We agreed it would be better for me to wait until he was further along in his pursuit of his own movement before committing to a watch from him. Before he left, as is our tradition, my wife made sure that he was adequately supplied with several pounds of kumquats and a jar of her kumquat marmalade.

Since that initial meeting, Josh has further expanded his operation and left his job in education to dedicate himself full time to the development of his own brand. He returned to my house on a couple of other occasions to discuss his progress and, of course, get more kumquats. On one occasion, I hosted a gathering for friends at my house so Josh could show what he was creating. At the time he was well on his way toward building his first in-house watch. He brought an unfinished prototype, along with a new member of his team, a young watchmaker who provided details about the movement.

Josh returned for another visit, and this time he brought the first nearly completed prototype for me to see. The movement design was nice, and the finishing of the **bridges** of the movement was unique. Most impressive was the multilayered dial with his **guilloché** pattern aligned so that the row of the weave was uninterrupted from one component to the next. It was a difficult design and an engineering feat.

Sitting on our couch, we spent some time talking about his project, but then the discussion diverted to other topics of mutual interest within the watch community. We were able to share stories about several different watch projects and the watchmakers involved. Some of the stories contained information that was not common knowledge. The two of us knew segments of the same stories, and we were able to fill in some of the gaps that the other was missing. The watch world is not very big, and the grapevine is small enough to allow the same incidents to be shared from different perspectives by different people. Eventually, Josh went home with pounds of kumquats and another jar of marmalade. We planned to keep our conversation going in the future.

To date, I have not committed to watches built by Keaton or Josh. The conundrum remains, if we do not support the growth of watchmaking in the US, who will? Yet these watches have a price associated with them that is not pocket lint. Purchasing one watch is good, but that alone will not assure continued growth of these watchmakers. They and others need broad-based support to be successful. The AHCI represents independent watchmakers around the world; however, the membership requirements are challenging for many watchmakers, especially newcomers with limited financial resources. The Horological Society of New York does an excellent job as a resource for general horological education and provides programs highlighting independent watchmakers, but that is not their primary focus. I have had several very preliminary discussions regarding the formation of a nonprofit group dedicated to the support of independent watchmaking in the US. I know that I do not have the ability, talent, or hands to be a watchmaker, but I am certainly interested in being more than just a client and cheerleader. Giving them support and better exposure to the watch-buying public in the US would be a great service. It might even encourage others who possess a notion or a passion to develop their own brands and take the leap into the field. Whether such a group comes to fruition will be a matter of time and further conversations.

The Perfect Gift

While many watchmakers and their family members and my watch friends have been to my house, support for my collecting, of course, starts with my family. On holidays, birthdays, and anniversaries, there is always the challenge of finding the right present for a friend or a loved one. When one collects watches, the price of a watch can be very intimidating or simply just not affordable for a gift giver. My mother resolved such a problem by giving my father one stamp to cover all the gift giving events for the year. However, with that concept in mind, there can be a different order of magnitude between the cost of a stamp and a watch. Of course, watches come in different price categories. "Less expensive" ones can give an equal amount of joy as very expensive ones, but even "less expensive" examples may not fit someone's budget. Yet with the desire to support the collector's passion, the gift giver searches for something related to watches. Books, a small set of tools, a loupe, and a branded item of clothing have been given to me as gifts and are much appreciated. One holiday season, my sons gave me a unique gift that I continue to enjoy: an antique oak ice box.

Over the course of history, many solutions were developed to preserve food, with cold storage being one of them. One storage device developed for the home was the ice box. It consisted of a compartment where a block of ice was placed and a main compartment for food storage. On the bottom was a tray to collect the drippings from the melting ice. My sons bought a two-compartment ice box that had a top section for the ice and a main section for the food. Both compartments had been lined with felt. The boys fitted a block of wood into the upper compartment and a wood shelf in the divided main compartment. The two pieces of wood were milled with grooves wide enough to hold the feet of collars used to display watches.

When they gave it to me, I was very excited, placed it prominently in our house, and immediately appreciated the significance of the ice box, as did my wife. I gave them a huge smile and profuse thanks while my wife groaned, with good humor, of course. I now had a display cabinet that must be filled. It was my duty and obligation to my sons to fulfill their unstated expectations. It is incumbent upon the recipient to use a gift to its fullest extent to express appreciation, right? So to please the boys—and only them, of course—I needed to find suitable watches to fill the ice box. Over time, I succeeded in doing just that. I have found watches that I happily mount on the collars and display in the ice box. It is a joy to lift the top hatch or open the door to admire the gems that sit there.

Despite her protestations, my wife is now an active participant in my journey and has absorbed more than a basic understanding of watches. More importantly, she is now able to hold up her end of a conversation regarding watches with anyone. She is a fine hostess and friend to those who have stayed or visited us. To be sure, she is most gracious in doling out her marmalade. Participating in my journey, she has met many of the foremost people in the watch industry, many of whom now call us friends. She has also contributed to my collection by surprising me with watches that, of course, instantly became the most important pieces in my collection. She has plotted and connived to present me with several watches, usually working with Chad.

The first one was given during the winter holidays—we celebrate both Hanukkah and Christmas. One year, hanging amid the branches of our Christmas tree, I found an Omega De Ville Co-Axial Chronograph Olympic Edition. I was speechless. It was the first watch I was to receive with the vaunted co-axial movement. I was only first starting to understand the significance of the movement, and it was long before we met George Daniels. I had admired the watch in the store on a number of visits, and when it was no longer in the display case, I just assumed it was sold. I admit I was a bit sad to no longer see it, but one cannot have everything. I had no inkling there was plotting afoot between Chad and my wife. Weeks later, I found the watch hanging on a branch of our tree. I was stunned. Not for a moment did I express any dismay about the conniving that took place between Chad and my wife. As subsequently asserted by George, its timekeeping has been consistently excellent, being plus/minus one to two seconds per day.

Several years later, we were visiting our son in Berkeley. That weekend coincided with my birthday (actually, my wife and I have the same birthday). On the morning of our birthday, we chose to go for a celebratory breakfast at a favored place. After placing our order (my choice was the Alameda, an insanely large meal that guaranteed that no other meal would be necessary for the rest of the day), my wife presented me with a pair of socks as a birthday present. She enjoys filling my sock drawer with interesting and funny pairs, so I naturally assumed they were more fodder for the drawer. However, the socks were heavy, and I could feel something wrapped inside the one sock. Reaching inside the sock, I pulled out an Omega De Ville Hour Vision. She did it again. During a previous visit to the Watch Connection, I had expressed interest in the watch. Chad must have alerted my wife, and once again, they went about their intrigue. I usually see Chad every one or two weeks. He was tight-lipped about the Hour Vision. I got not an inkling about what they had up their sleeves.

Seamaster Olympic Edition by Omega

The Hour Vision has a co-axial movement, by then the standard movement for most Omega watches. As it so happens, it represents another George Daniels connection; George was given the exact same model as a gift and wore it frequently. Sadly, I did not think to ask George, when we met, what his daily wear was. It was only much later that I read about his Hour Vision and saw pictures of it on his wrist. When I saw pictures of the watch itself, I could tell that he had worn it frequently, as the case had plenty of scratches. I am honored to share that with him. Good choice by my wife.

The first feature that brought the Hour Vision to my attention was its design, but its function is also interesting. The case is designed to allow the movement to be seen from different perspectives through windows built into the sides of the case in addition to the sapphire glass on the back. Although not marketed as a travel watch, it is easy to adjust the hour hand when changing time zones without affecting the minute hand or the central second. Unlike typical travel or **GMT watches**, the Hour Vision does not indicate the home time, but the convenience of this watch when crossing time zones still makes it very utilitarian. And, of course, the co-axial movement assures that the timekeeping is very precise.

De Ville Hour Vision by Omega

My wife continued to plot and connive, keeping a close eye on what I liked and appreciated and what fell in her price range. For example, although I acquired most of my Ulysse Nardin watches primarily because of the innovative engineering within the watch, there was also a stylistic aesthetic that attracted me. The brand also produced a line of simple, time-and-date-only watches in the Classico line. There was nothing special about the movement—it has a standard ETA movement and did not have any of the Ludwig magic within. The one that caught my eye was highlighted by a blue enamel dial with a sunburst-patterned **guilloché**. The Classico was offered in either a steel or a gold case. Although I like precious metal cases, this one looked better in the stainless steel case.

A friend had purchased the watch, and initially I was nonplussed when I saw it on his wrist. Tastes can change, or maybe it was because I saw the watch under the right lighting that showed off the dial work, but I grew to admire and desire the watch. The more I saw it, the more it pulled me in.

This was before I acquired the Marine Annual Calendar with its blue sunburst dial. The two watches have the same sunburst **guilloché** pattern, but they have quite different aesthetics. The blue of each dial is very different, with the Classico blue a more vibrant, electric blue compared to the more muted blue of the Marine Annual Calendar. There is debate in collector circles over whether a watch should or should not have a date window. Some detractors believe that the date window breaks up the harmony of the dial. In most situations the window does not bother me, and I accept it as a useful component of the watch. At times it is helpful to know the date as well as the time. In this situation I do think that the window detracts from the beauty of the **guilloché** somewhat, but not enough to lessen my enjoyment of the piece. It was all about the incredible blue of the dial created by Donzé Cadrans.

Once again, the co-conspirators went about their business. I expressed interest in the watch, and my wife started to make arrangements for another birthday present. In the interim, prior to my birthday, we took a trip to Germany. In Munich, we came upon a watch store that, of course, I had to enter. On display was a Classico with the blue enamel dial. My wife was happy and relieved when I pointed it out and commented wistfully about the watch. Under the lights of the display case, the dial glowed. It is always a great feeling when the recipient unknowingly expresses an interest in a planned surprise gift.

The plot worked perfectly. It was a birthday present and a total surprise. Chad and my wife were, once again, very proud of themselves. On the dial is printed "**Chronometer** Officially Certified." This means that the watch has been regulated to specific standards. In fact, as with the other two watches my wife bought me, the Classico is virtually spot on with regards to the measurement of time even after all these years. This one did not have a co-axial movement. What would George say?

My wife has picked very well because when all is said and done, the purpose of the watch is to tell time as accurately as possible. The ones she selected have done an excellent job in that category. There is a reason they are the most important watches I own.

Classico Blue Enamel by Ulysse Nardin

Chapter 12

Good Chocolate, Melty Cheese, and Interesting People

As mentioned earlier, over the years, my wife and I have been invited to events sponsored by watch companies in some very interesting and exotic places. The events might only last several days but typically when we travel overseas, we try to extend our time whenever possible to afford us the opportunity to explore the region.

On two separate occasions we traveled to China with the expressed intent of attending the Shanghai Film Festival. Each time the event lasted four days, during which we were able to tour Shanghai, a small city in China with a population of twenty-five million people. It made no sense to fly such a distance for only a few days, so on each visit we added time to see more of China. Besides, obtaining a visa to visit China is a challenge, and once we got ours, we figured we should maximize our opportunity. When we applied for the visas for the first trip, we had to account for all our anticipated whereabouts in China for the duration of our stay. When we finally got our visas, they were for ten years, so now we can essentially go and come as we please during subsequent visits.

On the first trip we toured Beijing, a city lost in a haze of pollution before heading for Shanghai. After the film festival, we traveled to the water city of Wuzhen, followed by visits to Suzhou and Hangzhou. Often during our touring, we would be stopped by locals asking us (in sign language) if they could take our pictures. Wanting to further Chinese-American relations, we always agreed. It was only toward the end that I came up with the idea that if someone asked to take our picture, we should return the favor and take theirs, to their utter delight. On our way home, we stopped for a brief visit in Taiwan, highlighted by the night market in Taipei (where we had incredible fried chicken and toured a football field sized market with every kind of trinket imaginable) and a visit to Sun Moon Lake.

On our second foray to Shanghai, once the film festival concluded, we flew to Xian to see the terracotta warriors. We traveled with a Jaeger-LeCoultre team member and accompanied her when she visited several of her clients. The cities where these clients live are not on a typical tourist's itinerary, but we had great dinners and saw amazing watch collections, ones worthy of their own museums.

Dinners were especially entertaining. The people we visited did not speak English, and we certainly know no Chinese. The Jaeger-LeCoultre representative served admirably as an interpreter. After several bottles of Moutai liquor, though, we enjoyed very animated conversation, hugging, and singing. The highlight of that second China trip, besides the watches, was the trip to Chengdu to see the pandas and try hot pot.

As a participant in these and other adventures, my wife understands there is the expectation that she will be asked to take part in the portions of the trips dedicated specifically to watches. During the "commercial meetings," she will either listen to the conversation or strike up her own conversation with some of the staff members. It also helps that during these trips there have been plenty of distractions other than watches. These distractions are needed since there is a concept of too much of a good thing. In 1817, a French novelist and critic with the pen name Stendhal became physically overwhelmed after visiting the art masterpieces in Florence, Italy. He wrote about it, and the condition became known as Stendhal Syndrome or Florence Syndrome. Whether Stendhal Syndrome is a real condition or not has been debated since the description was first published. That said, there are reports of tourists becoming physically or emotionally overcome to the point of seeking medical attention after seeing such masterpieces as the statue of David or during a tour of the Uffizi Gallery. When surrounded by horological marvels, one needs distractions to clear the mind and avoid such risks of developing the watch equivalent of Stendhal syndrome.

Another brand sponsored a trip to the Cannes Film Festival. Never in my wildest dreams did I think we would ever have the opportunity to go to the festival and allow the "A-listers" an opportunity to breathe the same air as us, so when the offer was made, we jumped. That is where I gave Catherine Deneuve her comeuppance (to be discussed later). We played pétanque followed by dinner at the famous La Colombe d'Or, a restaurant with great food and walls covered with amazing modern art by Picasso, Calder, Miro, Chagall, and others. A tour was arranged for us at the Fragonard perfume factory, and we made our own perfume at the Galimard factory, both establishments in the town synonymous with the perfume industry, Grasse. I do not wear cologne or perfume, but it was interesting to learn how they are made. The one I made I named "Freak." The bottle with the Freak and one of their own creations that was gifted to me (I'm sure not as balanced or fragrant as mine) remain on the sink in my bathroom. I only rarely take a spritz but frequently have fond memories when I look at the bottles.

When we went to the actual film festival to see a movie, we entered the theater by walking the red carpet, for which we had to be properly dressed. My wife had her makeup and hair done professionally. I put on my best suit and tie. We were ready to go, or so we thought. When we went to the lobby to meet our group to head to the festival, our host, Patrick Pruniaux, CEO of Ulysse Nardin, informed me that I needed a bowtie to walk the red carpet. That was shocking news, to be sure. How could I be so unprepared? Without missing a beat, Patrick ran back to his room and loaned me his spare bowtie. Disaster averted. Once properly attired, although the hotel was two blocks from the festival, we were escorted to our car, as the only way walk the red carpet and enter the theater was by arriving in a car.

We enjoyed our time on the Riviera to be sure, but I did not enjoy the experience of walking the red carpet. Frankly, I was very embarrassed. The crowds were not there to see me or my wife, though maybe they should have been excited to see her. I am.

Dream Vacation

During the course of this journey with watches, we have acquired quite a number of friends and acquaintances within the watch world who live in Switzerland. When I suggested to my wife that it would be fun to visit our friends there, I thought perhaps we could also arrange to visit some watch companies. After some discussion, my wife agreed to the concept of taking a trip to Switzerland for almost two weeks exclusively dedicated to watches and watchmakers. Several more conversations occurred before we started to make plans, as I wanted to be sure she would be okay with a trip so dominated by my passion. My wife steadfastly agreed to the trip with the caveat that she would get good chocolate and melty cheese and be able to meet interesting people and have good conversations. I happily agreed, and we started planning. The decision was to be there twelve days and hopefully avoid any symptoms of Stendhal Syndrome, as neither of us wanted to risk psychological trauma.

After we agreed on a general outline for the trip, we booked our flights and coordinated the itinerary with the people and companies we hoped to visit. Everyone was accommodating and helped us develop a great itinerary. We began in Zurich. There we wandered down the Bahnhofstrasse and came upon Beyer Watches and Jewelry. On the lower level of the store is the Beyer Clock and Watch Museum, a small but well-known museum that displays a portion of their private collection of time-measuring devices dating as far back as 3500 years. The collection tells the story of the measurement of time from ancient times to the development of clocks and watches by way of their incredible exhibition. This visit was unplanned but a great way to start our journey immersed in watches and the measurement of time.

The next day we drove to Lucerne. I had previously been to the city after graduating from college in the 1970s. At that time, it seemed that at every turn there was a store selling cuckoo clocks and music boxes built to look like Swiss chalets. Now those shops were selling watches. Another notable difference was that outside many of the watch stores were signs written in Chinese. It was a clear indication of who comprised a significant percentage of tourists and watch buyers. In Lucerne, we walked the Chapel Bridge, originally built in the fourteenth century but reconstructed after a fire in 1993. That pedestrian **bridge** is famous for painted panels depicting commercial life in Lucerne during the Middle Ages. No watch stores were depicted. We also paid our respects to the famous carving of the dying lion and made a brief stop at the Museum of Transport.

We next proceeded to Bern, where we were able to see the famous statues including the *Kindlifresserbrunnen* statue, the Child Eater of Bern, the picture of which Paul Gerber sent me. Before we visited the bears of Bern, we were lucky to join an English-language tour of the Bern clock tower, the Zytglogge. It is a clock originally built in the twelfth century. Astronomical measurements and indications were added to it during the sixteenth century. Before the tour, we saw the clock's hourly animation display in action, but when we were able to witness it from inside the housing of the clock, that was a special treat. Over the course of time, much has changed with regards to the construction of clocks and watches, materials used, miniaturization, the manner of storage, transmission of energy, and reduction of friction, all critical factors when building a time measurer. Learning about the Bern clock showed us, however, that the basic principles of time measurement have remained the same across the centuries. It would be hard to put this clock on the wrist, and I am sure its accuracy is not up to COSC standards. However, it is still working and telling time. Reflecting on my preference for watches over cars, how many cars will be functioning as designed nine hundred years after they were built? Timepieces are built to withstand the effects of time. Can car manufactures say the same? I rest my case.

As we walked the streets of Bern, we passed the patent office where Einstein was employed when he developed the theory of relativity, a theory that has important relationships to the measurement of time. Leaving Einstein, we came upon the Bern bears, who have been residents of the city since its early days. They had been exhibited in pits until they were given a new park in which to roam in 2009.

After viewing the bears, we drove to La Chaux-de-Fonds for our scheduled tour of the Ulysse Nardin Manufacture. Ulysse Nardin has two separate locations. Besides La Chaux-de-Fonds, they also have buildings in Le Locle. In the morning, we started at the La Chaux-de-Fonds factory. While waiting in the lobby for our guide, I noticed a box sitting on the unattended receptionist's desk. Curious, I strolled to the counter and looked at it. It was addressed to Patek Philippe. Clearly, I had no idea what might be contained within the box, but I am sure it was not brochures. Ulysse Nardin is affiliated with Sigatec, the supplier of the majority of silicium components used by the watch industry. I imagined that inside the box were silicium parts Patek Philippe had ordered from Ulysse Nardin. I am absolutely sure I was wrong.

It was during our tour of the Ulysse Nardin Manufacture that I had the opportunity to go to the haute horology department and speak with the watchmakers about my Stranger. I had to explain the story to our tour guide, much to the dismay of the watchmakers who were listening. I was laughing; the watchmakers were not. We then drove to Le Locle to continue our tour. Once we found our destination, we were given directions to a nearby building where Donzé Cadrans was located.

Donzé Cadrans is one of the, if not *the*, top creators of enamel dials, as well as dials with **grand feu** enamel, champlevé, and cloisonné. It produces dials not only for its owner, Ulysse Nardin, but for other brands as well. For a prominent supplier of such international renown, the building was very nondescript and the production room surprisingly small. We were escorted by the manager and watched as dials were placed into a small oven to be baked while others were stamped with the names of Ulysse Nardin, Lang & Heyne, Zenith, and Patek Philippe.

In one corner of the room, a woman worked diligently, hunched over her bench, creating a cloisonné dial that portrayed the image of a sailing ship for a Ulysse Nardin watch. The dial had sections outlined by gold wire. One section at a time, the woman added colored enamel to fill each space. We watched her carefully apply a dollop of enamel with a tiny brush, rinse the bristles in a cleaning solution, wipe it off on a dry cloth, and then put the brush between her lips to get the bristles to a fine point. She repeated the process over and over. My wife and I were surprised to see her so willingly put the brush into her mouth. Certainly, there must be a better way to get the bristles to the desired fine point.

In the 1920s, radium was used for luminescence on watch dials. Women painted the radium onto the numerals on the dial using fine paint brushes and "pointed" their brushes with their lips. Sadly, a number of these women developed significant illnesses directly related to the radiation exposure. Eventually the use of radium for luminescence was discontinued.

When we asked, it was confirmed that the enamel contained lead. Simultaneously, my wife and I had the same thought: chronic exposure to lead could result in neurological problems. We mentioned our concerns to the manager who was our guide. He looked at us and shrugged his shoulders. It was her choice. Should the young lady start acting oddly, we suggested that someone should check her lead levels. He nodded, and we moved on. Not much else we could do or say.

That evening we went to dinner with Patrik Hoffmann, at the time the CEO of Ulysse Nardin, and Susanne Hurni in Le Chaux-de-Fonds. It was at that dinner I first learned of the newly developed anchor **escapement** and saw the prototype that now graces my wrist.

At dinner with Patrik and Susanne, our conversation was wide-ranging. One topic did involve the watch on Patrik's wrist, the prototype for the anchor **escapement**. My wife's quest for good chocolate was also discussed in detail. Suzanne recommended we visit a small chocolatier, Jacot Chocolaterie. According to her, Jacot is the chocolatier that supplies the Swiss government with gifts for dignitaries. At the conclusion of an excellent meal and evening, we had made significant headway in our quest for excellent chocolate, and I had made a decision about the prototype watch.

The next morning, we went to the MIH in La Chaux-de-Fonds, where, to her credit, my wife did get engrossed in the exhibits. We spent a couple of hours enjoying the museum. I was sure to point out the case displaying the Trilogy. Unfortunately, there was no opportunity to meet Ludwig Oechslin.

Once done at the MIH, we had an appointment to meet Kari Voutilainen, so off we went to Môtiers. On the way, we stopped in Noiraigue to visit Jacot Chocolaterie, as instructed. We were sure to sample a variety of their wares and make a purchase sufficient to satisfy my wife's desires.

This was not my first meeting with Kari. By this time, we had exchanged a number of emails and met at several dinner events in Switzerland and in California, as well as at some watch shows. I have admired Kari's work for a long time and knew I wanted a watch from him, eventually.

When we arrived in Môtiers, we were early. Besides being known as the home of Kari Voutilainen, Môtiers is also known for the production of absinthe. We occupied ourselves in a store dedicated to absinthe. After learning its history, how it is made, and how it should be properly served, we were invited to try some. We were careful to limit how much we sipped. We did not want to meet Kari with absinthe on our breath. We also sampled absinthe-containing caramels, which we purchased along with a small bottle of the real thing. A very small bottle.

At the appointed time, we drove to Kari's house, where his workshop is located. Like Marco, his workshop was on one side of the building and his residence on the other. At the entry there were two doors, one to his workshop and the adjacent one to his residence. We were briefly introduced to his wife, who was heading out for a hike in the nearby woods, a favorite family pastime. Kari led us to the first floor of his atelier, where we came upon a rose engine machine, a machine which was familiar to us, and one my wife was proficient at operating. That led to a conversation about his dials and the people he employed. He revealed that of all the designs that he is capable of producing, one of his least favorites was the basket weave **guilloché** pattern. He said it was the most complicated to create and required utmost concentration—a tidbit I filed away for later use. He showed us other pieces of equipment and explained their individual uses, and then we climbed the stairs to the upper floors of his workshop.

We met his teenage son, dutifully working in the atelier alongside the other watchmakers, and observed the various stages of his production process. We then sat with Kari and had a nice conversation over a cup of coffee. I told him I wanted a piece by him. Exactly what model I wanted I did not know, but I wanted the right piece, a pretty common refrain from me. When I say that to a watchmaker, they usually understand what I mean: something special and meaningful to me and to the watchmaker. In truth, any watch from a watchmaker such as Kari, whose annual production is small, is special. We discussed options, and after some time, he recommended that I wait to decide, as he was going to be creating something special. The model he was referring to was the 217QRS, a model with his base Vingt-8 movement with the addition of a **retrograde** date.

As we sat and talked, I took what may be a pretentious step. I suggested to the master a project he might consider. I proposed to Kari the concept of a **monopusher chronograph**. I had the idea that all the **chronograph** functions would be controlled by way of the **crown**. He kindly listened to me, gave me a nice smile, and said he would consider my idea. This was years before I came upon the COS prototype by Richard Habring. I guess I was ahead of my time. Before we parted company, Kari kindly presented to me a copy of his book. I neglected to have him sign it. No matter.

When the 217QRS was announced, I jumped at the chance to order one. There were to be a total of thirty produced, ten each in three different precious metal cases. With Tim's input, I decided to order a platinum piece. That was the easy part. The challenges came when I was asked to decide on the dial color, whether to have Roman versus Arabic numbers, and what the **guilloché** patterns on the dial would be. The design decisions were stressful. The easiest decision was the color of the dial, salmon. I also knew I wanted some component of the dial to have the basket **guilloché** pattern, as I knew he so loved that pattern. I acknowledge I was being a bit of a troublemaker. I relied heavily on Tim's input regarding the design of the dial. Even after all this time, I still do not have confidence in my ability to make design decisions. I absolutely did not want to make the "wrong" decision for such a special and long-desired piece.

When the watch was finally delivered, it was breathtaking. All facets of the watch were incredibly beautiful. Inspecting it front and back with a loupe, I had no words but could only make utterances of delight. My only thought was, *Where does one go from here? This is a perfect watch.* The pinnacle of fine movement finishing was there in my hand. I am not convinced there is a suitable answer, but I have not been dissuaded from lusting after other watches.

217QRS Retrograde Date by Voutilainen

After we left Kari, we drove to Neuchâtel to Stephen McGonigle and his partner Cathriona's apartment. By that time, I already owned two McGonigle watches, and we had an established relationship. Their apartment overlooked Lake Neuchâtel and had a fantastic view of the distant snow-covered Alps. Unlike John, Stephen remained in Switzerland. He had a side hustle: he owned the only Irish pub in Neuchâtel. Cathriona managed the pub while Stephen continued to ply his skills as a watchmaker. Once again, the visit involved good food and lots of wide-ranging conversations. Sitting on their terrace, drinking wine and distracted by the vista in front of us, it was hard to follow the train of the conversation at times.

Stephen took us to his workshop, which was on the outskirts of Neuchâtel. It was a well-lit space located within an industrial complex. He shared his workspace with another Irish watchmaker, Stephen McDonnell, the person responsible for the Marin 3 prototype. Previously, when I learned of their connection, I asked Stephen McGonigle if Stephen McDonnell would consider making a watch for me. The answer was a polite "Not likely." Stephen McDonnell's preference was to remain in the background, doing what suited him, designing movements for others. He had no interest in developing his own brand. In fact, at the time we met, Stephen McDonnell was in the process of arranging to move his family back to their home in Belfast, Ireland. Stephen McGonigle explained the other Stephen longed to be back in Ireland, but also, he was tired dealing with the arduous regulations ex-pats were apparently subjected to in Switzerland.

Stephen McDonnell was very convivial when we were introduced to him. We discussed the Marin 3 in detail, and he explained his philosophy behind the **jump hour** and the use of his wife's nail polish for the indicator. He took particular pride in the degree of finishing he was able to achieve on the module. When we went into Stephen McDonnell's workroom, he was working on a CAD design for a movement; he was not willing to reveal with whom he was working. Ultimately, using deductive reasoning, I was able to guess the brand. However, he would neither confirm nor deny that he was working with MB&F to develop a new movement for a **perpetual calendar**. As it turned out, I was looking at the design for the heart and soul of the MB&F Legacy Machine Perpetual.

Although he would not tell us the specifics regarding his project, Stephen used the CAD drawing to give my wife her next in-depth horological lesson. He explained, utilizing the computer drawing, how a watch works. He showed her step by step how energy is transmitted through gearing from the **mainspring** to the **escapement**. Next, he explained how the **escapement** measures time. Patiently, he went through the process, and I could see the light shine bright in my wife's eyes as her appreciation for the art and mechanics of watches grew. To say the least, I developed a man crush on Stephen McDonnell.

I have often considered obtaining the Legacy Machine Perpetual, as it is a very innovative movement and one of the best **perpetual calendars** on the market. However, I find it a big watch for my wrist size and not comfortable to wear. Although I absolutely respect and marvel at the novelty of his creation and the knowledge that I had the honor of seeing the renderings in its nascent days, I still choose wearability over function. Since our meeting, Stephen McDonnell returned to Ireland and has been working behind the scenes with Bremont. I am anxious to see what Stephen will go on to create in the future.

When we left Stephen McGonigle's workshop, we drove further into the hills above Neuchâtel to visit Studio 7h38. Studio 7h38 is so named to honor the hour and minute of the birth of Luca Soprana's child. Located in a nondescript courtyard, the studio has been the site of significant watch designs and developments. The studio is run by Luca, along with a team of watchmakers and designers. They conceived and designed the Deep Space Tourbillon for Vianney Halter and a **chronograph** for Omega. On Luca's desk sat another one of their accomplishments: the prototype for the Jacob & Co. Astronomia Tourbillon. I'd read about it, as it was unveiled at the previous Basel Fair, but here was the original prototype.

The watch had a triple-axis **tourbillon**, globe, and dial on three of four axes rotating around the midpoint. The fourth axis had a diamond as a counterweight. I do not know the size of the diamond, but it certainly was not a chip. It was a huge watch, measuring 50 mm in diameter and standing 25 mm tall. It was a fascinating piece of watchmaking but clearly not one I could conceive of wearing, even if the price was not an issue. As I inspected it, with full permission, of course, the "crystal" dome (the prototype actually had a plastic cover) came off in my hand. It was not secured to the case, and no one seemed concerned. There I was with the prototype uncovered in my hand, watching the **tourbillon** spin while, the earth, dial, and diamond slowly rotated around the center pinion. It was fun, and I did not get into trouble or get a dirty look.

Studio 7h38 had the feeling of a commune. After touring the small studio and meeting the team, we stood in the courtyard outside, talking with Stephen and Luca. A Volkswagen Beetle drove up, and one of the members of the studio got out carrying a bag of groceries. Apparently, the car was available for use by any member of the studio.

Across the courtyard, we stopped for a bite to eat at a small restaurant. Sitting outside, we were adjacent to the entrance to a medieval castle, the Chateau de Vaumarcus. Stephen told us that the castle had suits of armor, a particular fascination of mine, and a one-bedroom accommodation. He suggested that Studio 7h38 might be able to arrange for us to sleep there for a night among the medieval furnishings. We put it on the list for a future trip to Switzerland.

This would not be the last time Studio 7h38 played a part in my journey. Several years after the visit to Studio 7h38, Tim showed me a watch with a movement I'd never seen before. The dial was engraved with the name Derek Pratt, a British watchmaker and contemporary of George Daniels. In a number of ways, they were of equal significance in the world of horology. Derek assisted George by making some parts for his famous watches. He also helped problem-solve an occasional technical challenge faced by George. Derek also built a number of significant watches under his own name.

Like George, Derek made every component of the watches he built. A **remontoire** is used by watchmakers to assure movement accuracy. It stores energy and releases it in pulses to the **escapement** in such a fashion to assure a **constant force** and timekeeping accuracy. Although used by other watchmakers in the past, he was the first to place the **remontoire** on the actual **escapement** in a **tourbillon** movement of a pocket watch. Apart from his own constructions, he was the creative force behind the original Urban Jürgensen & Sønner brand. Also, he was the first person to attempt to replicate John Harrison's marine **chronometer**, the H4, the first marine **chronometer** to accurately measure longitude at sea and thus improve navigation. Unfortunately, Derek was not able to complete the H4 project due to failing health. It was eventually completed after his death by Charles Frodsham & Company.

Sadly, Derek did not receive the notoriety he deserved during his lifetime. As a tribute, Derek's friends and family decided to release a very limited series of watches, no more than ten. The watches would feature the **remontoire** reminiscent of the one Derek built. The watch Tim showed me was the prototype belonging to Tom Bales, a friend of Derek's and one of the instigators of the project.

Thinking about the watch, I saw it as a possible companion piece to my Daniels. Whereas George was involved in the conception, design, and construction of his Anniversary watch, the Pratt piece was a true memorial project since Derek had died a number of years earlier. I was put in touch with another close friend of Derek's, Ron DeCorte, an American watchmaker from Ohio. For Ron and Tom, this was a passion project they had been trying to get off the ground for many years. After some discussion, Ron invited me to be part of the design process for the first watch, which, in turn, would be mine to purchase if I so desired. We had numerous late-night telephone calls to discuss various aspects of the design. At those times Ron regaled me with tales of Derek and their friendship. I came to learn this project was truly an international affair: Ron and Tom, both living in the States, seemed to be the directors the project that also involved John McGonigle, in Ireland, advising on the movement construction and finishing; Kees Engelbarts, originally from the Netherlands but now Geneva-based, responsible for **skeletonizing** and engraving; Joshua Shapiro in Los Angeles creating dials; and Luca Soprana of Studio 7h38, an Italian, constructing the movement.

Ron and I decided on the idea of making the case for the first watch from argentium silver, the material used to make the H4. We also decided the number 1 piece should have a dial engraved by Kees with the design inspired by the **bridge** covering the main **barrel** of the H4.

It was an interesting project, and I was assured by those involved in the project that it was going to be a truly unique piece. This was going to be something special. However, as time progressed, several problems crept in. The first dial was not acceptable to members of the project. It was rejected due to concerns about stability and because the finishing needed to be improved. Kees had to redo it from scratch. The argentium silver did not lend itself to a watch case and had to be abandoned in favor of platinum. Eventually it came time for me to decide if I wanted to purchase the piece. I started to get cold feet. I was concerned that it was money, a lot of money. Of course, I do not acquire watches with the concept of ultimate financial gain, yet the price of this watch gave me pause. I do not have an endless fund of money at my disposal. I have to consider each purchase with some degree of fiscal responsibility.

When the watch was completed, I was told, it would be announced to the world with a press blitz and much fanfare to be orchestrated by a person well known to the watch world. Finally, Derek's contribution to watchmaking would receive the appreciation he deserved. Over time, I saw no evidence of any publicity. Ultimately, I backed out of the project with mixed emotions. I was concerned for all involved that the watch would be left unsold. I did not want all the work to be for naught. That said, I subsequently learned that number 1 was sold to a collector in a different country. Sadly, the watch never received proper notoriety and remains in anonymity.

It turns out, my reticence to buy the Pratt watch was another fortunate decision. After the purchase of the number 1, an order was placed by another collector for number 2. However, seemingly out of the blue, a retailer in Dubai announced the availability of a limited number of Derek Pratt watches for sale. Those watches contained the same movement as in the prototype I had seen. On the dial, there was the name engraved, "Derek Pratt." They were also built by Luca and Studio 7h38. Whereas the watch I considered contained a central second hand, this one had a seconds sub-dial. That was the only difference. When this Pratt watch was announced, I contacted several of the people involved in the original project. They, to a one, said it was my good fortune not to have purchased the number 1, as its significance had been lost. In fact, the collector who had ordered number 2 canceled his order and had his deposit refunded, and the project folded. As far as I know, the person with number 1 is still okay with his purchase.

Perhaps in the future I will find a watch built by Urban Jürgensen & Sønner that contains a movement designed by Derek; meanwhile, I may have something close. Antony, my friend in London who sold me my De Ville Co-Axial, is also a Chopard enthusiast. Antony was excited about the Ferdinand Berthoud brand and was talking to me about the newly released FB3. He connected me with Ken Koshiyama, the international sales director of Chopard, who, as it happened, was going to be at the Chopard boutique near me. I arranged an appointment with him to see the Ferdinand Berthoud collection. I had some familiarity with the line but had never seen one in the metal, but knowing that they were considered very highly by the watch community, I was interested to see them. The meeting was scheduled to last for an hour.

At the appointed time, my wife and I went to the boutique and met Ken and the Chopard boutique staff. Ken placed in front of me a series of Ferdinand Berthoud watches. We went through the six pieces, and Ken focused on the newly released FB3. I thought I would be interested in the

FB3, but when he showed me the FB2RE, I was stunned. Lightning struck once again. It is an incredible piece. As we talked about the FB3, I kept putting it down and picking up the FB2RE. Housed in a white gold case, the dial alone was amazing. It is composed of multiple components covered with white **grand feu** enamel. Stunningly, the sloping edge of the dial had perfect enameling. I was told that the dial was very complicated to make, with a high failure rate. In fact, I later found out, because of the difficulty making the dial, the full complement of FB2RE watches were not produced. The movement was beautiful in construction and exquisitely finished. Interestingly, it had a **remontoire** and a layout that was very similar to the Pratt movement, though rotated ninety degrees compared to the one in the Pratt watch. This movement also has a **fusée** chain, unlike the Pratt, yet the two **barrels** for the **fusée** were in the same orientation as the two **barrels** in the Pratt.

FB2RE by Ferdinand Berthoud

Observing that I could not put the watch down no matter how much we discussed other models, after two hours my wife put me out of my misery and told me to order the FB2RE, which I ultimately did. With the FB2RE, will I have gotten the Pratt movement, albeit modified? Is it a situation similar to getting the Habring[2] Rattrapante in the IWC Ingenieur

Doppelchronograph? Was Studio 7h38 involved with this watch? I will have to wait find out the answers to these questions.

###

In the hills above the city of Neuchâtel, Stephen, Cathriona, my wife, and I went for a hike in the Creux du Van, a stunning rocky "amphitheater" formation. There we were fortunate to see a couple of the denizens of the natural reserve, alpine ibexes. Similar to when I visited his brother, John, during our hike, Stephen and I talked mostly about watches. We discussed the McGonigle brand, and he told me his thoughts for the future, particularly the plan to create a **minute repeater**. When the conversation turned to the greater world of watches, it was fascinating to hear Stephen's perspective. Like other watchmakers I have spoken with, Stephen was very complimentary about Rolex. He thought they made a very solid, well-built, and reliable watch. Despite that enthusiastic endorsement, I was not convinced to change my decision never to get a Rolex. He was also very complimentary toward Greubel Forsey. He thought their business model was something to admire and their watches were exceptional.

During our visit, we made sure to stop by their pub to lift a pint. Stephen and Cathriona helped me keep my promise to my wife. They took us to a restaurant where we had melty cheese. There we experienced fondue in the true Swiss fashion, dipping boiled potatoes, not bread, into the cauldron of hot melted cheese and washing it down with local wine.

After a couple of very congenial days with Stephen and Cathriona, we drove to Yverdon-les-Bains, a town at the tip of Lake Neuchâtel, to have dinner with Don Corson and his wife, Gabriele, at their home. By the time of this visit, I owned the Dresdener. Don and I had met a number of times in Switzerland, Philadelphia, and Los Angeles. On one of his trips to Los Angeles, Don came with his wife, Gabriele, and the four of us were able to meet for a lovely dinner. By the time of this visit, Don had sold a second Dresdener and built a watch with a flying **tourbillon**.

After being served a wonderful dinner, Don and I excused ourselves from the table, and he brought me to the living room to show me his latest creation, his **tourbillon**. The piece was very innovative. The **tourbillon** cage was elevated above the plane of the dial. Because the watch was in a titanium case, it was incredibly light. When I put it on, it felt like a toy, but it certainly was not. It was an engineering marvel. I did my best to follow his engineer-speak. It reminded me of when one of my sons, an engineer, was in college and we walked around the engineering building. I could not understand the titles of the courses I saw posted, even though the words were in English. I do understand the concept of a **tourbillon**, but building one, especially in such an innovative way, was a challenge to understand for someone without an engineering background.

The next day we visited another watchmaking friend who I have known for quite some time. Once again, we were served an excellent lunch, after which I was invited to see a new development he was working on. Before he showed me what was in his hand, he requested that I not discuss what I was about to see with anyone, ever. By then I was very used to hearing things not for public distribution, and I promised to keep the secret. With that, I was shown the movement he designed. It was composed of two **balance wheels** connected by a multiple-curved spring. He went on to explain how the two **escapements** would be in resonance through the action of the clutch spring. It was an attempt to ensure better accuracy of timekeeping by having two **escapements** influence each other's actions and defeat errors inherent in the performance of the individuals. I knew I was looking at something original and innovative. In the watch world there are very few watches that utilize the principle of resonance, and I already had the F.P. Journe Chronomètre à Résonance. I was told that he had more work to do before he would have a fully working movement with his invention. He knew he was going to need help to bring a finished product to fruition. Up to that point, no one knew about this project.

Subsequent to our visit, the movement was put in the hands of Luca Soprano of Studio 7h38. There, apparently Luca provided some design and technical input but did not produce a working model. Sometime thereafter, the movement concept and design was sold to Armin Strom, where the head watchmaker and developer, Claude Greisler, perfected the movement and incorporated it into a watch, the Mirrored Force

Resonance.

Having seen the initial movement and familiar with the watch's development, when I learned from Sebastian, the Armin Strom representative, that the watch was to be released in a limited run of fifty pieces in a rose gold case, I asked for the first one produced. I had the temerity to ask what was in it for my friend. Sebastian told me in confidence, of course, as part of the deal between with Armin Strom, my friend would receive some compensation for the first few watches sold. I wanted to support my friend. This was even more motivation to get the number 1. Happily, I was successful and received the first Mirrored Force Resonance watch ever produced. True to my word, until now, I have not revealed the origin story of the movement. It was only after receiving Armin Strom's permission I felt I could tell this story.

Mirrored Force Resonance by Armin Strom

Once again, getting the first rendition of a new model, especially when it contains completely new and revolutionary technology, brings with it certain challenges. Much like my adventure with the first Freak, until the watchmakers can truly test a watch in the field, they might not have a full understanding of any glitches in their creation. Such was the case with the Mirrored Resonance. It has traveled back to Switzerland a couple of times for adjustments. At one point, I had fun doing field tests on the movement, supplying Claude with performance data. I am not going to be presumptuous and say I am part of the quality team, but I am honored to consider myself an assistant field tester, if there is such a position.

Staying with the Preschers

The next day, we drove to Twann to meet Thomas Prescher at his workshop for a quick tour. We then went on a stroll around the town and, of course, had a coffee while we chatted. Afterward, we drove around the crystal-clear Lake Biel to Ipsach and were warmly welcomed to their home by Heike.

We had been invited to stay there for three nights and were provided comfortable accommodations in the basement—across the hall from their bomb shelter. Apparently, there was a period of time when citizens of Switzerland were required to include a bomb shelter when they built a house. Now the shelter served as a convenient storage room.

On the first night, Thomas and I drove into town to purchase some beer from a local brewery. It was quite the scene, and the beer we bought was supplied to us in plastic bags. It was a great accompaniment to Heike's sauerbraten.

Our visit to the Preschers was akin to visiting family. Their two boys had a room strewn with a huge number of Legos. I could have spent hours with them building whatever our hearts desired. Instead, I did the proper thing: I joined the adults and spent the evenings in the backyard engrossed in conversations ranging from honey to politics.

The Preschers had a great itinerary planned for us. On the first day, the four of us drove to the Ballenberg Open-Air Museum. When we arrived, I was determined to buy the tickets for the four of us. Even though the museum was in the German-speaking region of Switzerland, I decided that I could use my high school French to make the purchase. As I walked up to the ticket booth, I rehearsed my French, but when I stepped up to the window, out came something resembling Spanish. A failure in cultural literacy. Where I work, many of the people I deal with speak Spanish, and over the course of time I have learned some of that language. I am far from fluent, although my wife is. I successfully bought the tickets when I switched to English.

The Ballenberg Museum is composed of more than one hundred rural houses and structures relocated from different regions of Switzerland. It followed the same concept of preserving the past as do Old Sturbridge Village in Massachusetts and Williamsburg in Virginia. Within a number of the buildings, craftsmen demonstrated traditional arts and crafts, while farm animals roamed about. It was a great exposure to the different regions and cultures that contributed to the development of modern-day Switzerland.

In the middle of our visit in Ballenberg, we were startled by the sudden roar of jet engines that reverberated across the valley and off the surrounding mountains. The thunderous roars were from a couple of military jets that had taken off from an airbase close to the museum. It was an interesting contrast: a museum dedicated to centuries of traditional Swiss history with craftspeople plying their homespun crafts created with handmade tools versus ultramodern jet fighters screaming into the sky.

The next day, we drove through Bern into the Alsace region of France to a city called Mulhouse. There we went to the National Automobile Museum. Even though I am not a car guy, I have been to a number of car museums, and I can appreciate a fine automobile. This museum had the most incredible collection of automobiles I have ever seen and is considered one of the most significant automotive museums in the world. The rows and rows of vintage cars of different makes and models, especially Bugattis, were breathtaking. Starting with cars built in the 1890s, the collection spanned decades of car production.

The history of the collection is as noteworthy as the collection itself. It was started by the Schlumpf brothers, who owned a textile factory from the 1930s until the early 1970s. Instead of paying their employees a fair wage or investing in their company, they secretly used their profits to accumulate an incredible collection of vintage cars, especially Bugattis. Ultimately, when the Schlumpf brothers had to declare bankruptcy, the workers protested. One night the workers broke into the factory and discovered how the brothers spent the profits: they found the huge car collection. Fearing for their welfare, the brothers were forced to flee from their homes in the middle of the night. They escaped to Bern, Switzerland, just over the border from France, thirty minutes away. They never returned to France for fear of prosecution, leaving their former employees with the vast car collection and the factory building that subsequently was converted to a museum.

After leaving the museum, we went to see another unique exhibit in the region. In Kintzheim, there is the Montagne des Singes, Monkey Mountain. Housed within this outdoor exhibit, Barbary macaques roam free in a forested park. These monkeys are native to Algeria and Morocco and were on the cusp of extinction. A group was transported to this park and have thrived ever since their arrival more than fifty years ago. As we walked around the park, it was not quite clear who was the one observing and who was being observed. It was fun to see the monkeys living an unenclosed life in their naturalized habitat. The whole day was a truly memorable experience for all of us.

By the time of this visit, I already owned Thomas's Single Axis Tourbillon. Perhaps it's not surprising that throughout the duration of our time together, Thomas and my conversations would frequently return to the topic of watches. As the visit neared its end, we discussed the possibility of me obtaining a multi-axis **tourbillon**. I mentioned earlier that Thomas is very interested in steampunk and had designed several watches with a steampunk aesthetic. We discussed him creating a double-axis **tourbillon** in a case of that design for me, and before departing the Preschers's house, after our last breakfast together, we agreed to the project with a handshake and hugs.

Over the course of my horological journey, I have ordered several watches and waited a year or two, sometimes longer, to receive the final product. The question remains: how long is too long to wait? That is clearly an individual decision. I seriously considered ordering the Charles Frodsham Double Impulse Chronometer. It is inspired by the work of George Daniels, and I thought it would be a nice complement to my other Daniels-related watches. When I inquired about getting onto the waiting list, I was politely informed that the wait for a watch was seven years. I could put a modest deposit down and wait my turn. I asked if there was any way to lessen the wait time, as I am not getting any younger. The response was, again very politely, that royalty and billionaires were similarly waiting, so no, there was no way to jump the line. Fair enough. I did not place the order. That was when I purchased my De Ville Chronometer Limited Edition with the Daniels Co-Axial instead; a decent substitute and a salve for my Daniels pursuit. Regardless, when Thomas and I shook hands to solidify the agreement for the double-axis **tourbillon** project, I did not realize how long it would take for the project to come to fruition.

Many factors came into play on both sides of the agreement, and the project took much longer than anticipated to be completed. We originally agreed to the creation of a steampunk-influenced design for a double-axis **tourbillon**, but due to the challenges that we faced, we ultimately agreed to make a course change. Thomas and I came to an agreement that I would receive a triple-axis **tourbillon** instead. Just not any triple-axis but the first wristwatch ever created to contain a triple-axis **tourbillon**, the prototype Thomas built in 2003. **Tourbillons** have become relatively commonplace in the upper reaches of the horological marketplace. A triple-axis **tourbillon** was not thought to be practical in a wristwatch. The watch would have to be too tall in order to accommodate the three axes. Thomas patterned his design after a carriage clock built by Anthony Randall in the 1970s. After detail study, he was able to create the world's first triple-axis **tourbillon**-containing wristwatch employing a unique design. It is well worth the wait to get a true piece of history, one I am very honored to possess and will always treasure.

The Vallée du Joux

After a long farewell to the Preschers, we headed to the Vallée de Joux, where Romain Gauthier was expecting us. When I'd originally informed him of our travel plans, he invited us to meet with him at his atelier and then join him and his family for dinner at his house. As an added treat, he offered to arrange for us to meet with Philippe Dufour, his mentor, at Philippe's atelier prior to us joining Romain. When we drove to meet

Philippe, even with GPS, I had difficulty finding the correct building. After several phone calls, Philippe graciously stood on the small porch outside of his building to serve as a landmark for our destination.

Philippe welcomed us into the first floor of the building that housed his atelier and then escorted us into his workshop, a place I'd visited previously. In the intervening years, the workshop remained unchanged. The windows were open, and the lingering smell of pipe tobacco permeated the room among the unoccupied work benches and cabinetry, machinery, and displays. We adjourned to the kitchen, where we sat around a table and chatted. Similar to our meeting with George Daniels, I did not have a script or a preconceived agenda to guide the conversation. Philippe offered us some chocolates (not Jacot but Lindt), and for the next three hours, we talked about everything and anything, although we did concentrate on topics having to do with watches.

Characteristically, his loupe was perched on his forehead, and he adjusted it periodically. It seems that many watchmakers have a need to always have a loupe at the ready, typically positioned on their forehead. It may be a part of the uniform of a watchmaker. We discussed the juxtaposition of corporate versus old-school watch production after I mentioned my observation about the difference between his workshop, with open windows, wooden floors, equipment and tools strewn about, and the ultra-clean environment of major watch manufactures. He explained he and other independent watchmakers are only working on one or at most several watches at any one time. It is therefore easy to protect them from unwanted dust and debris. In contrast, in the manufactures, where they are producing tens of thousands of watches per year, it is necessary to maintain a dust- and contaminant-free environment. That said, I have heard stories of independent watchmakers producing watches with hairs left within the cases. Of course, I did have a small issue with a piece of lint in a watch from a major watch manufacture that is compulsive about dust control, utilizing the latest technology. Reflecting on what Philippe said, I flashed to George Daniels's workshop, which was not much different than Philippe's or some of the other independent watch shops that I visited, minus the pipe smoke.

In the course of conversation, Philippe talked long and passionately about the importance of watch finishing. Well recognized as one of the leading watchmakers in the world with a particular reputation for creating finely finished movements, it was fascinating to hear his opinions. There is a difference hearing from the man versus reading it in some article. He bemoaned the difficulty he had obtaining and maintaining assistants. His workshop had several workbenches; clearly one was his, but the others stood empty. He spoke of how young watchmakers would come, spend a period of time with him, and then move on to other positions. He knew they were using their time with him as a résumé builder.

Often when collectors meet a watchmaker, the conversation includes a discussion of the watchmaker's favorite brands. Philippe volunteered that, in his opinion, the A. Lange & Söhne Datograph was the best **chronograph** in the market. He waxed poetic about the quality and, of course, the finishing of the movement. He, like Stephen McGonigle, was very complimentary about Greubel Forsey watches. I believe he has participated in that company on an advisory capacity, but it was my sense he was being objective in his comments. We, of course, did not talk about prices. Generally, the price of watches does not enter the discussion when speaking with watchmakers; technical aspects, quality, and accuracy are the topics of interest.

Philippe told us about the several other companies he has assisted in some advisory capacity. Early in his career, he worked for Jaeger-LeCoultre, and since that time, I was told, he periodically served in an advisory capacity for them. It was helpful that he lived only a few kilometers away from the manufacture. He told us about a recent meeting with the senior staff of Jaeger-LeCoultre, where he urged Jaeger-LeCoultre to get back to basics; concentrate on their iconic watch, the Reverso; and give up the aggressive marketing of other model lines. The Reverso is closely associated with the brand; no other watch company makes anything like it. He advised them to do what they did best in order to separate the identity of Jaeger-LeCoultre from other companies. Interestingly, over the ensuing years, that is, in fact, what happened, with good success. They have not abandoned other model lines, but they have emphasized the Reverso line. If what Philippe said was true, then he was right with his advice, but I remain wistful for the next Duometre. It was our impression he was not speaking in hyperbole but rather just reporting facts.

Our conversation turned to the economics of watchmaking. He was very open about the challenges he and other watchmakers face when dealing with different marketplaces and collectors from different countries. He mentioned how watchmakers in the independent world do not have retirement plans and that some have to continue working long past typical retirement age, at least in some capacity, due to the need for financial security. It was an interesting observation. It got me to thinking about other types of artisans, such as jewelers, painters, sculptors, writers, and the like who work piece by piece and may not have been able to establish retirement plans. The first time I met Philippe, on the Purists trip to Jaeger-LeCoultre, in the course of conversation, he stated quite openly that the Simplicity was his retirement plan. In truth and possible naiveté at the time, the comment bothered me as I was still caught up in the idealism of the watchmaker plying his trade for the sheer beauty and artistry of the craft rather than in terms of earning a living wage and securing his future. That said, watchmakers are artists, and I have had conversations with artists who continue to make art well into an advanced age. When asked why they continue, their response is that they must. They make art because they feel that they still have more to say and have the inner drive. Maybe this is also true with watchmakers.

During our meeting, I did not reveal to Philippe that many years earlier I had the opportunity to order a Simplicity. I had been in communication with Philippe's wife and was at the point of selecting case and dial colors but backed out because the cost, even at that time, was far beyond my comfort level. To quote a friend, it did not pass the sleep test. It was around that time I had my first encounter with Philippe and the comment about the Simplicity being his retirement fund still echoed in my memory. He has the right to do what he pleases, but, chalk it up to naiveté, the business practice bothered me, and it might have influenced my decision. Even in retrospect, I have no regret that I did not order one. Certainly, from a financial perspective, it would have been a good idea but once again, at the time my economics did not allow for the purchase. I could not have known it would have been a good companion to the other watches I now own. That is the only reason it was a missed opportunity, not the fact that its value has appreciated so significantly.

Throughout our visit to the various watchmakers and the manufactures, we were told pieces of information we were asked not to share. It was not as though we were told nuclear secrets, but for them it was an important request. It became a standard joke between my wife and me: we would say something to each other and then get an uncomfortable look on our face, suck some air through our teeth, and say, "I probably shouldn't have told you that." Of course, we honored their requests and continue to do so even years later. In a similar fashion, Philippe did tell us he had plans to embark on a new project that would be announced in due time. As can well be imagined, my ears perked up. Though silence was promised, I knew I was being given a teaser. He would not disclose the particulars of the project, but he did give me a ballpark figure of the price; the number was not eye-numbing but still quite significant. I made it clear to him I would be honored to participate in the project if possible. Since then, I have had conversations with several other collectors who have some knowledge of this mysterious project, but nothing seems to have come to fruition—at least nothing that has made the press.

The three hours passed quickly. It was a surprise to us, and possibly to Philippe, that we had such a long visit. We told him we were going to be visiting with Romain Gauthier next, which led to another discussion about Romain and his watches. Philippe was quite complimentary regarding Romain's work. When asked about his plans for the rest of the day, he told us he was going to head to the woods and hunt for mushrooms. Philippe, Kari, Thomas, Stephen, and so many other watchmakers have expressed their love for hiking. I am not sure if it is because they are European and that is what they do or because they are watchmakers who spend their professional time in a tiny world and for relief seek refuge in the greater outdoors.

We bade farewell to Philippe, who left for his mushroom hunt, and then we made the short, easy drive to Romain Gauthier's factory. Due to the length of our visit with Philippe, we arrived later than originally planned, but knowing we were with Philippe, Romain kindly waited for us. Unfortunately, by that time, the staff had already left for the day. I wanted to meet the team and go behind the curtain to see what their finishing process entailed. I was interested to understand what made their product stand apart from most others when it came to finishing. As we walked around the workshop, Romain indicated the workspaces for the various watchmakers and described their processes while showing us the tools of their trade. Perhaps the next time we will see them in action. Even though there did not seem to be anyone in the factory except for us, machines were humming. They were producing specialized components for several brands Romain would not name. The machines were programmed, he said, to work continuously overnight.

The tour did not take very long. We then drove to his house, which was nearby, and were introduced to his wife, Ana, and their children. Having just spent three hours with Philippe Dufour discussing watches and then having time with Romain at his workplace also discussing the intricacies of watchmaking, we made sure our conversation focused on other topics, in deference to my wife and Ana.

Dinner was cheese fondue prepared by Romain, this time not served with potatoes but bread and vegetables. The meal included a cooking lesson for my wife; Romain taught her the traditional way to prepare fondue. One important component, she learned, was shaved Emmental cheese in the fondue pot. Romain and Ana also unknowingly contributed to the fulfillment of my promise to my wife for the trip: watches, great conversation, melty cheese, and a cooking lesson, complemented by excellent Swiss wine. Our needs were met and exceeded.

Of course, knowing that Romain had a very close relationship with Philippe, I gently inquired about the project that Philippe alluded to. With no more than a smile, Romain diverted the conversation toward other topics and left any commitment unstated. After we returned home, I sent an email thanking Romain and Ana for their hospitality. In the email I reminded Romain of my interest in the Dufour project, with the response being appreciative but, again, total silence on that topic. Regardless, I have wonderful memories from that day and feel honored that both Philippe and Romain, and Romain's family, were so generous with their time and honesty. A watch would have been great, but these experiences are worth much more.

The Last Leg

Our final destination for this trip was the Jaeger-LeCoultre Manufacture. I had been there previously, but this was my wife's first visit. Since my first time there, the building had expanded. Departments for producing high jewelry, engraving, and enameling were brought under the roof of the manufacture rather than being located in other buildings around the Vallée de Joux. Across the street from the entrance to the building were several beehives perched on a retaining wall. They were the source of the wildflower honey Jaeger-LeCoultre gave away. Although really good, I do not think that the honey will be a profit center sufficient to offset a portion of their watch production.

As my wife and I toured the Manufacture, we were struck by the conviviality among the staff. Walking around the hallways and on the stairways, there was a family-like environment as people greeted each other. We went from one clean room to another, donning coats and booties, walking on sticky matts to remove dust and such, in stark contrast to the environments we experienced at Philippe's, Stephen's, Thomas's workshops or others. It was during that tour that we visited the art department and saw the picture of the Pomeranian in the Santa suit that was destined for the case of a Reverso.

We went to the haute horology department for one of the highlights of the tour, where we met Christian Laurent. A long-time employee of Jaeger-LeCoultre, Christian established the **Grand Complications** workshop and was responsible for some of the brand's most complicated watches, the Sphérotourbillon and the Gyrotourbillon. Christian does not speak more than a few words of English, and my high school French is limited to several phrases. However, with the help of our tour guide, Christophe, Christian spent more than half an hour teaching us about the Tourbillon, Sphérotourbillon, and Gyrotourbillon in intricate detail. Christian's love of the brand and enthusiasm for his work was very infectious and did not require translation. It is one thing to learn from an expert, but we were learning from the man who had the vision to develop these movements. When talking with watchmakers, it is sometimes difficult for them to transmit information in a manner that the general public, even those with some knowledge about horology, can understand. Christian was able to make the concepts and the basics of construction completely understandable for Christophe and us.

Since that first meeting with Christian, we have had the opportunity to see him several other times. On one trip to the Shanghai Film Festival, when we went to our commercial meeting, Christian was there. He joyfully welcomed me and my wife with a big hello and hug. Once pleasantries were exchanged, he and I spent time hunched over a two-headed microscope studying the Reverso Tribute Gyrotourbillon. With the assistance of one of the team members, there was no concern about a language barrier. He was very generous with his time as we discussed the intricacies of the watch, an absolute marvel. Once we had fully discussed the Gyrotourbillon, we turned our attention to several other models on display. I truly believe that he was having as much fun as I was. It is my supposition that many of the clients at the commercial meetings are not detail oriented and have little interest in the innermost workings of a watch movement. It is easy to believe that meetings with those clients are taxing and less than fun for someone like Christian. Sharing knowledge with a willing recipient and having a technical discussion must be like a breath of fresh air.

A memorable interaction with Christian was when we attended the Venice Film Festival. Jaeger-LeCoultre was, at the time, sponsoring several film festivals and invited us to attend this one as their guests. As part of the event, Jaeger-LeCoultre hosted a gala banquet. At the cocktail reception we met Christian, and, again with the translation assistance by a staff member, he told us he was going to retire when he celebrated his sixty-fifth birthday. He and I are the same age, and I did my best to try to convince him not to retire. It seems that the rules for retirement are stricter in Switzerland than they are in the States. Retirement in Switzerland is mandated at the age of sixty-four for women and sixty-five for men. When I begged him to reconsider, he smiled and shrugged in response.

At the gala, Jaeger-LeCoultre chose to honor Catherine Deneuve. When we were newly married, I informed my wife that there was only one woman in the world for whom I would leave her, Catherine Deneuve. It took her quite some time, but eventually my wife decided she would leave me for Andy Garcia. Neither of us has ever lost any sleep because of these declarations. The event presented me with my first and probably only opportunity to see Catherine Deneuve in the flesh. Standing outside the banquet venue, we talked with Christian. Nearby was Catherine Deneuve, smoking a cigarette and engaged in a conversation with someone. My wife told Christian about my crush on Ms. Deneuve.

What my wife and I did not know was that she had done promotional work for the brand, and Christian knew her. He took it upon himself, despite my protestations, to invite her to take a picture with me. Everything transpired in French, so I have no idea what was said, but in no time, Christian escorted me to stand next to her. To be totally honest, my heart was beating out of my chest, my hands were tremulous, and I wanted to run away, except we were on an island and there was no escape. After crushing out her cigarette, she turned, and my wife was able to capture the moment of me standing in the vicinity of Ms. Deneuve. She looked at the camera with barely a curt smile while I appeared extraordinarily uncomfortable. Once the picture was taken, wordlessly, she turned away, and the moment was over. To be sure, she showed no sense of joy to have had the opportunity to dash off with me. I do believe the one who had the most fun in the moment was Christian. Once the excitement for all concerned dissipated, I came to the realization that Catherine Deneuve was never going to replace my wife. A truly wise and excellent grasp of reality.

Eventually, karma presented the opportunity for me to reveal to Catherine how my feelings for her had changed. When we attended the Cannes Film Festival, we stayed in the same hotel, Le Majestic. In fact, a number of celebrities stayed at the hotel during the festival. It was fun to have them see me. I am not excited to see a celebrity; I would be more impressed if they made note on social media that they saw me. My wife and I were standing in the lobby of the hotel when Catherine and her retinue walked by. I purposefully did not acknowledge her or even smile in her direction. I showed her. I am sure she was crushed.

When it came time for lunch, Christophe took us to a restaurant not far from the Jaeger-LeCoultre building. It is a poorly held secret that watch companies interact with each other behind the scenes. In the restaurant, watchmakers and executives from different brands sat together, enjoying a repast. I think it is safe to say they were not just talking about the latest football game or the weather. Well, maybe they were, but not exclusively. It is interesting that different brands seem to release new products with similar dial colors or features at roughly the same time. When was the decision made that green dials would be "the thing" for the year?

Continuing our tour of the manufacture, Christophe guided us around the building, going in and out of different departments. Everywhere we went, we were welcomed by the staff. Never did we feel we were imposing or bothering anyone. The staff was always willing to momentarily stop what they were doing to explain the task they were performing to us in French or English. I am sure they are very used to people touring the facility, looking over their shoulders and questioning what they are doing.

Toward the end of the day, we went to a conference room for a coffee and to sit for a spell. There we were given a special treat: Muriel Job joined us. Any watch manufacture is a factory. In order to produce the volume of product per year that the brand sets as its goal, there is the need for division of labor. The glorified image of hundreds of watchmakers bent over their benches, each creating one watch at a time is not a reality for any major brand. That concept may apply to an independent watchmaker or to the watchmakers working within the haute horology department of a brand, where a single person is responsible for the production of one or two watches at a time. For the more "routine" production pieces, the creation of watches requires a large series of steps. Each watch movement is carried along the production line from one technician to the next. At each stop, one or several components are added to the movement. Besides not having the dexterity to work on watch movements, working on a line and being responsible for the same thing repetitively is not something that I could do day in and day out. However, there are people who make one task their life's work. Muriel is such a person.

Christophe, once again, had to serve as interpreter for Muriel as she explained her responsibilities. She, and only she, is responsible for creating the essential terminal curve of the **hairspring** in every watch movement. This curve is critical to keep the center of gravity of the **hairspring** properly positioned and prevent a waste of energy. If not correct, the resultant deterioration of function would, in turn, affect the accuracy of timekeeping. The creation of the terminal curve can only be done by hand. In the vast Jaeger-LeCoultre Manufacture, only Muriel has that capability, one that she has perfected over her more than twenty years with the brand. Very simply, without her expertise, there would be no watches. What's more, she has the unique skill to be able to create the terminal curve in the **hairspring** of the gyrotourbillon. That particular **hairspring** is a sphere, something not found in other watches. She brought one such spherical **hairspring** for us to examine as she discussed her process. Her dedication to her job and the role she plays within the Manufacture was in evidence several years earlier when she broke her leg while skiing. Despite the full-leg cast she had to wear, she still came to work, propping up her leg as she plied her craft. She did admit to us that, after much encouragement from the administrators, she was considering training a junior associate in the art of the curve.

Once the tour was completed, we bade farewell to Christophe and headed to Geneva for our final night. The trip was a success. We met everyone we set out to meet, and the conversations were indeed interesting for my wife and me. Much was learned and many secrets heard, not to be revealed. Opportunities were discussed to add to my collection, though it would take time for those realities to come to fruition. Even with multiple conversations and experiences, neither of us developed any of the symptoms or signs of Stendhal syndrome. All that and we enjoyed melty cheese and ate excellent chocolate.

Throughout high school and college, our older son played the drums in several bands. It is his assertion one always needs more cowbell. With cowbells in mind and to memorialize our trip to Switzerland, my wife added to the list of watches she has given me. For my next birthday, she presented me with a Swatch GB285 Die Glocke Black Dial Floral Embroidery Leather Women's Watch. To date, I have not worn this watch, a fact not lost on my wife, but it is treasured nonetheless. I now have a cowbell.

GB285 Die Glocke by Swatch

Chapter 13
6 x 11.5 cm

When I am asked how many watches I have, my standard reply is I have more than I need but not as many as I want. In so saying, I have developed the guiding principle that I do not want *another* watch but rather *a* watch. There needs to be something special about a watch to convince me to take the plunge once again. There are numerous factors to consider when hunting for the next watch, though I must say what is not on my list of preferences is the presentation box.

One of the ongoing challenges I face when I purchase a watch has nothing to do with the watch itself but the presentation box that accompanies it. I am not clear what the thought process is about the presentation boxes that come with some watches. For me, and the vast majority of the other collectors I know, the only time the watch might be seen in the presentation box is when the retailer or the boutique first presents the watch, hence the name. In fact, it is a rare occurrence that a new watch is actually delivered to me in the box. Almost always the watch and the presentation box are given to me separately, at times days or weeks apart. Once the watch and box come home, they are separated and typically not brought together again. The watch is stored in one place and the box in a completely different location. Of course, when selling a watch, there is extra value given if the watch comes with the presentation box. In fact, it is of even greater value to some buyers if the watch also comes with the original tags, paperwork, and even the shipping box that contained the presentation box.

Many presentation boxes are of a size that is easy to store, however some of them are huge. Some brands seem to subscribe to the belief that if someone is going to spend a significant amount of money for a watch, they should receive a box reflective of the prestige and value of the piece. The size of the boxes that some companies send with certain watches is almost comical. The TAG Mikrotimer and the Parmigiani Bugatti were delivered with huge boxes. When either box is opened, the only thing seen is the cutout for the cushion that holds the watch. There is nothing else in the box. There is no room to store brand information, operation instructions, or warranty material. Nothing. It is not clear what drove the brands to present the watches in such huge boxes. Granted, both of these watches are rare and valuable, but is there truly an expectation that the owner would have the room or desire to display the watch in these large boxes? The fact is when the watches were delivered to me, each was handed to me in a small box used for transportation, and the presentation box was given to me at a later time. Both the Mikrotimer and the Bugatti were shopworn and needed to go back to Switzerland for servicing and reconditioning. So, too, the boxes for each were worn and partially damaged. They also needed to be reconstructed before they were given to me.

On occasion, however, with great fanfare, a watch will be revealed to me at the same time as the presentation box. Such was the case when I received a watch from Girard-Perregaux and its quite special box at the same time.

The Girard-Perregaux Presentation Box

Girard-Perregaux is a brand I have followed for quite a long time. They are known for the triple-**bridge tourbillons**. For quite some time I have eyed their world timer but never acquired one. I have a problem with most world timers. They are interesting. Their function is to tell the wearer the time in each of the twenty-four time zones; however, they typically do not correct for daylight savings time. That means for about half of the year, they are going to be incorrect by an hour. My obsessiveness could not tolerate that inaccuracy.

On the Purists tour to the Chopard Manufacture, our guide was Patrick Wehrli. At the time, Patrick, the son of Martin Wehrli of Audemars Piguet fame, was the international sales director for the brand. After the Chopard tour, three of us had an extra day to spare prior to our scheduled departure from Switzerland, so Patrick arranged to take us to the ski resort Gstaad. The area was beautiful. A short hike provided us with great vistas of the region. We enjoyed lunch and then, while strolling around the village, found our way into a watch store. It seemed that Patrick knew the salesman, who, for a special treat, brought out a Girard-Perregaux Opera Two for us to see.

Patrick has a deep appreciation of watches, and although he was representing the Chopard brand, he and I drooled over the watch. The Opera Two is Girard-Perregaux's **grand complication**, which means that it features a **minute repeater**, a **tourbillon**, and a **perpetual calendar**. Westminster chimes rang out the hours, quarter hours, and minutes when the repeater was activated. The clarity and musicianship of the chimes blew us away. It was the first time I'd heard Westminster chimes in a repeater. Since then, I have listened to several other watches with Westminster chimes, but there is nothing like the first time and the lasting impression it leaves.

The Opera Two was the first Girard-Perregaux that I unquestionably yearned for, but the retail price made it unapproachable. It is much easier to fully appreciate a very special watch such as the Opera Two when not distracted by thoughts about whether I have sufficient funds to permit a purchase and how to justify it to myself and my wife. It was just wonderful to have had the pleasure of experiencing such a piece.

A while later, the Watch Connection became an authorized dealer for Girard-Perregaux, and soon thereafter the company announced the release of a very special watch. Historically, **tourbillons** were hidden from view by the case back of the pocket watch. In 1867 Girard-Perregaux decided to make the **tourbillon** visible to the owner and released the "**tourbillon** with three golden **bridges**." The **bridges** that supported the **tourbillon**, the gear train, and the **barrel** were redesigned in the shape of arrows and became part of the aesthetic of the watch. It was a first in the industry and has served as a hallmark of the brand ever since.

323

In 1889 Girard-Perregaux was awarded a prestigious jury prize by the Paris Universal Exhibition for an extraordinary pocket watch named La Esmeralda. It was so named in honor of the jeweler in Mexico that sold the piece to the president of that country. In honor of the 125th anniversary of that very special watch, the brand created a wristwatch La Esmeralda. From the pictures, I was intrigued and asked to see it. Arrangements were made for Chad to receive the prototype, but only for two days.

When I got to see it and try it on, it was brilliant. The domed sapphire crystal allowed the light to hit the movement and dial in such a fashion that the watch seemed to glow. My wife was equally taken with the watch. It did not take long for us both to agree that it was a must-have piece. As the watch's release had just been announced, I was able to get a fun case number. Number 1 already had been promised, but the brand representative secured for me number 8.

The case of the original pocket watch from 1889 was ornately engraved. After making the down payment for the watch, I asked Chad whether it would be possible to engrave the case of my watch in a fashion to honor the original case design. Chad passed along my request to the company. There was some back-and-forth discussion between us and the most senior level people in the brand. They responded with what we thought was an extravagant price to do the case engraving. Without batting an eyelash I agreed, something I do not think they expected. I was playing the game—though, in truth, I did not know if I was willing to spend the sum quoted in addition to the significant cost of the watch. After I accepted their proposal, more conversation occurred, and ultimately the request was denied by someone at the highest level of the company. Interestingly, several years later they produced a version of La Esmerelda with a highly engraved case. Coincidence? It was priced substantially higher than mine. I guess the quote they gave me for my original idea was the true cost for the enhancement rather than one to disincentivize me.

When the watch was delivered to the store, Chad first brought it out and gave it to me. It was terrific. He next brought out a large cardboard box, inside of which was the presentation box for La Esmeralda. The watch is large, but the box is huge. I removed the presentation box from the shipping cardboard box and proceeded to unwrap the multiple layers of cardboard covering the actual box. The experience was similar to a Matryoshka doll, a Russian nesting doll: a box within a box within another box, etc. In the presentation box there were multiple compartments and cushions for several watches, slots for jewelry, and a magnifying glass.

The actual presentation box was a cube constructed from beautifully grained wood with Girard-Perregaux inscribed above a rendering of their triple-**bridge** logo. Looking at it, the looming question remained as to the purpose of such a large presentation box and what to do with it. With relief, I saw the box had a lock and key. When considering the design and functionality of a presentation box, the brands do give some thought to the needs of the collector. They want to make sure the watches are secure, so they supply a lock and key for the presentation box. I know if I were to store my watch in a locked box, no one would be able to get to the watch. Oh, they might take the box with the watch inside, but the key, which I would always carry with me, would assure nothing untoward would happen to the watch. If I subscribed to that thought process, I would need to have a separate facility to store all my watches in their boxes. My belt would then be weighed down by a very large key ring needed to hold all the special keys. I doubt that there is a master key for locks on the different boxes.

La Esmeralda by Girard-Perregaux

Getting Boxed In

As large as the boxes for La Esmeralda, the Mikrotimer, and the Parmigiani Bugatti may be, they are individually dwarfed by a Roger Dubuis presentation box I was shown. I was invited by the nearby Roger Dubuis boutique to see their Excalibur Spider Pirelli MT. It is a very limited edition built to commemorate Pirelli's 150th anniversary in the tire business. It is a huge watch that is not my aesthetic. What was even more stunning was the presentation box the sales associate placed in front of me. According to him, the box weighed forty pounds. Besides space for the watch, it contained two additional straps and **bezels** that were interchangeable. Certainly, those extra parts did not require a forty-pound box. Yes, the box had a small lock and key for complete security.

There have been several instances when a watch did not come with a presentation box. The Chameleon from Armin Strom came only with a shipping box. The Ulysse Nardin Anchor Escapement prototype was essentially bought off a wrist, and there was never an assigned box. However, when that watch was shipped to me, the shipping department insisted I receive a presentation box with it. They took it upon themselves to select the presentation box created for the Moonstruck. That choice was totally unnecessary and not practical but very thoughtful. The Moonstruck presentation box has an incorporated winder so the owner can store a watch in the large box, which has to be plugged into an electrical outlet to keep the winder running to keep the Moonstruck wound to assure the one thousand-year moon phase accuracy. What the shipping department failed to take into account was that the prototype has a hand-wound movement, so the included winder is useless. That presentation box has never been unwrapped. That box is stored right next to the identical one I received when I brought my Moonstruck home. My Moonstruck is stored on a winder, as I do want the moon phase indicator to be accurate, but it is a freestanding winder, not the one from the presentation box.

Probably the most useful and considerate packaging for a watch came from Svend Andersen. His astronomical watches, such as the Secular Perpetual and the Orbita Lunae, do not come in presentation boxes.

Instead, they come on Scatola watch winders. That makes sense. Their utility depends on continuous function that is assured by the watch winder, as long as the battery does not run down. In a similar vein, the Ulysse Nardin Trilogy set is shipped in a presentation box that has three battery-powered winders. That box also has sections for the critical instruction book and a tool kit, as if I am going anywhere close to one of those watches with a tool. Also useful is a box supplied by Parmigiani for the perpetual calendar. That box contains a winder that is battery powered. Different from the Moonstruck winder, which is fixed in place, the Parmigiani-supplied winder was easy to remove from the presentation box. I removed the winder, and the watch is now stored on it.

The watch that came with the most economical packaging is the MIH watch, which was delivered wrapped in a copy of the *Neue Zürcher Zeitung*, the local newspaper. The date of the newspaper corresponded to the shipping date. Truly an offbeat and typical Ludwig Oechslin minimalist approach.

Personal Preferences

When considering the purchase of a watch, it is always fun and memorable to find or create something unique. Engraving a watch case adds a personal touch to the watch. Watches with signatures engraved from Ludwig Oechslin and Michel Parmigiani and watches with "prototype" or "piece unique" engraved on the cases are all very special and unique.

Besides engraving, there are other ways to turn a production piece into a unique one. For a birthday present, I decided to buy my wife another watch. Over time, she has seen quite a number of watches, more men's than women's, of course, and she has developed a definite opinion about what aesthetics spark her interest. My wife does not like anything that is flashy and prefers to avoid diamonds when possible. She was attracted to a specific Ulysse Nardin Marine Chronometer with a mother-of-pearl dial. One variation had diamonds for the hour markers. That was a definite no. The other model, without diamonds, she liked. There was just one problem: the model she preferred came with a white strap and gasket on the **crown**. She was very emphatic about not wanting the white, and I agreed with her. Neither of us like a white case or strap. We see that combination as too much of a fashion or statement piece. The strap was an easy problem to solve. A replacement black strap was obtained, but there was still the matter of the white gasket on the **crown**. She agreed to accept it as is, but the Ulysse Nardin service department came to the rescue. They found a black gasket to replace the white one. I was sure to point out to my wife that it was a one-of-a-kind watch. She wears the watch happily, caring not at all about its uniqueness.

Marine Chronometer by Ulysse Nardin

My wife and I traveled to Paris to celebrate our twenty-fifth anniversary. During our exploration of the city, we visited the Place Vendôme. Housed around the square are several watch boutiques that we, of course, visited. I saw some interesting timepieces, but none tempted me. However, when we stopped in the Swatch boutique, I was attracted to the Diaphane One, an unusually complicated Swatch watch. Unlike the ones I wore years earlier, this had a mechanical movement. Uniquely, it had a **carousel** movement that rotated 360 degrees twice an hour. I was told, but have never confirmed to my satisfaction, that the movement was conceived and designed by a team at Breguet; interesting if true. I had previously seen one back home but had not fully appreciated its complexity. This one, however, drew my attention. The Diaphane model is a "limited edition" of 2,222 pieces. Although the 2,222 watches are not, in my mind, a real limited edition, the version I saw in the Place Vendôme was truly a limited edition. The "standard" Diaphane One has a single diamond embedded at the twelve o'clock position on the back **bezel**. The Place Vendôme boutique had 222 pieces produced with three stones on the back **bezel** instead: a garnet, diamond, and sapphire to replicate the colors of the French flag. That edition also is significant to me as it reminds me of the fun week we had in Paris. That was my anniversary present to myself. In the process of making the purchase, I tried to negotiate the price, but the salesperson was unable or unwilling to make any accommodation. Instead, he offered me the choice of several additional straps.

Diaphane One by Swatch

The matter of straps has been an ongoing issue for me. Unlike many people who claim to have small wrists, I do have a small wrist. My wrist measures 6.25 inches or 15.875 cm in circumference. Finally, I have come to realize that the correct strap size for me measures 6 x 11.5 cm. The straps that come with most watches are too long for me. At best, when I am forced to wear a watch with a standard-sized strap, the pin typically is in the last or next-to-last hole, with the rest of the strap wrapped around my wrist, kept into place by the minders. Typically, the watches I look to acquire are ones that have to be ordered. The amount of time needed for the watch to arrive can be months, if not several years. Even when it takes a considerable amount of time for the watch to be built and shipped, it can take even longer for the appropriately sized strap to arrive. Occasionally, I am lucky, and the strap is shipped before the watch, but this is not a common phenomenon. This has left me with a bit of a conundrum: do I accept the delivery of a watch with the wrong-sized strap? I can at least wear it with the protruding strap for the time being, annoying as that may be. Or do I refuse to take delivery of the watch until the correctly sized strap is mounted? This provides motivation for the company to have the proper strap delivered in a timely fashion.

Watch brands seem to focus on the production of the watch but the production of different-sized watch straps seems to be less of a priority. It is my bias that once the watch is paid for, supplying a different length of strap becomes less of a priority and more of a source of annoyance for the consumer, me. It is not clear to me why the watch companies seem to be reticent to stock even a small number of alternative-sized straps so their customers can be accommodated in a timely fashion.

It is fun to change out the strap (in the parlance, "put on new shoes"), as that can make the watch seem new or refreshed. Straps come not only in different lengths but in different hides or other natural or synthetic materials. Of course, given my propensity to receive watches that have "idiosyncrasies," this also seems to apply to straps as well. Besides receiving straps of the wrong size and waiting interminably for the right size to arrive, I received my Jaeger-LeCoultre Nonantième with a very rare strap. When the boutique let me know of the arrival of my Nonantième, I hurried to the boutique as soon as possible.

When they presented the watch to me, it was in its original protective wrapping. It is typically left to the purchaser to have the pleasure of unwrapping a new watch. After taking a few minutes to admire the piece and setting the time properly, the next step is to put it on, of course. I was talking with the boutique manager while I put on the Nonantième. I have been wearing watches of some sort for much of my life, and there is usually no challenge to strapping one on. It is the same as putting on a belt, also something that I have done for most of my life. I do it without having to look at what I am doing. Yet this time I seemed to be having a difficult time. The boutique manager offered to help me. Really? I certainly know how watches work and how to get the pin into the hole of the strap.

I admit to being a bit irritated by the suggestion that I might need help. I looked down at what I was doing and discovered the reason I was having so much difficulty. The strap was composed of two strips of hide, alligator on the front and cowhide on the back, sewn together. The top, the black alligator, had holes, but the underside leather did not. It was the first time I have ever seen a watch strap without through and through holes. The boutique manager was mortified and sent a staff member to get another strap. I, on the other hand, could not stop laughing. I sent a narrated video of the strap and my struggles to various members of the Jaeger-LeCoultre leadership team, including the US brand president and the CEO. They, too, fell over themselves apologizing, but I continued to see only humor in the situation. Of course, that strap length was of standard size. It took quite a while to get the proper short strap. When the short strap came, it had the required holes. It is now a standard joke I share with members of the brand: when I order a watch, will I receive one with holes in the strap or not?

The absence of holes notwithstanding, most of my watches are worn with leather straps, usually alligator. With the proper size, I can fit the watch to the snugness I prefer. Likewise, when the watch comes on a metal bracelet, I have it adjusted so it, too, fits as I like it on my wrist. With that in mind, at times, one makes choices in life that have unintended consequences. By mutual agreement, my wife and I decided to join Weight Watchers. To encourage compliance, Weight Watchers awards a sticker for every five pounds lost and a medal for every twenty-five pounds. I am very goal oriented, and before long, I became obsessed with the need to get more stickers and medals. However, as I lost weight, I realized a problem I had not anticipated. I not only rapidly lost weight around my waistline but from other parts of my body. My already thin wrists got thinner, an occurrence I did not think possible. Sadly, my watches on the bracelets began to hang loosely on my wrist. The watches on leather or crocodile straps could be adjusted by going to the next hole, but the metal bracelets not so. A very distressing side effect of a noble plan. That was evidence I needed to realize I had lost too much weight. Forget the fact that people were coming up to me and asking if I was okay, concerned that I had cancer or some other chronic illness. Forget that I was cold all the time, missing, as I started to say often, my fat layer. It was the loosely fitting watches, the need to get the bracelets adjusted by having an additional link removed that convinced me to give up on my obsessive goal to get more stickers or medals from Weight Watchers. I gave in to the obvious and gained back some weight.

Chapter 14
The Dark Side

Collecting watches has been a joy. The journey I have been on has been filled with excitement and pleasure. As is true with anything, with the brightness comes the chance of darkness. I have been fortunate to avoid most pitfalls, but it does not mean I am not aware of the risk of being affected by the dark side of collecting luxury goods.

On a trip to China for a conference, a colleague thought he would bring me a souvenir. He knew of my interest in watches and had a passing interest in them as well. Before he returned, he purchased a watch for me for a couple of dollars. The dial had IWC printed on it, but it was very easy to tell that it was a cheap fake, a knock-off. The watch had a mechanical movement and worked, but I have no idea about its timekeeping accuracy. It had **pushers** and **sub-dials**, as if it was a **chronograph**, but neither functioned. Pushing the **pushers** did nothing. It was goofy to say the least. The quality of the fake was poor; it was on the order of the "Rolexes" I had previously received from Thailand.

During my travels in the US and abroad, I have seen countless numbers of street vendors with rows and rows of watches labeled with the names of various watch brands. No one would ever think those watches were anything but what they are: fakes. I have seen advertisements for businesses that claim to have the ability to replicate any watch on the market. Of course, I have never seen anything built by those businesses, but my bias is they are most likely of dubious quality inside and out. I have never, even for the sake of curiosity, explored that part of the dark side of watch collecting. At least they are out in the open about their business model.

Unfortunately, the quality of forgeries has become much better. Some fakes are being marketed as the real item and are extremely difficult to distinguish from the genuine article, even by those with considerable knowledge and expertise. This, of course, is no different from what has happened for decades, if not centuries, in the art world and other luxury goods markets. The ongoing battle between forgers and experts will probably never end so long as there is financial gain to be had. Sadly, expertly executed fake watches, including "frankenwatches" (watches constructed from the parts of other watches in a fashion to mimic a coveted model) have been sold by reputable dealers and auction houses, some for huge sums of money. Some of the most notable ones defied the careful inspection of multiple purported experts. This is, once again, why I shy away from the vintage market and why I continue to subscribe to the philosophy of "buying the seller." Regardless of the source, the buyer needs to be extra cautious regarding the provenance and the authenticity of a potential purchase. Whereas any watch can be reproduced to a very high degree of accuracy, the risk still remains greatest when looking at pieces said to be from those manufactures most in demand by consumers.

Buying a preowned watch carries with it some risk, but so does buying from auction houses. Auctions have become a more common marketplace for high-value watches and a popular topic of discussion among collectors. Adding to the high-profile nature of the auctions, the press has increased its coverage of them and particularly of their results. This helps to further drive the speculative market. The general assumption is that auctions help to set the market value of watches, particularly those in high demand or exclusivity. Unfortunately, even this mode of valuation can be a sham process. It is a known fact that certain brands drive up bidding on specific watches from their company in order to acquire the watches for their own collection or to support the market perception of value, exclusivity, and demand not only for particular models but for the brand itself. Sadly, this merchandizing strategy and market inflation promotes the perception of watches as a commodity, with buyers making purchases solely based on the expectation of substantial financial gain rather than for the appreciation of the horological marvels they are. I guess it is human nature for people to look for the next greatest thing with making a quick buck in mind. When that happens with watches, it saddens me because it puts a cloud over something I as a collector prize and cherish.

Every once in a while, there is a watch that seems to be magical. The Prescher **tourbillon** is one of those where the **tourbillon** sits on a post seemingly suspended in air, with no source of power or regulation of time from the **escapement**. Of course, the mystery was answered by Thomas's patient explanation. Thomas built another watch called the Mysterieuse that shows time, month, date, and moon phase without the movement in evidence. The movement resides out of sight, located within the sides of the rectangular case. Then there are watches from several brands where the hour and minute hands seem to float in space with no connection to the center pinion.

Jaeger-LeCoultre marketed a line of watches called the Mysterieuse (quite different from Thomas Prescher's) in the 1950s to the 1970s. In those watches, the time was indicated by two spherical **indicators** for the hours and minutes. The **indicators** seemed to float around the dial unsupported. Cartier produced a mystery watch where baton minute and hour hands similarly seemed to float in the center of a clear dial. Vianney Halter creates his watches with a mystery **rotor** that seems to rotate at the periphery of the movement and not be connected to a center pinion. Magically, the rotator keeps the movement wound. Pulling back the curtain on these mysteries, they all function by way of transparent discs made of sapphire crystals on which the hands or **rotor** are mounted and are moved by gearing on the edges of the discs. Even knowing the truth of the illusion, it remains fascinating to see these watches in action.

I came upon such a piece produced by the Zodiac brand. The Zodiac Astrographic had a "floating" dot to mark the seconds and "floating" batons that indicated the minutes and hours. It came with several dial color options, but the blue-dialed version was the one that called to me and my credit card. I chose the blue because it was a nice shade and because it was the only variation that came (surprise) as a limited edition.

It was only months after bringing it home that I learned of the dark side associated with the brand name. In the late 1960s in Northern California, there was a serial killer who called himself the Zodiac killer. He was responsible for five confirmed murders although he claimed as many as thirty-seven victims. He was never caught. During his reign of terror, he sent letters to the press that contained his signature: crosshairs through a circle. His "signature" was identical to the Zodiac brand logo. In several cinematic portrayals of the killer, the suspect was seen wearing the Zodiac Sea Wolf. Why did the killer choose this image as his calling card? Did he own a watch or have any other interest in the Zodiac brand? The brand did exist during his time. One can only speculate, but it does give me something to think about every time I put on the watch.

Astrographic by Zodiac

During my journey, fortunately, I have never met someone as evil as the Zodiac killer. For the most part, throughout the years I have met nice people: members of the brands, watchmakers, and fellow collectors. Some are now friends, while others remain acquaintances. They all are friendly and enjoy sharing this passion. Every so often I have come upon an "interesting" person. I am sure any group has their share of people who, shall we say, have different priorities or expectations.

Near where I live is a small shopping area that lines the harbor. My wife and I were walking around the area one day when I noticed a new store. The signage advertised that it sold watches. Unfortunately, it was after hours, and the store was closed. A few weeks later, when a group of my watch friends and I were having lunch, I told them of my discovery, and we decided to drive over and check it out. We entered the store, as it seemed to be open for business, but no watches were in sight. A football game was blaring loudly on a television. We came upon a young man who seemed to be mystified when we walked in the open door. When we asked to see watches they had to sell, he seemed lost. He offered to call his father, who showed up a few minutes later. A big guy, he barreled into the store and asked us what we wanted to see. We asked to see any Omegas. He went into the back and brought out some watches, each in its own plastic bag, not brand issued. We then asked about Patek Philippe and then Panerai. In a quick moment, he went to the back and returned with several watches from each brand, again with each in its own plastic bag. While he was talking with us, two scantily clad young ladies walked into the store. He immediately told them to go into the back. We never saw them again. Not too much later, we thanked him and left the store. Before we got into our cars, we stood in the parking lot discussing our experience. Between fits of laughter, we all agreed that he was not an authorized dealer. Who knew the provenance of those watches? One member of the group was very knowledgeable about the Panerai line. He said several of the Panerais we were shown were fakes. We were not sure about the legitimacy other the watches in the plastic bags.

The conversation then turned to the young ladies. Hysteria broke out when it was suggested that the store was a front for a more adult-oriented business. The store did not last very long. We do meet all kinds.

The Need for Service

Sending a watch back to the manufacture, regardless of the reason, is at times like sending a precious possession into a black hole. Some watchmakers seem to have figured out that ongoing communication with the customer while the watch is in their hands for service is critical when trying to provide an excellent customer experience. Sadly, most companies have not an idea how to keep the customer updated regarding their repair and, in turn, leave the customer in the cold, unhappy with their interaction. I have heard numerous tales of watches sent to a service department and "disappearing" without word for months to over a year. It seems logical to me that providing excellent service could, eventually, lead to another sale due to the brand loyalty built from the prior experience. Because of the high incidence of negative service experiences, many consumers are hesitant to send their watches for service.

Since the beginning of my horological journey, the question of when a watch should be sent for service has been a topic of much debate. All machines require routine maintenance. Without that care, there is a risk of parts wearing out in an untimely fashion, resulting in mechanical failure. Watches are machines and thus require maintenance. Logically, watches should be serviced at an appropriate interval to assure optimal and accurate function. Cars require maintenance at least two to three times per year depending upon the mileage driven. A watch that is operating at full capacity twenty-four hours a day every day might need service every three to five years. Because of modern developments such as the use of special lubricants and the introduction of silicium components, service intervals have been extended to as much as ten years.

The determination of service intervals typically comes from the manufacture and is included in the instruction paperwork that accompanies the watch. Confounding the recommendation for service is the fact that not all watches are worn the same. Some watches are worn on a daily basis, while others may not be worn but once every few weeks to months. It seems logical that the watches not worn as often can go longer between servicing. That said, there is a definite longevity of the lubricating oil, which can deteriorate or dry out over the course of time and require attention regardless of the frequency of wear.

That said, the proper interval for service is still a topic of debate. Many watchmakers I have spoken with regarding this topic do not see the need for a routine "oil change." They believe a watch should be serviced when it shows it is needed. The indication to them is if there has been a deterioration in the accuracy of the timekeeping. If the watch is running much faster or, more commonly, slower, than previously, that is an indication it is time for the watch to take a trip to "the spa." Those who subscribe to the belief of routine servicing are of the opinion that taking the "wait and see" approach risks greater damage to the movement, which could be otherwise avoided. Currently, I tend to be in the camp that follows the "service when needed" theory. To date nothing bad has resulted from following that philosophy. One exception that I subscribe to has to do with the water resistance of a watch. If the wearer intends to wear the watch in the water, it is best to have the gaskets changed every few years to prevent very expensive water damage to the movement.

When sending a watch for service, the owner needs to be prepared for a wait lasting months if not considerably longer. Over the course of my journey, as occurred with the TAG Mikrotimer or the Reverso Squelette, a watch can be gone for a prolonged period of time and then, when returned, not be correct and have to go back for another stint. Sometimes the prolonged interval is well worth the wait, but other times it has left me nonplussed about the watch.

I purchased a Parmigiani Kalpa QF, case number 1 of a series of fifty pieces. It was a nice watch, and I was happy to get a Qualité Fleurier-certified watch, and a number 1 at that. When I visited the Fondation Qualité Fleurier, I already owned the Parmigiani QF. Filling several shelves near the technician's desk were rows of black binders that contained records of every watch tested, including mine. I was tempted to ask if I might see a copy of the test results for my watch. While it might have been interesting, I am not sure I would have understood all the technical details. Besides, the paperwork that came with the watch detailed the testing results, which was quite enough for me.

After several months of owning the Kalpa QF, I realized the watch was not performing within the parameters guaranteed by the certification. Still well within the warranty time period, I sent the watch back for evaluation and recalibration. After a number of months in Switzerland, the watch was sent back to me. On return, when I put it on, I saw that the watch was still not performing as it should. Back it went to the manufacture. Months went by, and finally I received word that my watch was on its way back. When it was returned to me, I was told the movement could not be calibrated to meet the specifications set out by the Fondation Qualité Fleurier, so the service department decided to replace it with a completely new one, and now it was functioning within standards. That was terrific except for one problem. Collectors want everything aligned: the watch, the box and the paperwork. When I finally received the watch, it was indeed keeping time as expected, but the certification paperwork I had from the Fondation Qualité Fleurier was for a movement whose serial number did not match the one in my watch. The watch had to be returned to Fleurier once again to undergo testing and receive its certification paperwork. This last trip to Switzerland did not take nearly as long as the others, but the whole process from start to finish took more than fourteen months. By the time it was over, the excitement and enjoyment of the piece had faded, and my faith in the QF's stated standards of quality was tarnished. Ultimately, I sold the watch. To be sure, the buyer benefited from my experience and patience.

To their credit, Parmigiani admitted the shortcomings of their service department and sought to make amends to me. Their proposed solution was to offer me a very gracious accommodation on another watch of my choice. I selected the Toric Perpetual as the "apology" watch. Not one to miss an opportunity, I asked if the company could do something to make the watch extra special. They offered to have the crystal on the case back engraved with Michel Parmigiani's signature, something only offered on the most exclusive, high-end pieces. Of course, I accepted the offer. The watch has worked without problem, and although it is not certified by the Fondation, it functions well within their parameters of accuracy. It is a joy to wear, and to make it even better, I do have a unique piece. Despite the bumps in the road I experienced with the Kalpa QF, I continue to be a believer in the brand.

Waiting for the return of a watch from service can try one's patience. Fortunately, I have other watches to wear. Long ago I learned that there is nothing that I can say or do to expedite the service process. All I can do is wait and find humor in the situation. The fact is when dealing with fine watches, one does learn the true meaning of time. There can be an upside if the service takes a long period of time. When the watch is finally returned, the joy is much like strapping on a new watch. In fact, it is a less expensive way to experience the high achieved when bringing home a new watch. Most of the time.

Toric Perpetual by Parmigiani

Safe and Sound

Security is a major concern for me, as it is, I am sure, for all watch collectors. When I started collecting and owned a few watches, I was not very concerned about security. I knew the watches had some value, but none of them were Rolexes, so I figured none of them would be a target for the bad guys. I rationalized that the watches were "just stuff," and if any were taken, they could always be replaced. However, as time progressed and my collection grew, I started to acquire rare and irreplaceable timepieces. Encouraged by my wife, I realized I could not afford to remain blasé. I became more situationally aware when choosing a watch to wear. If I was concerned about where we were going and I wanted to wear something special, I would, at a minimum, choose to wear a long-sleeved shirt or sweater. I have never had the need to broadcast which watch I have on my wrist. Avoiding unwanted attention is always a guiding principle.

Some collectors, whether out of practicality, personal preference, financial reasons, or security, limit the number of watches in their collection. They only purchase another watch if they have made room for it by selling one. Limiting the number of watches in their possession certainly makes it easier to safeguard them as compared to a collection that is ever growing. As a side note, another benefit of limiting the number of watches in a collection is avoiding the problem of storage space for the presentation boxes. Even though I see the advantage of such a strategy, I have never tried it or given it much thought. If I sell one of my treasures to acquire another, I might be happy with the new one, but I will not have the other, a fact that will disturb the harmony in my collecting conscience.

When considering measures to provide safety and security for a watch collection, it is natural to assess the risk of damage as well as theft. The usual concern is geared toward what others might do, but there needs to be an understanding of the role the collector can play with regards to the risk of damage to the collection. Putting on and taking off a watch can be a risky endeavor. As demonstrated by the accidents involving my Vacheron Constantin Copernicus and Don Corson's Dresdener, having added protection for a watch might be useful to prevent such tragedies. Most watches come with pin buckles. A minority of watches are sold with deployant clasps. That is unfortunate because it is easier to carry a watch with a deployant, and the watch is less likely to be fumbled and dropped than one with a tang buckle. Hook the deployant around a finger until it can be securely placed on the wrist. Should there be difficulty securing the deployant, there is less likelihood for it to slip and head to the ground. It is a mystery to me why a deployant is not standard issue on all watches. Before wristwatches, pocket watches were usually attached to an item of clothing by way of a chain. No doubt one of the main purposes for the watch chain was to prevent the watch from hitting the floor should it be fumbled. Of course, the deployant is more expensive than a tang buckle and might increase the cost of the watch, but the security it supplies certainly makes it a worthwhile investment. I usually do not ask for a deployant when negotiating a purchase, although maybe I should, but I did ask for one when I was negotiating the purchase of the Jaeger-LeCoultre Tribute Reverso Minute Repeater. The reason I gave for wanting it was security. They understood and agreed to my request.

As my collection grew, I received several requests for interviews from podcasters. My watches and I have also been the subject of several magazine and online articles. I have been interviewed at the suggestion of brands in support of their advertising campaigns, and I have had my name included in several print ads. In all these circumstances, I agreed to the requested interviews with the caveat that my identity be obscured as best as possible. At times, I permitted my first name to be used, but I do not publicize my last name, where I live, or my occupation. In fact, in several articles written about my collection I was referred to by a fictitious name. In the past I used to occasionally post pictures of my latest acquisitions on social media. More recently I have minimized my social media exposure out of concern about security. I understand there is very little, if any, privacy when it comes to the internet, but I certainly do not want to make it easy for anyone to find me. Even with these efforts, it is not always easy to mask one's identity, as evidenced when I was asked if I was the one who spoke about my visit with George Daniels while I was visiting an Omega boutique.

As my collection grew, I knew that the loss of these gems would be devastating. When I came to that realization, I knew I could no longer keep them in my house unprotected. My wife and I discussed our options. Of course, one possibility was to sell the expensive pieces, and I would not have to worry. That clearly was not ever going to happen. The next was to install a safe in our house. My perception of a safe is that it only serves the purpose of slowing down a burglar at best. Many smaller safes can be carried off and opened later. A truly worthwhile safe would require installing an industrial-size vault. Years ago, Robert, the prior owner of the Watch Connection, offered me one of his safes when they were moving locations. After some discussion, my wife and I decided against the offer. A large safe would have to be kept in the garage, and although it could not be carried away, it might invite curiosity and possibly some unwanted visitors. We decided for our needs it was best to store the watches in a safe deposit box in our bank.

It truly was a sad day in my watch-collecting journey when I packed up my watches and deposited them in the safe deposit box. When I walked out of the bank the first time, I realized my journey had, in a sense, come full circle. I started out with money from my father, in part derived from his stamp collection, some of which had been stored in a safe deposit box.

There was minimal solace derived from the realization. Watches, like most finely crafted objects, are made to be enjoyed. The ability to admire the artistry, enjoy the experience of winding them, feel the watch on the wrist, and hear the steady tick-tock of the movement is what makes them a joy to behold. Locking the watches away in a bank deprives me of the joy I'd previously experienced on a daily basis, but one does have to face the reality of the world in which we live and the risks of an unguarded collection. That said, as I locked away my precious gems, I reaffirmed that no watch of mine would be a "safe queen," and I would strive to wear the watches stored at the bank.

I have done business at the same bank for years, but it is only since placing the watches in the safe deposit box that my wife and I have become known to the bank staff. We are now regular visitors. When we visit the bank, at the first sight of us, the bank staff starts the paperwork to allow us access to the safe deposit box. They are surprised if we are there for any other purpose and if we do not ask for access to our box. Once we are in the private room with the watches, we are sure to wind some pieces while we return some for safe storage and take ones to be worn until our next visit.

Regardless of the reason, selling or otherwise parting with a watch is a sad day, even if the watch is sold to provide funds for the purchase of another. It is truly a dark moment in the journey to have one watch leave the fold.

My wife remains mystified that I sold the Maurice Lacroix, my first watch, the one I bought to maintain a connection with my father. It is true I bought the watch with the belief it would be a longtime keepsake. I sold the watch because it ceased to appeal to me. Although the physical watch is gone, the significance of that first purchase has not diminished; it was and always will be my introduction to the world of mechanical watches and the start of a collection, watches and not stamps. Ultimately, that was the nod to my father. Over time, I have sold other watches in order to cull the herd. Typically, I used the funds from the few successful sales toward another purchase. The first time I selected several watches to sell, it was relatively easy to pick out the watches that no longer appealed to me. The second time, however, it was a much more difficult task—so much so that

I asked Tim to help me make the selections. He was able to look at my collection of watches objectively and decide which ones did not complement the others. Of course, his recommendations were influenced by his bias toward the independents, but I trust his opinion. He was going to be the one to market them, so I am sure some of his calculations involved picking watches he thought were marketable. I did not agree with all his recommendations, but we were able to come to an agreement on six watches. Even though all six did not sell, the process of selecting them was very distressing for me. Selling a watch is stressful. Though I may part with the physical item, I still have the memories associated with those watches, and sometimes those are as important as the watches themselves.

I was asked if I had an interest in selling the Reverso 101. Although no dollar amount was ever mentioned, I was told I stood to receive much more money than I had paid for the watch. The offer came by way of a trusted source, and I took it as valid. The offer was tempting, as it would clear up some debts I had. However, if I sold the watch, I would no longer have the watch. It was one of only five, and number 1 at that. If I sold it there was certainly no way I could replace it, should I so desire. I gave the possibility some thought but in the end could not pursue the offer. If ever I needed confirmation that I am a collector, I felt the decision to keep the watch over the real possibility of making some money fit well with the definition. On the practical side, however, there is some degree of comfort to know there is value in the watches should there ever be a need for funds.

Even though I have sold a few watches, I do not regret selling any of them. In a similar vein, I have not mourned watches I have not purchased. When I was a teenager, I suffered through the breakups of several relationships. My father accused me of wearing my heart on my sleeve and reminded me there were many fish in the sea. Similarly, there are many watches to choose from, and passing on the option to purchase a watch is not to be regretted. Over the years I have had the opportunity to purchase some that have gone on to become extraordinarily valuable in the secondary market. I had the opportunity to acquire a Dufour Simplicity and a Richard Mille RM005, to name two. I did not act on the Simplicity for a simple reason. The price of the watch at the time, though a fraction of its current value, was not something I could afford. Even though, in retrospect, it would have been a nice complement to the other watches I subsequently acquired, regretting the decision not to buy the watch is a useless emotion. Hindsight is 20/20. The Richard Mille did not appeal to me as it was a redress of a Parmigiani movement, and it just did not "speak" to me. That it now has a value five times what I would have paid is unimportant to me. If I did not make a connection with a watch, the possibility of future appreciation of its value is meaningless. These are but two examples of a number of watches I have been offered or considered over the course of time. What is done is done, and wishing for a different outcomes neglects what the pocketbook dictated and the sleep test allowed at the time. Certainly, as time passes, other opportunities will continue to occur. There are many fish in the sea.

Chapter 15
Retirement

Early in my journey, I had several watches and wore them interchangeably in any setting. The first time I assigned a specific role to a watch was when I received the Freak. When I first brought the Freak home, I knew it was a very special watch. It was then, and it is now. There had been nothing like it in many different respects. As it was the first very special watch I acquired, I felt that it was not the kind of watch that could be worn in just any setting. I designated it to be a watch worn on special occasions, especially those with my family.

As time passed and I began to acquire other watches, I started to assign each to the type of role it would play. Some were fit for doing chores, such as yard work, or going to the pool. I did not feel it was a good idea to wear a precious metal-cased watch or one that was rare or unique on those occasions. Likewise, the "special" and unique watches were more suited to date nights, visiting friends, or attending watch get-togethers. On those occasions I chose not to wear a ceramic-cased watch, a "beater," or a bulky sports watch. An additional variable to consider when choosing the watch for the day was the outfit selected. Should I choose to wear a long-sleeved shirt or sweater, I was more willing to wear something more precious or unique, as the sleeves would add a layer of protection for the watch and lessen undesired attention.

Going to work added a complexity to the daily decision regarding which watch to wear. Most days when I wake up, one of my first thoughts goes to the selection of the watch for the day. There are a number of variables that I have to consider when making that decision. When going to work, I had to, as best as possible, anticipate the plans and activities for the day. If I anticipated being very active, I knew that protecting the watch from accidental bangs or scratches was less feasible. In those situations, I usually selected one in a steel case that was a more "common" model rather than a unique or special piece. Should the day be one when I was going to be primarily at my desk, then I was more likely to pick a watch that was in a precious metal case or even one of the rare or unique ones. Doing desk work made the chance of accidental bangs to the case much less likely. Should I have a lot of meetings on my schedule or if I was going to attend a conference, I was sure to select a watch that would provide entertainment should the meeting or lecture not be engaging. These are the ones designated as "conference watches," of which a prime example is one with a **tourbillon**.

Weekends posed a different challenge. Daytime was often filled with errands, chores, and sporting activities, as well as cruising watch stores and boutiques. The evenings might include a visit with friends, dinner, or the theater. On those days I often selected a watch for the day and a different, special one for the evening. The weekends gave me the opportunity to choose a watch I was not comfortable wearing during the work week. As my collection grew, my desire to wear all of my watches did not change. I would, at times, stress about which watch to wear. Which ones had I not given adequate wrist time recently? It is a good thing that my watches do not have feelings and cannot give me guilt at being neglected.

Regardless of the day of the week, after a quick review of the activities planned for the day, a decision had to be made about which watch would be the appropriate choice. It was a crucial decision because once the watch was selected, I would be able choose my clothes. If the watch had a brown strap, then I knew my belt and shoes were going to be brown. If the watch had a colored metal, then the belt needed to have a colored-metal buckle. Last was selecting the shirt and pair of pants to complement the accessories already planned.

On occasion, I was faced with a quandary about the choice of watch due to the adjacency of two diverse activities. On weekends, my wife and I often participated in a group trail run that mixed walking or running off-road with beer and bawdy songs. The group was known as the Hash House Harriers. I typically wore my Bell & Ross ceramic watch so I did not have to worry about any accidental trauma to the watch and was still able to read the time despite sweat-streaked glasses. In fact, for all the trail runs I have attended, the watch still looks as good as new. The strap does not, but the case is free of scratches.

One day, midweek, I was at work and decided to go for a trail run scheduled to start right after I finished my workday. I knew I did not have sufficient time to go home to change, so I brought my running clothes with me to work. When I headed out to the trail, I realized I was wearing a nice watch. I did not want to go out on trail without a watch. Heresy. In general, I do not carry my phone on the trail, yet I want to know the time, so I decided to do the run wearing a special watch. For the hour plus, I was more concerned about protecting the watch than I was about following the trail. Fortunately, the watch came through unscathed. The watch I wore on the trail is an interesting piece; the Parmigiani Ovale Pantographe has a fascinating **complication**. It was designed by Michel Parmigiani after a vintage pocket watch he restored that had telescoping hands.

Ovale Pantographe by Parmigiani

The case, as suggested by its name, is oval, and the minute and hour hands telescopically expand and contract as they go around the dial so that they remain equidistant from the edge of the dial. This is truly a unique **complication**, not something seen in other watches regardless of the geometric shape of the case. The magic of the telescoping hands is made possible by a series of cams located in the center structure on the dial. Beautifully constructed and finished, it certainly is not built for trail running.

When I anticipated I had a busy schedule at work and there was a greater risk of an accidental scrape or bang, I would make my choice for the watch of the day from a group of watches typically in steel cases that were designated as work watches. Included in that group were the Omega watches my wife gave me and the Ulysse Nardin Classico blue enamel. Another member of that group is an Omega Speedmaster 50th Anniversary Professional Moon Watch.

Speedmaster 50th Anniversary by Omega

It is my opinion, and the opinion of others as well, that every watch collection should contain a Speedmaster, a.k.a. Speedie. It is an iconic watch of the Omega brand and speaks so much for the world of mechanical watches; after all, it was the first watch worn on the moon. At a local museum, we saw an exhibit of the work of artist Daniel Arsham. One piece that fascinated me was a life-size casting of an astronaut pictured as if he were walking on the moon. There he was, in his moon suit with helmet, oxygen supply, and gauges representing the height of scientific achievement of the time, and there, strapped on his right wrist, was the casting of a mechanical watch. In the face of modern science able to land a man on the moon, there was a mechanical watch using two-hundred-year-old technology. The interplay of timekeeping and scientific advancement was not lost on me. I am not sure how many visitors to the museum had the same experience as I, but it was a true revelation.

Another "work" watch I preferred was a little one in a 34 mm case, the Ulysse Nardin Michelangelo Rectangular Triple Date Moon Phase. Wearing a small watch, such as this or the Paul Gerber Retro Twin Power Reserve on one day, and a large watch like the Audemars Piguet Polaris the next is fun. Luckily there is no such thing as "wrist confusion." Many collectors limit themselves to certain case sizes with the belief they cannot wear anything bigger or smaller when often they can. Who cares what other people think? Looking at the Ulysse Nardin Michelangelo Rectangular, it is much more delicate in appearance than my other watches. It has **sub-dials** made from mother-of-pearl, not typical for men's watches, that give life to the dial. It is powered by a Piguet movement that, I was told, is finicky. Indeed, it has needed to travel to the service center several times for calibration, which was not easily performed because special tools are required. Small and delicate, it is not a watch that would typically be considered in a category of a "work watch," but the distinction is arbitrary, and it is a personal choice anyway. This is a watch I acquired for the simple reason that I found it pretty. As interesting as the watch may be, the strap has an unusual feature. In order to adjust the date and moon phase, a **pusher** is needed. A small cylinder containing the **pusher** is supplied with the watch. The strap, in turn, has a pocket constructed between the layers of alligator and leather to hold this cylinder so that the **pusher** is always at the ready should the need arise to adjust the **sub-dials**.

Michelangelo Rectangular by Ulysse Nardin

Before I became obsessed with watch collecting, a watch was nothing more than a tool needed on the weekdays. Cell phones were not as common, and there was not the tendency to use them to tell time. On the weekends I found it liberating to take off my watch on Friday evening and not replace it until Monday morning. It was glorious to not have my existence governed by the dictates of time. After falling down the horological rabbit hole and having watches I did not feel comfortable wearing at work, the weekends were transformed into the time to wear my special watches.

My father worked beyond his eighty-seventh birthday. By extension, it was my assumption that I would follow his lead and work well beyond typical retirement age. The concept of retirement seemed foreign to me. My family could not conceive of me not working, and they, too, figured I would work as long as I was physically capable. As it turned out, that was not to be. When I celebrated my last milestone birthday, I came to the realization I had graduated college fifty years ago and had been on a treadmill ever since. It was a shocking reality. I decided I would not take the path I assumed I was destined to follow. Instead, I chose to embark on a new journey. It was time to retire from my career. When I broached the subject of retirement with my wife and family, they were overjoyed and enthusiastically supported the decision.

When I started to consider the possibility of retirement, I started to think about how I would occupy my time. That was answered pretty easily: take better care of myself, do some consulting, and write a book. Soon after that I became obsessed with the concept of recording my journey in the world of watches. I started making copious notes but did not start typing until I had dropped the microphone and fully retired.

It is a well-known tradition that after a certain number of years of service to a company or as a token of esteem upon retirement, the celebrant receives an engraved timepiece. This tradition dates back to the railroad industry in the early to mid-nineteenth century, when the gift of a railway watch was highly prized. But what to give the watch collector? The collector will always accept another watch, but the gift giver might feel challenged to pick the right one.

No, I did not receive a watch at the time of my retirement, and that is okay. Nonetheless, major life events are frequently memorialized by a special gift. For men, often the gift is a watch. My wife celebrated several of my birthdays and holidays with the gift of a watch. More special was the Freak cake she arranged for me. Otherwise, I have not acquired a watch to celebrate a special event. I have enough reasons to buy the next one. That said, I thought that since this was a once-in-a-lifetime event, I would buy myself a special "retirement watch." As it turned out, it did not happen.

At the time of my retirement, I had several watch projects in process, and it seemed artificial to label one particular project as "the retirement watch." The process of collecting is a continuum, and I saw no reason to think my interest or passion for watches was going to diminish. I have had a number of friends declare that they are done with collecting, only to show up at the next get-together with a newly acquired piece. That said, some people actually tire of the hobby. Some either do not acquire another watch, choosing to enjoy what they have, or they sell off their collection. That will not be me.

Entering the next phase of my life, retirement, I knew the demands and structure of my days would be different. In anticipation of this change, my wife and I more than several conversations regarding how this change would affect my horological journey. As a basic concept, I knew I still had the passion to continue to explore the world of watchmaking and watches.

The first obvious effect was I had more time to pursue my interests. The staff at the bank were used to seeing us access the safe deposit box on Saturdays. Now when my wife and I go into the bank on random weekdays, we are often received with the observation, "But it is not Saturday. What are you doing here today?" It is always good to keep our friends in the bank on their toes.

One of the immediate ramifications of retirement has been the repurposing of watches. Without the previously established daily and weekly structure, there is a need to evaluate the designation of various categories and their particular roles in conjunction with my new existence. I needed to figure out when to wear different categories of watches. I still want to wear all my watches and not suffer the slings and arrows of guilt should I not wear any watch at least on occasion.

Retirement brought a new consideration for the watch of the day. One of our goals for the golden years is to take better care of ourselves. We try to go to the gym three times a week and go on long walks at least two days a week. Going to the gym carries with it a certain degree of risk of personal injury due to overexertion or accident. More importantly, there is a risk of damaging a watch from a falling weight or misuse of equipment. We no longer go on the trail runs. The walks we take, though sometimes on trails, are more sedate and likely to be on paved surfaces. Nonetheless, one still must be cautious regarding the choice of watch in case there is an untoward occurrence. These activities mandated the need to assess my watches for the category of "gym watches," ones that are robust and carry with them less implications should there be an untoward event.

A watch that immediately fit this category is the Bell & Ross Military Ceramic piece. Joining it is the St. Gallen Rescue Watch. It is a very sturdy watch, if any watch can be considered as such, with what I will call a unibody constructed case. The case is constructed in such a fashion to allow easy removal of the rubber straps for cleaning should the need arise. The strap even has a hole in it so that it can be hung up to dry after cleaning. The model I acquired was one produced in a limited series, as indicated on the dial, for the Purists group. The series was limited to 188. I received number 6 even though it was not a Ulysse Nardin. At the time the watch was released, I was asked to co-author a review of the model for the magazine *International Watch.* To date, it is the only published article I have written regarding watches.

St. Gallen Rescue

I added the citation for the original publication to my list of professional articles on my curriculum vitae. It served more as a joke than anything else. Adding it to my curriculum vitae was my way of subtlety commenting (truly only to myself) about how people pad their curriculum vitae to give the appearance of great academic achievement.

After the gym or a walk, I not only shower, but I also change watches. The watch chosen for the gym or the walk is certainly not the one to be worn the rest of the day. I now consistently wear a minimum of two watches during the course of most days.

In the past, it was a rare occasion for me to change watches midday, except if I was doing trail running or other activities not suitable for a nicer watch on a weekend day. The self-imposed stress of having adequate opportunities to wear one of my "special" watches has lessened. I now have greater freedom to wear those watches at other times during the week as well as the weekend. I recently had the chance to see Roger Smith's Pocket Watch No. 2. It was being exhibited by an auction house in preparation for its sale. While inspecting the piece, which was incredibly marvelous, I was told that the watch had never been wound by the owner.

Roger was invited by the auction house to inspect the watch as well as give a talk about it. When Roger saw the pocket watch, he asked permission to wind it, which, of course, he was given without hesitation. Here was a very important watch that had not been wound in years. That is the absolute definition of a "safe queen." It saddened me to know that the watch was not being appreciated to its full potential. To visit that incredible watch, I wore my Series 2, which is wound and worn even though it rests in the safe deposit box when not in use.

Another new reality from my retirement: I am now able to cruise the boutiques and watch stores with increased frequency and regularity. Of course, that puts me at greater risk of temptation. I certainly have to be on guard to prevent myself from being swept away by another pretty face— a dial, I mean. I admit to the fact that I do have watch ADHD and have, at times, jumped from one must have to another. Faced with the watch ADHD diagnosis, I cannot be expected to be cured from this affliction in a day, if ever, regardless of my employment status. Truly one has nothing to do with the other. There are no medications to treat this condition, but I do know there is a need for better control, especially now that I risk greater exposure to many more options. However, self-control can only go so far.

At the last Watches and Wonders, Chopard released a watch that was brought to my attention. My friend in London told me about the salmon-dial L.U.C. 1860 he ordered. He suggested I might want to consider the watch as well. Soon thereafter, other watch friends also spoke of it and suggested it was the kind of watch that would suit me. I have followed the Chopard brand and have been aware of their watches for many years. I have been to the Chopard Manufacture with the Purists, and I have met the co-president, Karl-Friedrich Scheufele. However, none of their products called my name—that is until the Ferdinand Berthoud FB2. Even though the Ferdinand Berthoud line is a separate entity, it is still under the umbrella of the Chopard brand and still overseen by Karl-Friedrich Scheufele.

The more I read and thought about the 1860, the more I realized I had the capacity to say no to temptation only so often. The salmon dial was beautifully finished with **guilloché** decoration of the central portion of the dial in a lucent steel case, a Chopard development.

L.U.C. 1860 by Chopard

It is a small watch at 36.5 millimeters in diameter, but it would be a nice break from some of my larger watches. When I spoke to my friend in London, who is well known to the Chopard brand, and then to the local boutique staff, I was told there were only going to be limited number produced this year. The worldwide response to the watch has been overwhelming, and the possibility of getting one was a year or two off, if that. However, as it turned out, someone my friend knew had received an allocation for one but decided to postpone his order. After some discussion, it was decided at the highest levels, I am told, to offer the allocation for that watch to me. It is really nice to have good friends. How could I say no? This model is a reissue of a prior model, but in this one a date window is not present, something cheered by many Chopard enthusiasts. I must admit I agree; the watch dial design is better for its absence.

Some people say that when retired, every day is like Sunday, but some stores are closed on Sundays, so instead, I believe every day is like Saturday. That said, the calendar does not agree. There are seven days in the week, but since retiring, it is at times difficult to remember what day it is. The obvious solution to the problem is to get a watch that displays not just the date but also the day.

I have several watches that display the day of the week, the MIH, Parmigiani Toric Perpetual, Ulysse Nardin GMT +/- Perpetual and the IWC Doppelchronograph. True, they are useful and fit the need, but remembering the watch ADHD I suffer from, I do want variety. Enter Watches and Wonders, when Vacheron Constantin released a version of the Patrimony Retrograde Day-Date. The release of a boutique exclusive with a salmon dial (again) and a platinum case occurred soon after I retired and my inability to remember what day of the week it was became more acute. What to do? A watch with a bi-**retrograde** movement is uncommon. I did see an Oris Artelier Pointer Day Date around the same time, which also has a day of the week **sub-dial**, but it does not compare to the design of the dial, the elegance, and the fine finishing of the Vacheron. Order placed; watch received.

Patrimony Retrograde by Vacheron Constantin

My wife and I have been told that when building a collection of art, a guiding principle is to have three pieces from a particular artist. I do not know why this is a thing, and we have not always followed that advice. I guess having now obtained my third salmon-dialed watch in a white metal case (the Voutilainen, Chopard 1860 and the Vacheron Patrimony). I should move on to another color combination.

Over time, I have joined several watch enthusiast groups and organizations, but I have had trouble attending their get-togethers and lectures. No longer tied to a work schedule, I have found that attending these events has become feasible, as has meeting friends for lunch during the weekdays, with or without my wife. I can now afford the time to advance my learning and understanding of watches, as there is always more to learn. In that regard, I now have opportunities to read and study the various books about watches and watchmakers I have accumulated over time. In the past I read several, but there are many more on my bookshelves waiting for me. The time has come.

For sure, the one thing I can guarantee will not occur during this new phase of my journey is that I will be taking watchmaking classes or tinkering with watch movements. A number of years ago a friend, knowing of my interest in watches, gave me two vintage watches he had no use for. He suggested I could learn how to take apart and reassemble a movement with them. At that time, I had a passing thought that it would be a fun learning experience. The watches, however, have remained on my desk, undisturbed. I took the master class where I popped the **jewel** at the Jaeger-LeCoultre Manufacture, not an auspicious start to my thought of putting screwdriver to movement. Subsequently I have attended several additional "classes" sponsored by Jaeger-LeCoultre, Ulysse Nardin, and Vacheron Constantin. I did not send any other **jewels** flying but did lose some screws. What I recognized was that over time, my skills with a screwdriver and tweezer have not improved whatsoever. It is painfully evident that watchmaking is not in my future. There is a reason I do what I do and watchmakers do what they do, and those paths will not cross.

When I retired, one goal I set was to continue to do some consulting. Sure enough, the day after I retired, I received several calls asking for my services and since then have received more requests. The consulting work I am doing is an extension of what I did for the past forty-plus years. When I do consulting, I charge an hourly rate. Usually, when I am so engaged, I wear a **chronograph** to measure the time spent. The chosen **chronograph** cannot be a typical **monopusher**, as those models do not have a restart function, except for the Habring^2 COS pilot.

Most of the consulting engagements involve reading a varied quantity of files. I find that the best time to do this reading is when I am traveling. On an airplane flight there is undisturbed time convenient for doing this work. When flying, I am frequently crossing time zones, and so a travel watch is a handy accessory. Combining the two functions, a **chronograph** with a travel watch, would be incredibly useful. To date I have not acquired a watch that pairs the two **complications**.

The Ulysse Nardin GMT +/- remains my favorite travel watch, and I have suggested to several members of the company multiple times the possibility of creating such a piece with both **complications**, to no avail. I once posed the question of the feasibility of adding a **chronograph** to the Ulysse Nardin GMT +/- on the Purists site. In response, I received a detailed explanation from one of the members why this was technically not possible. Nonetheless, I remain hopeful that this is not an impossibility if only a designer at Ulysse Nardin would take an interest.

When I announced my retirement, a common topic of discussion involved our plans to travel. Not restricted by the dictates and obligation of schedules, work assignments, and projects, we have been liberated to travel when and wherever we wish. Fortunately, I have several watches designed for travel across time zones. Besides my favorite GMT +/-, a number of my other watches from Ulysse Nardin have the same GMT function, but traveling with gold-cased watches is not usually the best idea. The Jaeger-LeCoultre UTT is another option, but again, it is in a gold case, although white gold is not as noticeable. I did fancy the Parmigiani Hemispheres when it was first released. It has the uncommon feature of having an independently set second time zone. Most GMT or travel watches operate such that a **pusher** moves the hour hand forward or backward (depending on the model) with a separate indicator of the home time. In the Hemispheres, both dials can be controlled by the main **crown** at three o'clock; however, the second time zone can be adjusted independently by the **crown** at two o'clock. There are parts of the world where the time zone is changed in half-hour increments. I must be prepared for every eventuality. Another useful feature of this watch is that it has separate day-night **indicators**, one for each of the time zones displayed. That is more useful for the traveler than might be first thought.

It is good to know whether it is day or night at home to prevent middle-of-the-night phone calls or texting.

Hemispheres by Parmigiani

After Parmigiani released the Hemispheres, MB&F released the LM 1. It, too, had two dials that were independently set by way of the single **crown**. In the publicity material circulated upon its release, Max Büsser claimed that the LM1 was the first watch with two independently set time displays. My mother used to religiously do the *New York Times* crossword puzzle. On one occasion, she discovered an error in the puzzle and sent a letter to that effect to the editor. In return she received an acknowledgment and a "You Got Me" certificate. Seeing Max's statement about the LM1, I sent him a note telling him the LM1 was not the first, citing the Parmigiani Hemispheres, Franck Muller Master Banker, and the F.P. Journe Résonance as examples to make my point. Max emailed back with an acknowledgment of his error, but I did not receive a certificate.

Before retirement, my days were long and replete with scheduled meetings and appointments. The dictates of time ruled the day. In such circumstances it is debatable whether to think of a timepiece as an aide or an enemy. There never seemed to be enough time during the day to complete all the necessary tasks. This meant that the obligations of the job extended into the evening hours at home. Evening relaxation was not a foregone conclusion.

Anticipating retirement came with the expectation of being freed of the dictates of the clock. Once the initial incredulity of not having to go to work subsided, I started to settle into a new normal and realized that time still plays a significant role in my existence. With less structure to the day, sometimes I need a reminder of an upcoming event. The Jaeger-LeCoultre Memovox Timer is very useful for such scenarios. It can be set to a specific alarm time within a twelve-hour period, or it can be set utilizing a countdown feature. It was produced in a limited quantity of 250. I was able to secure one through the boutique, but I did not get number 94 because the limited edition was labeled "One of 250"; hence there were no individually numbered pieces. I was happy to get the watch knowing that it was a limited edition and in great demand, even though it did not read "Number 94"

Over time there have been many different Memovox models produced, and I have admired some, but the added countdown feature and the color combination made this a piece that I wanted as a representative sample of the product line. The Ulysse Nardin Sonata also comes with alarm and countdown functions, but it is a bulkier watch and cased in gold, so I am bit more protective of it during routine wear.

Memovox Timer by Jaeger-LeCoultre

Years ago, my wife asked me whether I was going to continue acquiring watches once I retired. I remember shrugging as my answer. Ultimately, I tried to reassure her by saying I was not sure, but I could always sell one watch in order to get another. Now retirement is upon me, and I enjoy all my watches. The thought of selling a watch continues to be anathema. Yet I enjoy the process of discovering a new watch and pursuing the hunt and the ultimate victory of acquisition. A friend described the process somewhat differently, labeling it as "retail therapy." Regardless of the term, the likelihood of turning off the enthusiasm for the next watch is slim to none. One does have to modulate, but, as stated, there continue to be many fish in the sea.

I have told my wife I do not want to fail at retirement. I have read that one in six retirees eventually return to the work force. I do not want to return to my prior profession. In what other area do I have any experience? By way of the fifty years in my profession, I have extensive experience working with people and have intimate knowledge regarding the concept of customer satisfaction. I spent my career being very detail oriented. I have extensive management experience; I was in charge of a department with more than thirty staff. Also, I have sales experience, having worked in the Watch Connection. Over the last twenty-plus years, I have accumulated a modicum of knowledge about the world of horology. All that considered, I spoke to friends at several boutiques and floated the idea of me working with them. To a one they gave me a positive response. With that in mind, one evening, on a lark, I researched job opportunities in a holding company that owned a number of watch brands. To find out more detailed information, I read that I had to create an account with the company. I created an account but went no further. At the moment I saw it more as a joke and figured the people reading my application may not appreciate the joke, as it was serious business for them. I put aside the computer but kept my account active. Maybe one day I will return to it, complete the application, and send them my résumé. Who knows?

After all, I am sure of one thing: this journey will never end.

Acknowledgments

I would like to thank everyone who has made my journey so very special. Too numerous to mention (this is not an Academy Awards acceptance speech), everyone who I have met along the way has added something to my experiences and knowledge, not to mention my collection. Although my pocketbook may not always share my enthusiasm, I treasure all that you each have brought to me as we have traveled together.

In the process of creating this book, I especially want to thank my friendly readers who have left their imprint on the text; Michael Roeder, Tim Brown, Mohannad Abanomy and Scott Goldman, your input was invaluable. For insights and the title, thanks to Richard Haier, and thanks to Rick Rabbin for his legal expertise.

A huge thank you goes out to Justin Morton of J Morton Photography for the magnificent images of the watches.

This book would not have been possible had it not been for the guidance, expertise, and patience of Lisa Shiroff of Tasfil Publishing along with her team. She lit the path to the successful conclusion of a dream.

Most importantly, there are no adequate words that can express my gratitude and love for my co-editor and life partner, my wife. She has tolerated my craziness and has been a willing, though dubious at times, companion every step of the way of this journey. Thank you.

Glossary

Amplitude: The number of degrees an **escapement** rotates per beat in either direction.

Anglage: A process of finishing the sharp edges of components of the movement by beveling them to a specified angle.

Annual calendar: A watch that displays day, date, and month. It takes into account months that have thirty or thirty-one days and requires adjustment only at the end of February to account for either February 28 or 29 (leap year).

Barrel: A cylindrical structure that contains the **mainspring**.

Balance wheel: A weighted wheel that rotates to and fro with a certain **amplitude**. It contains the **hairspring**, which serves to return the wheel to neutral and limit the **amplitude** of the swing.

Bezel: The rim of a watch case that holds the crystal covering in place.

Bridge: A part of a watch movement that holds other components in place. Typically made of metal but can be composed of other material.

Carousel: Much like a **tourbillon**, it rotates the whole **escapement** and **balance wheel** 360 degrees to defeat the negative effects of gravity. Usually it takes an hour or more to make the rotation, whereas the **tourbillon** takes typically a minute to rotate the **escapement**.

Chronograph: A stopwatch used to measure the passage of time that consists of an independent second hand and dials that count elapsed minutes and hours.

Chronometer: A watch movement adjusted to measure time within certain standards of accuracy.

Complication: Any additional feature of a watch beyond seconds, minutes, and hours.

Constant force: A mechanism that regulates the supply of power to the **escapement** in such a fashion that the release is consistent throughout the **power reserve**.

Crown: Typically located on the side of the case, it is used to wind the watch and set the time.

Ebauche: A basic unfinished watch movement massed produced and supplied with the expectation that it would be modified, finished and cased by the watchmaker or company.

Electroplating: A process to electrochemically apply a metallic coat onto a base metal component.

Equation of time: A calculation that defines the difference between solar time, as indicated by the position of the sun, and mean time, that is indicated by a timepiece.

Escapement: The components of a watch movement that take the power stored in the **mainspring** and divide it into segments that then measure time.

Escape wheel: Part of the watch balance. A toothed wheel that rotates and controls the movement of the pallet fork, thus measuring a unit of time.

Flyback: A special component of some **chronograph**s that, when activated, resets the counters while the **chronograph** remains activated to allow continuous measurement of time intervals.

Foudroyante: Otherwise known as "flying second." An independent dial that divides a second into equal parts, allowing for accurate time measurement.

Fusée: A chain that is wound around a conical spool or a cam that gradually unwinds to release energy to the **escapement** used in place of a **mainspring**.

Grand complication: A watch movement that contains a **tourbillon**, an astrological indication (e.g., moon phase), a chiming feature (**minute repeater**), and a calendar function (**perpetual calendar**).

Grand Feu: An enameling process in which silica and, as required, additives are heated to high temperatures on a metallic base in multiple layers.

Guilloché: Decoration typically applied to the dial but can also be applied to other components of the watch, usually involving engraving of a metal surface.

GMT watch: A watch designed for travel across time zones. Can be set to indicate time at home and at current location.

Hairspring: A component of the **escapement** that oscillates within the **balance wheel** with a specific frequency to measure an interval of time. Typically made of a metal alloy or silicium.

Indicators: Markers typically on the dial that indicate the seconds, minutes, and/or hours.

Jewel: Stones, typically synthetic rubies, used in a movement as a bearing to decrease friction at contact points.

Jump hour: A watch display where the minute is displayed by a running hand and the hour is indicated by a stationary hand or digital display. When the minute hand completes its sixty-minute sweep, the hour indicator "jumps" to the next hour on the display.

Lugs: Projecting portions of the case that support the mounted strap or bracelet.

Mainspring: A thin length of metal alloy that, when wound and under tension, stores the energy used to power mechanical energy.

Minute repeater: A mechanism built into the movement that, on demand, strikes, by way of a hammer striking a gong, the hours, quarter hours, and minutes of the current time.

Monopusher chronograph: A stopwatch that has all functions controlled by a single button or **crown**.

Perlage: Decoration of the surface of watch parts typically consisting of an overlapping circular pattern.

Perpetual calendar: The module in a watch that displays the month, date, and day so that it accounts for the various numbers of days in each month. Unlike an annual calendar, it is programmed to account for the number of days in February and leap years.

Power reserve: The amount of energy remaining in the **mainspring** to power the movement.

Pusher: A button that projects from the side of the case, used to activate a function of the watch such as starting and stopping a **chronograph** function or activating a chiming mechanism.

Rattrapante: Otherwise known as a split-second **chronograph** or a doppelchronograph. A **chronograph** that has two second hands to measure the passage of time. Pressing a pusher stops the first hand while the second one continues to measure the passage of time.

Reference number: The designation by the watchmaker or company of a specific completed watch movement, usually composed of a series of numbers and/or letters.

Régulateur: A watch where the hands for hours, minutes, and possibly seconds are on different segments of the dial and rotate around different points.

Remontoire: A small wheel placed on or near the **escape wheel** that stores energy from the **mainspring** and releases its bursts to the **escapement**. Used to assure a **constant force** of energy and improve the consistent accuracy of the timekeeping throughout the **power reserve** of the **mainspring**.

Retrograde: A linear display, typically in an arc, that can read time or another indication such as the day of the week or the month. At the end of the arc, the indicator jumps back to the beginning rather than completing a full circle.

Rotor: A weighted structure that serves to wind the movement, typically in response to the movement of the wearer's wrist.

Skeletonization: A process to remove nonessential material parts from the plates of the movement, leaving only the weight-bearing essential elements in place.

Sub-dial: Secondary dials or registers apart from the main dial. Used to indicate seconds, **chronograph** elapse time, or other indications.

Tourbillon: Invented to counteract the deleterious effects of gravity on an **escapement**. The **escapement** is mounted in a cage that rotates 360 degrees in a predetermined period of time, typically a minute. A double-axis has the **escapement** rotate in two planes and a triple in three.

Verso: The underside of a movement.

Vibration frequency: Measurement of the number of oscillations of the **balance wheel** in a given period of time. Typically measured as hertz (Hz) or vibrations per hour (vph).

Watch Index

Watchmakers and Watch Industry Professionals Index

About the Author

Mitch Katz lives in Southern California with his wife and his two rottweilers, Blood and Jaws. You can connect with Mitch at Mitch@Tasfil.com.

* 9 7 8 1 9 6 4 0 1 4 5 3 1 *